The strange death
of Socialist Britain

Patrick Cosgrave

The strange death of Socialist Britain

POST WAR BRITISH POLITICS

CONSTABLE · LONDON

First published in Great Britain 1992
by Constable and Company Ltd
3 The Lanchesters, 162 Fulham Palace Road
London W6 9ER
Copyright © 1992 Patrick Cosgrave
Patrick Cosgrave has asserted his moral rights
ISBN 0 09 471430 4
Set in Linotron Plantin Light 10½pt by
Servis Filmsetting Ltd, Manchester
Printed in Great Britain by
St Edmundsbury Press Limited
Bury St Edmunds, Suffolk

A CIP catalogue record for this book
is available from the British Library

For Elizabeth Ward

Contents

Illustrations

Illustrations supplied by Hulton Deutsch Collection

Introduction

Writing in a considered way about contemporary British politics – that is to say, covering the last generation – is a relatively novel practice in this country. Traditionally, the contemporary mode has been confined to memoirs and to journalism. The universities, in general, tended to treat with suspicion that discipline which we now call political science. Historians, in particular, believed for most of this century that contemporary matters could not be treated in a scholarly way; and publishers took the view that there was no market for books about modern politics, unless they were of the 'instant' variety.

In the last thirty years, however, all this has changed. It has come to be believed, both in the universities and in the ranks of the interested general public, that serious appraisals can be made, even of comparatively recent events. It is fair to say that among the most powerful influences, on what amounts to a sea-change in the way the thinking British consider political writing, was brought about by the inauguration, after the 1945 General Election, of the invaluable, and now famous, series of election studies emanating from Nuffield College, Oxford. The first Nuffield study, which appeared in 1946, was by R. B. McCallum and Alison Readman. The name which, however, is most associated with these works is that of Dr David Butler. Dr Butler wrote the 1951 and 1955 studies single-handed. Since then he has been assisted by various collaborators. There are, in my view, many faults to be found in the Nuffield method, but it is nonetheless necessary to say that the various volumes are indispensable reading for anybody seriously concerned with the evolution of politics in this country.

The British tradition of political writing – and I am considering a period of two or more centuries – has been very different from that of France, Germany, or the United States. In those other three countries the belief that contemporary affairs could be analysed at a level at once popular and scholarly was of long standing. Perhaps the best known of foreign writings is Alexis de Tocqueville's *Democracy in America*; but *The Federalist Papers*, written by the various Founding Fathers of the infant American republic, are not only contributions to the political polemic of their day, but scholarly contributions in their own right: but then, their authors, while being politicians of weight, were also scholars. American awareness of the sheer intellectual power of the Founding Fathers was gracefully illustrated by President John F. Kennedy when he played host, at the White House, to a vast gathering of the most powerful minds in the United States. 'This', said the President 'is the most significant intellectual gathering to have come together in this House since Thomas Jefferson dined here alone.' The British have never accorded such respect to thinkers. In nineteenth century Germany, scholars such as Ranke and Treitschke were not merely given the formal reverence due to great scholars, but found their advice sought by politicians and statesmen and their books selling in very large numbers. The British, on the other hand, have been constantly suspicious of thought expressed on paper, though they have often been admiring of, and susceptible to, political oratory, as witness such careers as those of the two Pitts, Charles James Fox, Edmund Burke, and George Canning. Nonetheless, the tendency was to see the speech as a political act and not as a product of a contemplative intellect.[1]

To be sure, there were exceptions, both among British politicians and among British scholars. The third Marquis of Salisbury, Foreign Secretary and Prime Minister variously between 1874 and 1902, wrote lengthy and pungent essays on matters of contemporary political interest: most of them, taken individually, would be substantial enough to form small volumes today. What is more, they can be profitably read today as models of knowledge and lucidity. Salisbury's nephew, Arthur James Balfour, who succeeded him as Prime Minister and was subsequently Foreign Secretary, was a scholar of no small repute, and one of his finest works was a study of Treitschke.

Among the British scholars who applied themselves with effect to the study of the affairs of their time, two names stand out. The first is that of Sir John Seeley. Seeley was the first holder of the Regius Chair of Modern History at Cambridge University. Indeed, it could be said that the power of Seeley's advocacy and the popularity he enjoyed among the literate public of the day created that Chair.[2] Seeley first gained a major reputation as a religious writer with his study of the life of Jesus Christ, *Ecce Homo*. But he went on to become a formidable historian, notably with *The Expansion of England*, about which he made perhaps his most famous remark, that the British Empire 'was acquired in a fit of absent-mindedness'. Seeley set himself to construct a policy out of this fit, and he succeeded beyond his wildest dreams. For *Expansion*, and the essays collected in *The Growth of British Policy*, provided a systematic justification for the British practice of empire. Like Graham Wallas, who wrote influential books at the turn of the century – and is now perhaps best remembered for his extraordinarily prescient analysis of the rise of Japan to the status of a world power[3] – Seeley sought to create a system of thought out of a series of often accidental experiences.

Seeley and Wallas alike – there were others, but these two are the most eminent – believed in the practical application of scholarly work. They were both meticulous in their study of the material available to them but they both also believed that their books should have a practical application to public affairs and that they should influence politicians. The British historians who succeeded them, however, tended to seek to emulate Leopold von Ranke, whose conviction it was that the study and writing of history should be undertaken for its own sake and that pure objectivity in historical and political scholarship could be achieved. Only in *Die Grosse Machte* (The Great Powers) did Ranke seek to prescribe courses of political action. Seeley it was, however who, in *The Growth of Political Science*, gave the title to what in the second half of the twentieth century has become an academic discipline of its own, separate from the study of history.

The burgeoning of this separate discipline was greatly influenced by the coming into being of vast amounts of new information of a kind intrinsically different from that available to historians who lived and worked before the twentieth century. For example, we now have available to us mountains of statistics, political, economic and demographical. We have public opinion polls, and we have the sub-discipline of sociology.

The writer of contemporary political narrative – or biography – falls, alas, between two stools. The historians tend to deride his work because, in the nature of things, it cannot be based on archives, while the massive amount of information available to the political scientist is virtually indigestible to a biographer or, say, the author of a book on the life of a particular government.

The Nuffield Studies, to take the most notable evidence of the fissure, invariably open with an account of events between the general election under scrutiny and the election before. But these narratives are always superficial. They bear little relationship in terms of quality to the subsequent pages, loaded as they are with facts and analysis. One feels, somehow, that the hearts of Dr Butler and his various colleagues are not in the business of studying the more obviously dramatic aspects of political events.[4] Apart from the studies of various general elections, the Nuffield school is perhaps most substantially represented by a book which Dr Butler produced in collaboration with Professor Donald Stokes, *Political Change in Britain*[5]. As well as the unrivalled knowledge which Dr Butler has of the facts of modern British political history, which makes anything written by him required reading for the serious student, this book, based on more than a decade's research, was unique for its time in drawing together a vast amount of disparate material. It also stated an ambition – to use the sociological material on which the authors worked to make political predictions. The foremost of the predictions was that, for demographical reasons, the Labour Party had become – in Harold Wilson's phrase – the natural governing party in the United Kingdom. Alas for Dr Butler and Professor Stokes their immense labours did not substantiate the prediction. Thus, it behoves anybody who studies politics in this country to be extremely wary in handling all the voluminous material available to our generation, which was not available to earlier generations; and to resolve, having made a synthesis of it, not to use it to predict the behaviour of the British electorate.

The distinction between the writing of history and writing about current – or recent – affairs was brought to an acute point by a circular issued by the Department of Education and Science on 14 January 1991. The Secretary of State's judgement was that nothing that had happened in the past thirty years could be considered as history. The whole tenor of the document, which runs to some forty pages,[6] is to suggest that, while it was not impossible to teach current affairs, the subject should not be considered as history. It follows from the judgement made by Mr Kenneth Clarke that the history of modern times cannot be taught in a considered and scholarly way, but that a clear separation should be made between the past and the recent past. I happen to think that any political subject can be written about and taught from an historical perspective; by this I mean that every attempt possible should be made to handle the available evidence with objectivity. The danger of separating the last generation from more distant periods is that the student, whether at school or university, may fail to see the threads in the seamless robe of history. There is no reason why the events of the last thirty years cannot be treated with the same critical discrimination as periods in the more distant past on which we may have much more intimate, and detailed documentation.

The whole question is one of attitude. Political history should be approached with acuity. The teacher, or the writer, should do his or her best to describe matters and motives fairly. But he or she should not conceal the views they hold; nor should they seek to impose those views on the student or reader. It is unfair to students and readers for any writer to impose a wholly artificial distinction between the recent and the more distant past. There is no reason why contemporary, and recent, political affairs should not be taught and written about in a scholarly fashion. The great sin is to apply one's own prejudices, without making clear that they are no more than prejudices, and to seek to influence rather than describe. The luminous understanding of the great scholars may sometimes be found, in the light of subsequent knowledge, to be wrong; but what they have written will, nonetheless, guide the future.

I have described the way in which I see different traditions of political writings in different countries. It is perhaps not without significance that the three writers who seem to me to have produced the most effective combination of the historical approach and that of political science were none of them British. Professor R. T. McKenzie was a Canadian.[7] Professor S. E. Finer[8] and Professor Samuel H. Beer[9] are American.

In the pages that follow I will consider the history of British politics since 1945 within an historical and narrative framework. The first period is 1945 to 1951, in which year the Conservatives returned to power. The second period runs from 1951 to 1979. During this period, allowing for the brief hiccup of the Heath administration from 1970 to 1972,[10] governments of both major parties sought, with minor changes, to administer the revolution which Clement Attlee had bequeathed to them. The final period runs from 1979 to the time of writing. During that period Margaret Thatcher set out to reverse the policies introduced after the war by Attlee and the consensus that, broadly speaking, existed between 1945 and 1979. Mine is, thus, a story of revolution, followed by consolidation, followed by counter-revolution.

The long historical perspective of the period since 1945 can and should, however, be looked at in a larger context. Over the period two things of major importance occurred. The first was the loss of – or, perhaps more properly, the abdication from – empire. The second was the ineluctable burgeoning of a concern with welfare – the state of society rather than of the nation. It is true, of course, that there was also evidence of a pervasive economic decline, and this evoked increasingly despairing concern from 1960 onwards.[11] I have preferred, however, first to stress the matter of welfare because it was to become increasingly apparent that it was more than anything else the burden of the welfare

17

state that made it more and more impossible for Britain to pay her way, given the vast subsidies required by nationalised industry more and more dominated, as the years went by, by the trades unions.

The revolutionary dream was that strategic industries could be run more efficiently and more profitably by central government than by private capital, and could thus make the contribution required to pay for the Welfare State. An important factor here, and one which contributed greatly to the tightening stranglehold exercised by the unions on the economy, was the commitment on the part of both major parties to a policy of full employment. From the moment Edward Heath was elected Leader of the Conservative Party in 1965 one of the principal – and sometimes the only – bones of contention in the House of Commons was which party could more effectively bring down an unemployment figure steadily encroaching on the dread figure of one million. When, in 1968, the figure *did* pass the million mark Heath became convinced that he could win the next General Election, for it was perceived wisdom that no government could hold on to power while unemployment was rising. It is necessary to recall here that most of the older senior politicians of the day had vivid memories of the dole queues of the thirties.

Nobody could have predicted then that after 1979 a government, headed by a Prime Minister who had no serious folk memories of the 1930s, would calmly preside over an unemployment figure well in excess of three and a half million and go on to win two further General Elections. Victory in three successive General Elections was of course not unknown for a party: the Conservatives won in 1951, 1955 and 1959. But victory in three successive elections by a single leader was without precedent this century and Mrs Thatcher's triumphs up to her resignation in 1990 ensured her a place in the record books as the longest-serving Prime Minister this century. The capacity to keep her nerve in the face of unemployment figures more than three times greater than those in the face of which, in 1972, Edward Heath decided to reverse the free-enterprise policies on which he had been elected in 1970, was crucial to the success of Mrs Margaret Thatcher's counter-revolution. It enabled her, further, to outface and crush the major trades unions.

Before Mrs Thatcher – indeed, almost immediately after the 1945 General Election – the Conservative Party had decided to accept the main principles of the legislation of the Attlee government. Indeed, it was regarded by the leadership of the party as a *sine qua non* for regaining power to convince the electorate that the party had sloughed off the capitalist policies of the thirties and had wholeheartedly accepted the pursuit of welfare along collectivist lines. Churchill himself was not greatly interested in policy formulation and he scarcely bothered to read the plethora of documents setting out the new, and supposedly enlightened, Tory approach to social and economic matters. The great policy review was, in consequence, carried out under the aegis of R. A. Butler, who gathered around him at the Conservative Research Department and at the Conservative Political Centre[12] a large number of exceptionally talented men and women. Some of these – they included Reginald Maudling, Iain Macleod and Enoch Powell – had served with distinction in the war and therefore had a self-confidence and maturity such as enabled them to converse on equal terms with their superiors.

There was no question but that, after the shattering defeat of 1945, the Conservative Party was in dire need of a moral and intellectual renaissance, and over the years since its return to office in 1951 the years of Butler's ascendancy have acquired the status of legend. It can be argued, however – and I do believe – that the electoral importance of the propaganda attending the policy revisions has been greatly exaggerated. By 1951 the Labour government – most of whose senior Ministers had served in Cabinet from 1940 onwards – was exhausted. On the policy front the Labour Party had run out of steam, nearly all of the undertakings in its 1945 manifesto having been implemented. Conversely, Conservative batteries had been recharged by six years in opposition. It is true that Churchill had by 1951 taken little opportunity to bring forward able men and women from the younger generation so that, when he re-entered Number Ten, Downing Street in 1951, the faces around the Cabinet table were, for the most part, familiar. The generation that was to dominate Tory politics in the later fifties and throughout the sixties and early seventies had yet to emerge.[13]

But we must never forget that the post-war years marked the foreclosure of the Empire. It might be supposed (to use Seeley's formulation again) that an empire acquired in a 'fit of absent-mindedness' could be got rid of with relative ease. Indeed, the pain of losing India having been got over, British politicians in the following years were more than happy to congratulate themselves on the fact that the ending of the imperial era had been accomplished so smoothly. It was not until the late sixties and the seventies that this myth was destroyed. For the most part Britain's former colonies fell into poverty, dictatorship, and often chaos. The continuance, moreover, of the imperial idea as enshrined in the Commonwealth ensured that British governments were perilously slow even to begin to deal with what is now one of the most intractable and dangerous of the nation's political problems – immigration from the 'new', or coloured Commonwealth, and the consequent presence on the island of large pockets of immigrants alien to British culture.[14] Further – and perhaps even more importantly – there was a psychological detritus of empire. Successive governments, while patting themselves on the back for their part in the efficient transition from Empire to Commonwealth, nonetheless continued to believe, and to behave, in accordance with that belief, that Britain remained a world power on the old scale. It was fundamental, for example, to the foreign policy of Anthony Eden, which was unquestioningly followed until the late sixties, that British diplomacy was based on three power sources – Britain and her Commonwealth, the United States of America and Western Europe.[15] The notion that the Commonwealth would loyally follow Britain's lead was one soon to be overthrown, and the later decision to apply for membership of the Common Market demonstrated a new belief that this country had, for survival's sake, to become part of the proto-federalist EEC.

Again, economic exigency required the withdrawal of military forces which had been supposed to play a crucial part in South East Asia and the Persian Gulf. The most shattering of all the experiences which were to reveal Britain's inadequacy was the failure of the Suez invasion in 1956. The process of adjustment to the reality of the fact that Britain was, in world terms, no more than a marginal power was a distressing one. It was not until the middle seventies that British governments, having abandoned grandiose undertakings which they had neither the means nor the will to fulfil, began to understand that a medium-sized power could, precisely by operating on the margins, procure for itself a fulfilling role. Britain, of course, had a crucial military role to play as a member of NATO. She had – and has – an important part to play in minor, but still significant, theatres such as Central America and, more recently, in the major confrontation with Saddam Hussein in the Gulf. Even in a country as far distant as Afghanistan, Britain, through the provision of military aid, was able to have an effect on the civil war which followed the Russian invasion of that unhappy country. Nonetheless, the long years of illusion had a profoundly debilitating effect on the economy and on British politics. In psychological terms it seems to me that, albeit insensibly, the collectivist ambitions of the Welfare State were steadily replacing the dreams of empire.

All great historical movements have deep roots. It would therefore be wrong to suggest that the election – or re-election – of any particular government has determined a major change in the historical direction of any national life. Nonetheless, it is fair to choose the election of the Labour government in 1945, and the Conservative government in 1979, as turning points in modern British history. The Labour revolution of

1945 grew out of the perceived memory of discontent and injustice in the 1930s. The Conservative counter-revolution, which began in 1979, grew out of a national perception of the fact that the post-war consensus – signalled by the policies of the Churchill government of 1951 – had failed. At one time it seemed to those who wished to sustain the consensus through increased prosperity that the answer would lie in membership of the European Economic Community. At the time of writing, however, the nations of Western Europe are faced with a cataclysmic upheaval in Eastern Europe and the Soviet Union, an upheaval that seems likely to draw Western Germany, the most economically powerful member of the Community, into an increasing preoccupation with Central Europe, to the detriment of her Western commitments.[16] Such a preoccupation by the Federal Republic is bound seriously to weaken economically the international organisation in which the United Kingdom has invested so much capital and energy. One thing is clear: whatever is to happen to this country will be deeply affected by the development of events as far afield as the Urals, and even Central Asia. Britain's markets are uncertain. This island, however, has, throughout its history, depended less for its domestic economic stability on its own resources – severely limited as they are – than on its capacity to maintain healthy international financial relations. The collectivist state created after the war was ultimately destroyed, not merely by domestic profligacy, but by the severe loss in international power occasioned by the cost of the Second World War. Any future domestic policy, whether it is collectivist or capitalist, must come to terms with that fact, however unpalatable.

To tackle the uncertainties which lie ahead for the next half century requires, however, an unforced conviction of what the nation is, and what the nation is about. The Conservative Party led by Margaret Thatcher enjoyed a considerable measure of success in destroying a consensus which, in any event, was becoming increasingly discredited by the mid-1970s. But there is no new general agreement in place. The incipient capitalism of the Thatcher years has not yet put down roots, and the unpredictable course of international events makes it all the more difficult so to do. Nonetheless, this is not principally a study in international relations: exchanges between states form only a backdrop – though an essential backdrop – to my argument.

It is a truism to say that when governments close to a general election adopt policies similar to those favoured by the opposition they endanger their position. This happened to the Home government of 1963–4. All except rhetorical references to socialism were dropped, and the essential stress of Wilson's case was on the argument that Labour would perform more competently in power than a tired thirteen-year old administration. This was almost exactly the same appeal made by the Conservatives in 1951: most of the government's policies were accepted, but, it was argued, the Tories would be more efficient in their management. Further back, during the General Election campaign of 1945, the caretaker Conservative government led by Winston Churchill adopted many of the policies advocated by the Labour Opposition led by Clement Attlee.

The ideological rift between the parties did not open until Edward Heath was elected Leader of the Opposition in 1965. A decade later Margaret Thatcher opened it more widely and, on the other side, Michael Foot became Leader of the Labour Party in 1980 and turned the rift into a chasm. After Foot's disastrous defeat in the 1983 General Election his successor, Neil Kinnock, sedulously set about moving his party towards the centre, if not embracing all the ideals which have come to be known under the rubric 'Thatcherism'. Only history can judge the extent to which he imitated the policies of Margaret Thatcher and, subsequently, John Major.

CHAPTER ONE

A Peaceful Revolution

(1945–1951)

On 3 May 1945 German envoys, nominated by Hitler's successor, Admiral Doenitz, arrived at the headquarters of General Montgomery at Luneberg Heath. An intimation as to their future was given by the fact that Montgomery refused to shake hands with them. Earlier in the day he had telegraphed to Churchill that he intended 'to get from it [the delegation] the unconditional surrender of all German forces . . .' He did so in a matter of minutes.

The war in Europe was over. Churchill hoped to prolong the existence of the wartime coalition after VE (Victory in Europe) Day until, at least, VJ (Victory in Japan) Day, and, if he could, throughout the period of post-war reconstruction.[1] This, however, proved impossible: Clement Attlee, not to mention his more vociferous colleagues, convinced that they would win a General Election, were determined to get on with the creation of a socialist Britain. Churchill reluctantly put in hand preparations for a General Election.

The Allied leaders – Churchill, Truman and Stalin – had, after the German surrender, sent a message to the government of Japan requiring an unconditional surrender. The Emperor rejected it out of hand. On 6 August 1945 the United States Air Force dropped an atomic bomb on Hiroshima.[2] Still Japan would not yield. Two days later, therefore, a second atomic bomb was dropped on Nagasaki. The following day Emperor Hirohito surrendered unconditionally.

However, Churchill was by then no longer in charge of affairs. The British General Election had been held on 26 July. Churchill had been hoping for a Conservative majority of between 80 and 100. But, as his Private Secretary, John Colville recorded in his diary, the result was the worst for the Conservatives since 1906.[3] Labour was returned with a majority over all parties of 146. The Conservatives were reduced from

585 to 213: it was small consolation for Churchill that his own majority in Woodford was a substantial 17,000. His wife, who felt strongly that he needed a rest, observed to him that defeat was a blessing in disguise. 'If so,' Churchill replied, 'it is a blessing very heavily disguised.'

Attlee, three weeks later, observed to Colville that he had expected, at the very best, a majority of 40.[4] Reflecting on his shattering defeat later, Churchill wrote that on the day of the election he had awoken just before dawn 'with a sharp stab of almost physical pain'. This arose from an intuitive conviction that he would be beaten:

> All the pressure of great events, on and against which I had mentally so long maintained my 'flying speed', would cease and I should fall. The power to shape the future would be denied me. The knowledge and experience I had gathered, the authority and goodwill I had gained in so many countries, would vanish. I was discontented at the prospect, and turned over at once to sleep again.[5]

It was now Attlee's opportunity to shape the future. The Conservative Party was in complete disarray. Clementine Churchill, her daughter tells us, would have preferred Churchill to resign as Leader of the Party, for it was clear that the verdict of the electorate had not been cast against him personally: he was still held in the highest esteem. The condemnation, rather, was of the pre-war Conservative Party, held responsible by the people for the depression of 1929–31 and the exceptionally painful unemployment of the pre-war years.

Churchill, however, was determined to hang on, though, having retreated to the South of France for a painting holiday immediately after the election, he did not enter the new House of Commons until the following January, an abstention which made the plight of his party even more wretched than the General Election result itself. Nonetheless, there was no move to choose a new Leader. Churchill's prestige was too high, and the power of his office too great to allow of challenge. It was true, all the same, that the disorganised character of the Opposition added considerably to the ability of the Attlee administration, buttressed by its massive majority and the clear evidence of overall numerical support among the people,[6] to proceed with the most radical reconstruction of British government and society seen since the dissolution of the monasteries by Henry VIII.

Labour's ambitions were, indeed, extensive, not to say grandiose, and, for the following three years they could not be gainsaid. A National Health Service, free at the point of use, was to be created.[7] Most major industry was to be taken into public ownership according to the principles of the Labour Party's constitution, which required 'the common ownership of the means of production, distribution and exchange . . .'[8] In its political essence the Labour programme required a hitherto unprecedented control of the state and of society from the centre. As Douglas (now Lord) Jay, a Junior Minister in the Attlee government and subsequently to serve in cabinets headed by Harold (now Lord) Wilson, observed, 'The gentleman in Whitehall really does know best'. It was significant, therefore, that for some years the Attlee government retained the whole apparatus of wartime controls, including food rationing: such controls, however irksome to the public, were entirely in keeping with the way of thinking of the Labour government. The abolition of controls was eventually to become the centrepiece of Conservative opposition, summarised in the title of the 1950 and 1951 manifestos (both written by Churchill himself) *Set the People Free*.[9]

The twin Labour themes of nationalisation and welfare were thus, inextricably, intertwined. In the view of Labour theoreticians the nationalisation of the means of 'production, distribution and exchange', was a good in itself. But it was also, of course, intended to be the method by which the dreams of collectivised welfare, to which Labour politicians had aspired since before the First World War, would be fulfilled.[10] While, after 1945, Churchill continued to be regarded both in his own party and in the country at large as a titanic figure, the Conservative Party was held in considerable disrepute, largely because it had been Conservative governments which presided over the years of depression between 1918 and 1939. The Labour Party had been in government before, either alone or in coalition, but had never before enjoyed a majority, let alone such a splendid majority, as that which it enjoyed after the General Election of 1945.[11]

To the Labour Cabinet and its supporters, 1945 ushered in a new dawn. To the Conservative Party, the very size of the Labour victory dictated a change of course: a party so readily and easily victorious, having fought against the undisputed hero of the War, had to be imitated rather than challenged. Thus it was that the Conservative opposition accepted the broad terms of the Attlee revolution. From 1945 to 1950 – when Labour's majority was reduced to sixteen – almost the sole Conservative argument was that they would be more efficient at running a mixed economy than were Labour Ministers. On the hinge of this argument depended everything that happened in British politics until 1970, and perhaps even for another nine years. It is worth recording, however, that the 1951 government headed by Churchill was able to keep its promise of efficient economic management: it sharply reduced the proportion of national income taken by the State.[12]

However, for six years it seemed almost impossible to challenge the Labour Party. For the first five years Labour's majority in the House of Commons was sufficient to carry all before it. The House of Lords remained, broadly speaking, Tory, but in no adamantine fashion. It was agreed as a convention that no legislation which the Labour government favoured would be seriously opposed, but only criticised as to its detail by the opposition. The then Conservative Leader in the Lords, Lord Salisbury, explained the reasoning behind his tactics to Dr Janet Morgan in 1970:

> The Conservative Peers came to the conclusion that where something was in the Labour Party manifesto we would regard it as approved by the country . . . If they produced something that wasn't in the manifesto, we reserved the right to do what we thought best . . . We passed on Second Reading nearly all the nationalization bills – in the one case of the Iron and Steel Bill we went rather further as we didn't think they'd a justified demand. So we put in an amendment not to put it into force till after the election. The Labour Party accepted that.[13]

Labour's ascendancy, at least until 1950, was not merely practical – because they commanded a real majority in the House of Commons and an effective majority in the House of Lords – but intellectual. Lord Blake once observed that nothing is so powerful as an idea whose time has come.[14] There was what amounted to almost a tidal wave of opinion in favour of Labour ideas. Though it was later to be assumed that the Labour Party's socialism was Marxist in origin, it is fair to say that it owed more to Methodism in general and Clement Attlee's experience of social work in the East End of London before the War in particular.[15] It will be a contention repeated throughout this book that powerful personalities – and Attlee, for all his self-effacing mannerisms, was a powerful personality – can have profound influences on events.

An important distinction, however, must be made between the Labour Party in victory and the Conservative Party in defeat. On the one hand, Labour had the advantage, in 1945, of having Cabinet Ministers who had served with distinction throughout the War: this was in marked contrast to earlier Labour governments – those headed by Ramsay MacDonald – whose members had no executive experience before taking office. On the other hand, in the election campaign itself the Conservatives suffered from two marked disadvantages. The first was that the tide of ideas had been moving towards the Labour Party's plans for social amelioration; the second was the vivid folk memory of massive unemployment presided over by a Conservative government in the thirties. Throughout the history of the twentieth century the British electorate has consistently shown itself to be predisposed towards ideas for improving national welfare, unless the state of the nation – in war or peace – has seemed to require harsh measures, either to achieve victory in war or to revive the national economy.[16] Mrs Margaret Thatcher gained enormous benefit from 1975 onwards from a national conviction that rigour in administering the economic affairs of the country was a necessity, not just an option.

Nonetheless, however complete the Labour victory of 1945 seemed to be, there was an underlying conviction in both parties that a Labour government was somewhat unnatural. The post-war Conservative Party felt only the need for cunning adaptation, and no need for fundamental change. In the aftermath of the Attlee victory, R. A. Butler's father wrote to him to congratulate him on retaining his seat;

> I was prepared for a Socialist majority, and saw some advantage in it, on the domestic as opposed to the foreign front, but did not think it would be so sweeping . . . Be of good cheer. The wheel turns and will come full round.

Butler himself was of a like mind to his father. Lord Devlin recalls him as comparing the Labour victory of 1945 to 'a bout of the measles which the country would have to suffer but from which there was no doubt the British people would ultimately pull through'.[17] It is probably true to say that young Conservatives were less inclined than Sir Monty Butler to accept the theory of the full circle. Nonetheless, there was an unforced conviction that Conservatism would ultimately prevail, even at the price of a fairly substantial adjustment to the policies of the Labour Party. There was then, and remains within the Conservative Party, a conviction that the natural order of political affairs in the United Kingdom dictates the continuance of Tory government. Whereas, in the nineteenth century, it was widely accepted that office would be shared between the Liberal and the Conservative parties, both being of remarkably similar opinion, in the twentieth century the Labour Party was generally assumed to be, and to some extent felt itself to be, a bunch of interlopers. Moreover, between Ramsay MacDonald and Clement Attlee a series of Labour leaders seemed not only unsuited for power but not particularly interested in acquiring it. Arthur Henderson, George Adamson, William

27

Clynes and George Lansbury were all considered to be chairmen of a parliamentary collective rather than serious contenders for the post of First Lord of the Treasury and the occupancy of No. 10 Downing Street. It was not until 1965 that Harold Wilson had what Tories regarded as the audacity to proclaim Labour as 'the natural party of government'. Even then Wilson's claim was to prove to have a short shelf life.

It is one of the great paradoxes of British political life since the achievement of full male and female adult suffrage in the 1920s[18] that the domestic aspirations of the electorate have been more in tune with the policies of the Labour Party, while the willingness of the same electorate to accord power to the Conservative Party has been most marked. It may well be, therefore, that there was something of wisdom in the post-1945 Conservative appeal to the people which essentially rested on a claim to efficient economic management.

Three Chancellors of the Exchequer served in the Attlee government. They were men whose policies differed as much as their temperaments. The first, Hugh Dalton, is described by Peter Jenkins as 'roistering'.[19] He was appointed on 27 July 1945. His whole idea of economic policy consisted of government-led and taxpayer-financed expansionism. After an indiscreet remark to a journalist in November 1947 about the contents of a budget speech he was about to make in the House of Commons, he felt obliged to resign his office and never returned to government.[20] Dalton was succeeded on 13 November 1947 by Sir Stafford Cripps. Cripps was a millionaire of Socialist conviction and deep personal austerity. He founded and financed the Labour Party newspaper, *Tribune*. (In later years *Tribune* became the vehicle of dogmatic left-wing opinion and was, for a time, edited by Michael Foot. That was not a development that would have pleased Cripps.) Cripps, who has never been the subject of the major biography which he deserves, seemed positively to relish the regime of financial stringency which he was obliged to introduce because of the failing British economy. He was succeeded, in turn, on 19 October 1950 by Hugh Gaitskell. Gaitskell's brief administration was characterised by the coinage of the word 'Butskellism'. This combination of the names of R. A. Butler and Gaitskell was held to denote a similarity of aims, beliefs and policies between Chancellor and Shadow Chancellor. Its use continued when the Conservatives returned to power in 1951, and long after Gaitskell succeeded Attlee in 1955. It may be said to have maintained its vogue even after Gaitskell's death in 1963 and his succession by Harold Wilson. Butler, of course, continued in office until 1963: he retired from the House of Commons when offered the mastership of Trinity College, Cambridge in 1965.[21]

It should be said here that one of the most distinguished political writers of our time, the late Peter Jenkins,[22] discounts the whole idea of a post-war consensus on policy between the parties.[23] He rightly points out that there were important differences between Labour's conduct of government – and particularly in the matter of management of the economy – between 1945 and 1951 and those of successive Conservative governments thereafter. He draws attention to the fact that after the 1951 General Election the Churchill government 'set about dismantling the panoply of war-time and post-war controls which Labour had relied upon to plan production and arrange fair shares in conditions of austerity'. This dismantling was, of course, what Churchill meant by the slogan 'set the people free'. There were also differences of some significance on matters of monetary policy, the convertibility of sterling, state controls and the distribution of wealth. Mr Jenkins prays in aid for his argument that there was no real consensus, other than what he describes as the Post-war Settlement, consisting of agreements on policy made between the coalition parties during the War, Hugh Gaitskell's biographer, Philip M. Williams[24] It is true, as I shall describe shortly, that the Conservative opposition disliked the National Health Service reforms introduced by Aneurin Bevan, and that the steel industry became a political yo-yo between 1945 and the present day. But most of the differences between the two major parties, once the Attlee revolution had been implemented, were tactical. Mr Jenkins also quotes Edward Heath, who said in 1971 that 'there never *was* a consensus . . . The parties never came together in their policies. Even the idea of "Butskellism" was sloppy and inaccurate'.[25]

However, when Butler replaced Gaitskell as Chancellor after the 1951 Conservative victory, Gaitskell confided to his diary:[26]

As to their [the Conservatives'] policy, so far of course apart from the Bank rate, etc. they have really done exactly what we would have done, and have followed the same lines on controls, economic planning, etc. It is possible that they will change later and go in for relying much more on monetary and budgetary influence. This will mean cutting something, at least food subsidies and perhaps more. But on the whole I think it unlikely. Butler is on the extreme left of the Tory Party and is shrewd enough to understand that what they have got to do while in office is to live down the reputation inherited from their periods of office in the thirties. What the intelligent Tories will, of course, want to do is to be able to say to the electorate when the election comes, 'No war: no unemployment: no cuts in social services. Just good

Government.' If I am right about this they will want to stay in power for three or four years, and I do not really see why they should not.

I need not refer to the debate on the Address which is available. On the whole I think that they have behaved reasonably well in not trying to make out that we had hidden the facts from the nation.[27]

I will shortly discuss the real differences that there were between the Labour and Conservative parties. But, with the exception of steel, on all strategic matters there was little to choose between the 1945 and 1950 governments and those of 1951, 1955 and 1959. The fundamental fact of the matter is that Attlee and his colleagues having introduced a revolution in both policy and attitude, the Conservatives accepted what they had done. Consensus is the only word to apply to such a development.

As I have already observed, the one single, major difference between the Labour and Conservative parties was on the question of the steel industry. While, broadly speaking, Conservative governments from 1951 to 1964 were willing to accept what the Attlee government had done, the steel industry represented a fundamental test of valour to both parties. It is useful, therefore, here to review the dates of acquisition and deacquisition by and from the state of that, until recently, unhappy industry.

It was not until 1949 that Attlee and his colleagues got around to the business of nationalising the steel industry. This was done through the Iron and Steel Act, 1949, and was in pursuit of both the constitution of the Labour Party and the 1945 manifesto. The proposition which lay behind the Act – which took effect on 1 January 1951[28] – was that all manufacturing industry was better handled by the state than by private business. At the time of nationalisation the British iron and steel industry was run by five major firms: the Conservative opposition immediately undertook to return the industry to its original owners. Thus the Iron and Steel Act of 1953 denationalised the industry, though the Churchill government agreed to set up the Iron and Steel Board, which would supervise the activities of the private companies. The Labour manifesto for the General Election of 1964 promised that steel would be renationalised. However, the Labour majority being only three, the position of Harold Wilson was a somewhat parlous one, given that two Labour MPs, Woodrow Wyatt and Desmond Donnelly, had made clear their determination to vote against a Bill to bring the steel industry back into public ownership. After his much more substantial victory in the General Election of 1966 Harold Wilson brought in a further Iron and Steel Act, which did just this.

Sensitive to the choppings and changings of policy which had so damaged the security of the metals industry, the Heath government of 1970 decided to leave well alone. When Mrs Thatcher won the General Election of 1979, however, it was her settled determination to return iron and steel to private ownership. Her task was more difficult than that of Churchill in 1951. It was open to him simply to restore the industry to its previous owners. But by 1979 the original firms had ceased to exist. She was helped, however, by two important factors. The first was the increasing uncompetitiveness of the public corporation, British Steel. The second was the steelworkers strike of 1980. This strike – like the later strike by the National Union of Mineworkers – gave her the moral authority to act as she wished. So it was that, under the aegis of Ian (now Sir Ian) MacGregor, the industry was fined down; many mills were closed; and the industry was sold off to small shareholders. It is worth observing that, albeit on a much smaller scale than when it was first nationalised, the British steel industry is today one of the most efficient and competitive in the world.

Given the Labour government's conviction that industry – and particularly manufacturing industry – could be run more efficiently by the state than by private individuals, it followed that Labour's ambitious social programmes would be paid for out of industrial profit.[29] It was not until the 1970s that it was realised that this aim was impossible of achievement.

It is convenient now to consider the Labour revolution which followed 1945 in four different segments, before considering how all of them came together to form a coherent pattern.

First, essential to the whole of the programme of the Attlee administration was the matter of nationalisation. Nationalisation was not unknown before 1945, but after that date it became part of the life-blood of government.[30] In 1946 the Bank of England was nationalised. In the same year both the coal industry and civil aviation were also nationalised. The following year electricity and public transport were nationalised; and a large number of private transport firms were taken over by the state. A British Transport Commission was established. The Docks and Inland Waterways, a number of hotels,[31] railways, London Transport, road haulage and road passenger transport were all drawn into the net of the state. In the Transport Act of 1962 the Conservative government of the day reorganised the system of central administration – but no denationalisation was suggested, let alone propounded.

In 1948 the gas industry was nationalised. Iron and steel has already been mentioned. Thus, when Churchill returned to power in 1951 most of the major manufacturing and utility industries were in the hands of government.

The second segment of Labour's policy concerned social matters. Here, the vital commitment was to the creation of a National Health Service. The Conservatives were not unwilling to consider a substantial improvement to the vestigial provision of health care for the general public made before the war. Aneurin Bevan was the driving force behind the enactment of a Statute that provided whatever health care was required free at the point of use. The Act further made provision for removing general hospitals from the control of local authorities and for their administration by regional boards under the direct supervision of the Ministry: again, the 1951 government accepted this radical change and it was not until 1986 that a beginning was made on its abolition. Bevan believed that the highest conceivable cost of providing a free health service would be £300 million a year.[32] He was not sensible of two problems. The first was – and is – that any wholly free service generates unending demand. The second was that advances in medical science which were not predicted in 1945 – or even in 1942, when a committee of all the Coalition parties proposed health service reforms – were to create the expertise to treat many illnesses and medical conditions previously thought incurable. There arose, therefore, an almost insatiable demand for research and facilities unimaginable at the time of the passage of the National Health Service Act.[33] It is with these demands[34] that Mrs Thatcher wrestled from 1979 to 1990, and which her successor, John Major, faced on becoming Prime Minister.[35] Argument about the National Health Service became critical in 1989, when the consensus on its structure, as between the main political parties, broke down completely.

Third, in 1946 the Labour government imposed controls on private landlords by means of the Furnished House Rent Control Act. The provision of rented accommodation by private individuals was hedged in with further restrictions in 1949 by means of the Landlord and Tenant Rent Control Act. Rent tribunals were given the authority to determine reasonable rents and their powers were extended to unfurnished accommodation. The Conservative governments of the 1950s did make substantial changes to both these Acts, but the private rented sector has never recovered the level of activity it enjoyed before the war. The Wilson governments of 1964 and 1966, moreover, imposed further restrictions, which were relaxed, but only partially, by Conservative governments from 1979 onwards. The pattern is once more clear. With few exceptions – steel being the most notable – the post-war governments headed by Churchill, Eden, and Macmillan made little or no dramatic change to the structure of domestic policy and administration introduced by the government elected in 1945.

It was generally recognised, of course, that the Labour Party had a special relationship with the trades unions and special obligations to them.[36] This constituted the fourth segment in the Party's revolution. In the Foreign Secretary, Ernest Bevin, Attlee had as a senior Cabinet member probably the most powerful trade unionist of the age. Bevin had been brought in to government and the House of Commons by Churchill in 1940, largely because of his trade union power base: he was then General Secretary of the country's largest trade union, Transport and General Workers.[37] As long as the war lasted Bevin stuck loyally to his political last: despite a certain amount of militant pressure, the TGWU remained steadfast in support of the government until the conflict was over.

With the election of a Labour government, however, the trade union movement required some compensation, not merely for their wartime efforts, but for their support and financing of the Labour Party from its inception. During the 1945 election campaign itself Labour gave to the unions the most important single pledge in their manifesto – the provision of full employment. The Conservative Party, and Churchill as Prime Minister in the caretaker government which succeeded the break-up of the coalition, rapidly followed suit. But his promise was far less convincing than that of Attlee, for it was a series of Conservative governments which had presided over the disastrous unemployment figures of the thirties. Neither the Attlee government, nor any of its successors, was able to achieve full employment as the ordinary citizen might understand it: a truer meaning of the phrase might be 'an acceptable level of unemployment'. As long as unemployment was kept below the magic figure of one million it was found to be politically acceptable. The figure exceeded one million by 1969, and Harold Wilson lost the General Election the following year. This encouraged the myth that a government could not win an election while unemployment was rising, and this myth, combined with his own memories of hardship in the thirties, persuaded Edward Heath to change his policies in 1972 in order to expand the economy. It was not until the advent of Margaret Thatcher that it was found that an unemployment figure as high as three or more million was no necessary bar to winning General Elections.

It was a fundamental part of Labour belief that the controlled economy was the key to growth and the provision of full employment: full employment meant the provision of jobs for all but those who were judged unemployable, either through disability or inclination, and those

33

changing jobs and temporarily on the dole. In consequence the 1945 government maintained until almost the end of its life the various wartime restrictions on individual freedom – the most unpopular of which was food rationing. By the time the President of the Board of Trade, Harold Wilson, began the dismantling of the control system, it was too late to procure electoral success. Just as Churchill had been unconvincing in his promise to provide full employment in 1945, so the Labour Party was unconvincing in its promise to abolish controls.

The Labour governments headed by Clement Attlee in 1945 and Harold Wilson in the 1960s and 1970s did provide legislation which conferred enormous privileges on trade unions. But trade union privilege went a long way further back. In 1901 a court decision in the House of Lords ruled that a trade union could be sued for damage to an employer caused by a strike. In 1906 the incoming Liberal government, in pursuit of an election promise, passed the Trade Disputes Act. This piece of legislation freed the unions from any liability for damages caused to an employer by reason of industrial action. In 1927, however, the Trades Disputes and Trade Unions Act made illegal the sympathetic strike, whereby workers in one factory could strike in sympathy with workers in dispute at another. In 1946 the Attlee government repealed the 1927 Act. Other measures taken in pursuit both of the government's social aims and in deference to trade unions included the National Insurance (Industrial Injuries) Act of 1946, which provided insurance for workers injured at their place of employment or contracting disease as a result of that employment.[38] When Churchill returned to power in 1951, moreover, he felt constrained not to follow the advice of colleagues who told him that the trade union movement was becoming dangerously powerful: he preferred the line of appeasement in industrial disputes. This often made life difficult for R. A. Butler as Chancellor of the Exchequer, for Butler was constantly worried about the dangers of wage inflation.[39] Thus began what was to become a rampant growth of trade union privilege which was the main cause of the downfall of the Callaghan government in 1979.

The Labour government of 1945–51 was, however, more fortunate than those headed by Harold Wilson and James Callaghan in its dealing with the trade unions. It was widely accepted that the tremendous cost of the war – which, among other things, totally extinguished the United Kingdom's overseas investments – made life difficult for any peacetime British government. The Western allies, moreover, had decided not to seek financial reparations from a defeated Germany, since it was generally believed that the reparation extracted from Germany after the First World War had contributed greatly to the instability which caused the rise of Hitler.[40] Further, the unions felt that Labour was very much their government; and were more than willing to stretch a point in negotiations with the first Labour government to enjoy a working majority. These two factors, combined with his general policy, gave Clement Attlee considerable leverage in industrial negotiations.

It is hard, coming towards the end of the century, to appreciate quite how fervent was the belief of the Labour movement in the supposed panacea of nationalised industry. Indeed, for all its very considerable achievements in the implementation of the social policies outlined in the 1945 manifesto, and for all that its successes were such as profoundly to alter the domestic economic and social structure of the United Kingdom, it is reasonable to say that ambitious programmes such as were undertaken between 1945 and 1950 were immensely damaging to the overall economic health of the country and laid upon Britain a burden which has not, at the time of writing, been fully lifted.

This was because of the truly horrendous economic state in which Britain found herself after the war, and of the immense complexities of her international political and economic situation. In 1945 the Lend Lease system, by which the United States had substantially fuelled the British war effort, was ended on the grounds that it was no longer needed. The United Kingdom found herself, because of the wartime liquidation of nearly all of her foreign assets, with no useful income from abroad. Yet, in addition to the provision which had to be made to compensate the owners of industries about to be nationalised, and the cost of the welfare state, Attlee committed himself to sustaining the Armed Forces at the wartime level; to paying for an indefinite period the cost of the occupation of large tracts of Germany – most significantly using the British Army of the Rhine. A part of Berlin was also occupied, and administered, at the expense of the British taxpayer. The Cabinet decided, further, to develop a British nuclear deterrent, without informing Parliament of the considerable expense that would be involved.[41]

Though perfectly agreeable to the ending of Lend Lease, Attlee and Dalton were not entirely insensible to the economic difficulties which Britain faced. Although they believed that, in the medium term, the greater productivity which centrally-managed industry would create would generate the revenues required to implement the social programme, to cover themselves in the short term they negotiated, following the end of Lend Lease, substantial loans from the United States and Canada. Two years into Attlee's first term two things had happened. The first was the clear evidence that the USSR had acquired an empire in Eastern Europe and posed a serious military threat to the West. The second was that the Western European countries were making no progress in repairing their economies, through lack of means.[42] General George C. Marshall, American Chief of Staff throughout the War – and at this time Secretary of State – therefore designed a programme of economic assistance which came to be known as the Marshall Plan. This aid was also offered to, but rejected by, the USSR. The Plan, which Churchill called 'the most unsordid act in the history of relations between nations', provided for the injection of massive sums of money, even now impossible to assess, into the infrastructures of the Western European economies: Marshall Aid did not consist of a series of loans, but of gifts, and no requirements were made as to how the flood of dollars should be spent.

Marshall Aid was suspended in 1950, on the grounds that it was no longer needed. However, though a ruined Germany made efficient, and indeed brilliant, use of what she received, and France was not far behind her, for the United Kingdom the aid merely provided a breathing space. The Attlee government remained in an economically intensely difficult situation until its fall in 1951.

In July 1947 sterling was made convertible. The following month convertibility was suspended because of a run on the pound. Runs on the pound became common, and in 1949 it was devalued from $4.03 to $2.80. In 1951 Bank Rate was increased from 2 per cent to $2\frac{1}{2}$ per cent. Any rise in Bank Rate was regarded then, as a rise in interest rate is regarded now, as an indication of an economy in serious trouble. The situation with regard to Bank Rate was to become a great deal more serious after the 1951 General Election, as the Churchill government strove to grapple with the economic legacy of Labour.

Throughout nearly six years of increasing economic vicissitudes the Attlee government clung grimly to the main planks of its programme of reform. But the parlous financial situation compelled it to take contradictory measures which were unpalatable not only to Labour Party supporters, who had hoped for a new economic dawn after the 1945 election, but also to the general mass of voters. In 1948 there was a freeze on pay and dividends – the precursor of the pay and prices policies of the 1970s. The Monopolies Commission was established with a view further to restraining the operations of private industry (all nationalised industries, were, of course, by their nature, monopolies). The freeze administered a severe blow to the aspirations of many of those who had voted Labour in 1945. Moreover, it was followed by a series of budgets not of any great dramatic importance in themselves but which nonetheless created profound irritation. It would be tedious to summarise them all, but their nature can be expressed in a single sentence which Hugh Dalton uttered to John Carvel, Political Correspondent of the *Star*, and which destroyed his career: '. . . the principal points would be – no more on tobacco; a penny on beer; something on dogs and pools but not on horses; increase in purchase tax, but only on articles now taxable; profits tax doubled'. These imposts may today seem trivial, but to a population reduced almost to penury by war and desperately looking for some relief they seemed intolerable. They also lent themselves to newspaper dramatisation. 'PENNY ON BEER' 'TAX ON POOLS AND DOGS LIKELY', ran the *Star*'s headline.[43]

However, in spite of the contradictions between aspirations and resources, the 1945 government was, in one vital respect, fortunate. Its two most powerful members – the Prime Minister and the Foreign Secretary – had tremendous influence within the Labour Party, and had the priceless experience of serving in the inner war Cabinet between 1940 and the end of the War.[44]

Ernest Bevin had been found a safe seat in a by-election in 1940 because Churchill, when discussing with Attlee which Labour politicians should join the coalition government of 1940, and what positions they should occupy, made it clear that he wanted the General Secretary of the Transport and General Workers Union in the Cabinet, so that the unions would be thoroughly supportive of the war effort.[45] Strictly speaking, Ernest Bevin's responsibilities in the War Cabinet were confined to keeping the unions in line. But Attlee, as Churchill's deputy in the coalition government, observed that Bevin involved himself in every question that came up in Cabinet and performed impressively. By the end of the War Bevin, who was on secondment from his union for the duration of the conflict, had lost his taste for trade union affairs and much preferred to continue in politics. His deep ambition, now that he had served his purpose as Minister of Labour, was to be Chancellor of the Exchequer. He was astonished – as was virtually everybody else jostling for position in the first Labour government to enjoy a majority – when Attlee offered him the post of Foreign Secretary. Bevin accepted with delight, for he had never thought of the Foreign Office as being within the range of possibilities open to him. He referred to it as 'a turn-up in a million'.[46] But Attlee's reasons were succinct. He said, 'Britain was facing a difficult position as a great power which had temporarily been gravely weakened. It needed a very strong personality to counterbalance this as far as possible.'[47]

This, then, was the formidable figure who took on the international problems of a greatly diminished United Kingdom in 1945. The axis on which the Labour government functioned in the post-war period was that of Attlee and Bevin. They had each other's absolute trust and Attlee had the steel to support Bevin in conclusions about not merely foreign affairs in the conventional sense but in international economic relations.[48] Moreover, both Hugh Dalton and Herbert Morrison had a desperate desire to be Prime Minister, and constantly intrigued against Attlee,[49] as indeed they had done before the war. As so often, the truth of a great relationship can be illustrated by what might seem to be trivial. Sir Frank Roberts recalls that Bevin was one day considering a paper concerning a relatively unimportant matter, and asked Roberts to get the Prime Minister on the telephone. Roberts protested that it was something too insignificant for such a consultation. Bevin replied, 'Better get Clem's agreement. I value his judgement and if things should go wrong we will be better off if he has agreed.'[50] The perfect trust that obtained between Prime Minister and Foreign Secretary depended on such attention to detail. The Prime Minister knew that if he was challenged by Morrison or Dalton he could rely on Bevin; and Bevin knew that if he got into difficulties – and his ebullient and egotistical temperament often did get him into difficulties – he could rely on Attlee.

The problems and complications that Ernest Bevin faced on becoming Foreign Secretary were either horrendous or complicated, or both. He tackled them all with a certain rough zest, and the skill of a man who had spent many years in trade union negotiations. They can be divided into two. The first concerned the economic position of Britain in the international field. The second was concerned with the military security of post-war Europe.

He had a formidable capacity for the practical. When George Marshall proposed the Marshall Plan, Bevin immediately negotiated with France and the Allied Administration in Germany the formation of the Organisation for European Economic Cooperation.[51] Bevin's proposals were essentially concerned with the channelling of American munificence in proportion to the needs of individual Western European countries.[52] Bevin also had to face the enormous cost of Britain's military responsibilities overseas. The coalition government had undertaken to preserve democracy in Greece. A civil war between Communists and Democrats broke out in that country immediately after the Second World War had ended, and Britain was financially responsible for keeping the promises the coalition government had made. Bevin concluded that Britain could not afford to meet its obligations, but he persuaded President Harry S. Truman to use American muscle and financial weight to turn the tide against the Communists in Greece. His arguments led directly to the enunciation of the Truman Doctrine, by which Stalin, having absorbed most of Middle and Eastern Europe into the Soviet Empire, was warned that he would not be allowed to extend his fiefdoms any further on pain of war.

Then there was Palestine. The United Kingdom had governed Palestine from the end of the First World War under a mandate from the League of Nations. The principal problem she faced was, of course, the unceasing conflict between Arab and Jew in the area which now comprises Israel and the territories occupied by Israel after the Arab-Israeli war of 1967. The ambitions of the Zionist movement for nearly a century had been to create in that area an independent Jewish state. At the end of the Second World War, and as knowledge of the slaughter of Jews in Nazi Germany came to the horrified attention of international opinion, pressure grew for a mass Jewish immigration to Palestine. Bevin acted swiftly to try to curtail this immigration, which he believed would make it impossible for him effectively to exert his famed conciliatory powers to bring about an agreement between Arab and Jew. In the event he found the task impossible. Furthermore, the expense of maintaining the British mandate was more than the British economy could bear and thus, in 1948, he announced that Britain was surrendering her Palestinian mandate, handing the whole problem over to the successor to the League of Nations, the United Nations Organisation, and withdrawing her troops from the area. The war between Jew and Arab followed, the Jews were victorious, and the state of Israel was established. It was immediately recognised by the USSR and the USA. Britain did not recognise Israel until the end of 1949.[53]

Bevin was a vital influence on the creation of the United Nations: the first General Assembly met in London, although the detailed drafting of the UN Charter was carried out in San Francisco. It is interesting to observe that, for so rough-hewn a man, Bevin entered on his tenure at the Foreign Office in a spirit of idealism. He believed that the creation of the United Nations would bring peace to the world, and he believed, also, that it would be possible to continue the wartime alliance of Britain, the United States and the Soviet Union, with the eventual addition of France, to serve this end. The scales fell swiftly from his eyes, as Stalin proved obdurate in argument and tightened his grip on the nations of Eastern Europe. He became convinced that the USSR posed a serious military threat to Western Europe, and that it was therefore necessary for the United States to maintain a defence force on the European continent, for it was only the Americans who could provide the muscle to resist any Soviet thrust. His concern was that substantial sections of American public opinion, convinced that their country's job had ended with the defeat of Hitler, wished to bring their forces home. He and Attlee feared that Truman would be succeeded by an isolationist President.[54]

The question was how a defensive shield could be erected, and how the Americans could be bound to Britain and Europe with hoops of steel. The matter became urgent in 1948 because of events in Germany. The conquered city of Berlin had been divided for purposes of administration between the USSR, the United States, the United Kingdom and France. But the city lay well behind Russian lines, deep in the territory of what was to become the German Democratic Republic. Stalin decided to seal all road access to Berlin. The Americans were uncertain what to do.

Bevin persuaded them to organise, in conjunction with Britain, the now legendary Berlin Airlift. It was made quite clear to the Russians that any attack on planes flying supplies into Berlin would be met by counter-attack. After some months Stalin gave way, but this exercise of power convinced all the Western Allies that the USSR did indeed pose a threat to the freedom of Western Europe and the Blockade was therefore instrumental in concentrating minds. Minds being concentrated, the hitherto tricky negotiations on the creation of a Western military alliance were speeded up, and resulted in the creation of the North Atlantic Treaty Organisation. Bevin persuaded first France and Belgium, and then Canada and the United States to join him in the creation of NATO, with a headquarters in Brussels, and a Supreme Commander who would always be American (but whose Deputy would be chosen in turn from the other participating powers). Thus, on 4 April 1949, the defence of the West was institutionalised by the signing of the North Atlantic Treaty.

Behind Bevin, however, there was always the steadfast and powerful figure of Clement Attlee. Attlee was underrated when he became Prime Minister. His reputation grew steadily after his retirement, and then declined somewhat. There is no question in my mind, however, that he was one of the greatest Prime Ministers of the century. It is ironic, however, that a government which came to power on a programme essentially domestic had its most dramatic successes in foreign policy and, in its domestic policies, sewed economic dragon's teeth for the future. Given that the senior ministers in the government of 1945 had served in the wartime coalition government, and then in a peacetime government which confronted huge problems, both at home and abroad, with resolution and no little skill, it is hardly surprising that by 1950 they were exhausted. The following year the Conservative Party was returned to power, to rule for thirteen years.

CHAPTER TWO

The Consensus at Work
(1951–1955)

Even with the combined benefits of hindsight and of contemporary diaries and papers, it is hard to appreciate how shattering was the blow inflicted on the Conservative Party at the hands of the electorate in 1945. It seemed inconceivable to most Conservatives – and even to many Labour supporters – that the British people would turn out of office the man who had been their inspiration and the embodiment of their will for the five years of his leadership. Beyond that, however, the task facing the Labour opposition was statistically enormous: in the event, they were to record the largest swing against a government since records had begun. It is, of course, impossible to make an exact comparison of figures between 1945 and the previous General Elections going back to 1924.

That year saw a comfortable Conservative victory, but it was succeeded, first by a minority Labour government following the General Election of 1929 and then by the break-up of the Labour Party and the creation of a National government following the financial crash of 1931. This government, though dominated numerically by Conservative members, had as Prime Minister the Labour Leader, J. Ramsay Mac-Donald.[1] Infirmity caused MacDonald's resignation in June 1935 when he was succeeded by Baldwin. Although the rump of the Labour Party who had refused to serve in the National government made a remarkable recovery in the General Election of November 1935, the Conservatives remained in power with a comfortable majority and, from 28 May 1937, a new Prime Minister, Neville Chamberlain. Because of all these changes, and the swings of allegiance which accompanied them, it is impossible to make direct comparisons between the success of the Conservatives in 1935 with that of Labour in 1945. Suffice it to say that the enormity of the task faced by the party led by Clement Attlee in 1945 can be appreciated only when one bears constantly in mind the divisions which had racked Labour from the time of the formation of the first (minority) Labour government in 1924. An appreciation of the extent of Labour's recovery from all its earlier divisions added to Conservative depression when the party was beaten by a Labour majority of 146.

However, Attlee and his colleagues had several advantages which their rivals did not appreciate. In 1940 Winston Churchill was able, as his predecessor had not been, to form a genuine National government for the prosecution of the war. He was determined that it should be National and belief in the genuineness of his determination enabled him to bring Attlee and the senior Labour leaders into his Cabinet and the lower reaches of the government.[2]

They served efficiently and, in the main, loyally. As a consequence, by the end of the war, the electorate knew that senior members of the Labour Party had contributed mightily to the progress and consumma- tion of a victorious war – one which had begun with the real possibility that Britain might be overwhelmed. Hitherto – and given the failure of pre-war Labour governments – it had been a potent weapon of Conservative propaganda to contend that the vision represented by British Labour was a foolish and even malign one; whereas the Conservatives were the party of efficient and good government. It was impossible to pretend, at the end of the conflict, that such as Clement Attlee, Ernest Bevin, Stafford Cripps, Arthur Greenwood, Herbert Morrison and others were people into whose hands it was unsafe to entrust the future of the nation. Yet, Churchill and the Conservative Party were foolish enough during the 1945 campaign to try to frighten the nation with the prospect of a Labour government. There were many examples of a propagandistic and tactical style which has not infre- quently served the Conservative Party well. But the most notorious example of the employment of an argument at once demeaning and unbelievable was that of Churchill himself. As always throughout his political life, Churchill reacted to a fight with gusto and was more often than not inclined to abandon wise judgement.

On 4 June 1945 he was due to make (on radio) the party political broadcast which was to be the centrepiece of his election campaign. The script, written with the collaboration and under the influence of Beaver- brook, was ready on 3 June. He showed it to his wife and daughter. Clementine Churchill begged him to cut out his harsher references to the Labour Party.[3] After further consultation with Beaverbrook, however, the Prime Minister yielded to the advice of his old friend – who was, after all, both a great journalist and the creator of a great and immensely popular newspaper, the *Daily Express*. This is what he said:

No Socialist Government conducting the entire life and industry of the country could afford to allow free, sharp, or violently-worded expressions of public discontent. They would have to fall back on some form of Gestapo, no doubt very humanely directed in the first instance. And this would nip opinion in the bud; it would stop criticism as it reared its head, and it would gather all the power to the supreme party and the party leaders, rising like stately pinnacles above their vast bureaucracies of Civil Servants, no longer servants and no longer civil. And where would the ordinary simple folk – the common people as they like to call them in America – where would they be, once this mighty organism had got them in its grip?

The comparison of the party of men who had served patriotically with him through five years of war with the Gestapo was not merely in bad taste: it was unacceptable to the electorate, and suggested that Churchill and the Conservative Party had served their purpose. [4]

Rhetorical errors in the Conservative campaign were, however, though important – they attracted all the news coverage – far from the whole story. Here we come to Attlee's second great advantage. It was the popular belief that the Labour Party had captured the spirit of the times, and were in tune with the aspirations of the people. There had been hard times in the 1930s, and for these the Conservative Party was blamed. The Labour politicians who had joined in the National government of 1931 had all departed the scene and their record did not sully the escutcheon which Clement Attlee wore into battle. The proven competence of the leaders of the Labour Party encouraged the belief that a new social world could be brought into life. Many older voters, moreover, remembered the promises of David Lloyd George after the First World War that the government which he headed would 'build a land fit for heroes to live in'. They also remembered, bitterly, how their hopes were blasted. The dominant element in the coalition government which won a massive victory in the 1918 general election was Conservative; and that was not forgotten either. [5] The impulse in 1945, therefore, was to give a new party a try, particularly given the ameliorative character of the social aspirations of that party. [6] Following their defeat the Conservatives did exactly what every democratic party which receives a trouncing in a General Election but which wishes, nonetheless, to return to power, does. They began to imitate the victors. There had, after all, been a good deal of work on post-war reconstruction done by Labour and Conservative politicians working together from 1942 onwards. On this material R. A. Butler and his supporters seized between 1945 and 1951. [7]

It thus came about that when Churchill returned to power in 1951 certain assumptions were common to both parties. The 1951 victory (which followed the near victory in the General Election of 1950 when an exhausted Labour Party saw its massive plurality reduced to a mere 16 seats) inaugurated a period of substantial consensus on philosophy and policy between the two parties. I believe Mr Howard[8] is correct when he observes that a great deal of Butler's work was cosmetic rather than fundamental. But the fact of the matter remains that, once in office again, the Conservative Party concentrated on administering the system which they inherited with efficiency and did not seek in any fundamental way to reverse what Labour had done. Certainly, a number of economic controls on the citizen were abolished: but the Labour government had begun that process itself. Certainly, the steel industry was denationalised. Certainly, the proportion of national income taken by the State was to be reduced. For the most part, however, the parties remained in no more than tactical disagreement until the mid-1960s.

It has already been mentioned[9] that Churchill had a lifelong liking for coalitions. He exerted every effort to hold the wartime coalition together until at least the fall of Japan and pointed out in his memoirs that, having been first a Tory, then a Liberal and then a Tory again, he could hardly be described as a party man.[10] Indeed, there is hardly any time in Churchill's career, with the possible exception of his challenge to the MacDonald government over the question of independence for India, when he would not have joined a coalition whoever headed it.

With this attachment to the idea of coalition went certain views about the structure of government. In the creation of the 1951 Cabinet he was influenced both by his notions about administration and by his experience of governing in wartime. Churchill's wartime method had been to operate with an Inner Cabinet, but also to group departments outside the Cabinet under the hegemony of senior Ministers, and he tried to employ this method again in his first peacetime government. This is the way in which every British coalition has operated since the beginning of the First World War. Although the 1951–55 government was a successful one, its administrative methods did not survive. There was, further, his liking for having non-political, or virtually non-political Ministers in government. There was a strange, and rather piquant, contrast between Churchill's ferocity in political debate, especially during election campaigns, and his constant and often anxious search for conciliation in government.

There were no fewer than seven peers in the 1951 Cabinet.[11] Of these only two, Lord Woolton and the Marquis of Salisbury, could be said to have been politically experienced, and Woolton's experience dated back only to the 1945 General Election. Earl Alexander of Tunis, the former commander of British forces in North Africa and Italy, went to Defence.[12] Lord Ismay, formerly Churchill's Chief of Staff and a general, became head of the Commonwealth Relations Office. The Pay-master-General, with a wide-ranging brief to interfere with government departments, was Professor F. A. Lindemann, who was elevated to the Lords as Viscount Cherwell.[13] Lord Leathers was named as Minister for Co-ordination of Transport, Fuel and Power.

Although the number of peers at the very peak of government caused a certain amount of anxiety to the House of Commons and the public alike, the anxiety was not extravagant since, given the mores of the day, the presence of peers in a Cabinet was not thought unusual or something which should excite protest. Concern about the appointments was related, nonetheless, to a more general worry about the composition of the government. It was rightly felt that the most senior Ministers had worked particularly hard in the war. Certainly, they had had the chance to recharge their batteries between 1945 and 1951, but they were still by now six years older and, with the possible exception of R. A. Butler, the new Chancellor of the Exchequer, there was no fresh young blood in the higher reaches of the government. The (probably unconscious) reason for this seems to be that Churchill, seventy-eight by the time he returned to office, preferred to surround himself with familiar faces and did not want to take the trouble to make new acquaintances.[14] In general, the 1951 government was an administrative mess, and Alexander and Ismay, in particular, were hopeless at their jobs: both men being soldiers they had little taste for the political world. Lindemann, eschewing the wider responsibilities which he was supposed to discharge, set himself the sole aim of fulfilling one of his most cherished ambitions, the creation of a United Kingdom Atomic Energy Authority: in this he succeeded.[15]

The economic situation which the Churchill government inherited was not parlous merely, but extremely dangerous. Butler has told us[16] that he did not expect to be Chancellor of the Exchequer, and that he had thought Churchill would appoint Eden, who was anxious to obtain ministerial experience on the domestic front. Eden was Churchill's pre-sumed, and virtually anointed, heir, and he was acutely conscious of his total lack of domestic experience.[17] In retrospect, Butler's fear that he would not achieve the office for which he felt admirably suited, and that that job would go to Eden, seems preposterous. Churchill himself had been a long-serving Chancellor of the Exchequer, and was in a position shrewdly to appreciate Eden's economic illiteracy. Butler's underlying conviction was not merely based on his appreciation of Eden's known desire to move from the Foreign Office, but upon a belief that Churchill despised him. The reason for this was that when, in 1941, the Prime Minister offered him the Presidency of the Board of Education (later to be the Department of Education) the offer was made almost in a spirit of apology. Churchill could not believe that any talented Minister would willingly accept a job which did not directly involve him in the war effort. Butler, far from being reluctant, expressed eagerness to take on the Board; and the Prime Minister was somewhat shocked. In the event, Butler produced a major reform of the schools system in Britain.[18] However, Churchill knew high talent when he saw it; he was aware of the dangerous economic waters that lay ahead; and he was convinced that Butler was the man to navigate them.[19]

For the most part Butler was given as much authority in the economic field as he had enjoyed when reformulating Conservative policy during the Attlee years, and to assist him he had Sir Arthur Salter, a former Oxford Professor of Economics and the Prime Minister's favourite economist.[20] On the positive side, and before tackling the economy, Butler was able to draw on the work he had done in opposition, when he had set out to achieve two things. The first was to bring into the service of the Conservative Party highly intelligent young people with an appetite for philosophising about post-war policy. The second was to devise a series of what he called 'charters' on every major subject of policy. There was a charter on economics; a charter on industrial relations; a charter on Welsh affairs; a charter on Scottish affairs, and many others. Although it can be questioned how fundamental Butler's review of party policy was, it was an indisputable fact that the charters gave the Conservatives a modern image which was of great use to them in the general elections of 1950, 1951 and 1955. In 1955, for the first and last time since the war, the Tory party won a majority of seats in Scotland. This was due in very large measure to the sense of hope which Butler's work engendered. In 1951 it seemed unlikely that the elderly gentlemen who led the Conservative party could create a feeling of the possibility of a better future similar to that which Labour had excited in 1945[21] Nonetheless, and largely as a result of Butler's work, in 1951 the Conservatives did it. It is a striking fact that so much was owed in terms of popular success by the Conservative Party to a man who was remote, intellectual and diffident.

Throughout his long career, in which he held, at one time or another, every senior ministerial post save that of Prime Minister, Butler could never command enthusiasm from a public audience. He was, however, a masterly speaker in the House of Commons, and he needed to be, given the situation he faced after the General Election of 1951.[22] 'Finance, of course, at the moment overshadows everything,' said Harry Crookshank to the House of Commons on 13 November 1951. 'We are in a desperately serious position.' As Dr Anthony Seldon says, 'He was not exaggerating'.[23] The dollar deficit – that is, essentially, the amount of money the United Kingdom owed to the United States which had to be paid in dollars not sterling – was expected between 1951 and 1952 to amount to $500 million. The balance of payments deficit was standing at £375 million. The Treasury was wrong about the dollar deficit: two months after the election Treasury civil servants reckoned that the deficit would be $1200 million. Moreover, the 1951 Conservative Party manifesto stated an ambition not merely to repair, but to improve, the social provisions made by the Attlee government. So grave was his view of the situation after he had seen Butler's summary of what he had found at the Treasury, that Churchill was moved to write privately to Attlee enclosing a copy of a report brought to him at his London home by Sir Edward Bridges and Sir Norman Brook[24] – a most unusual step for a Prime Minister newly in office to adopt toward the Leader of the Opposition. His object was to try to ensure that the Opposition would sustain rather than hinder the government in the measures it felt necessary to take to rescue the nation from its difficulties. Attlee behaved as Churchill wished.[25] The spirit of the wartime coalition had not altogether died, although parliamentary clashes between the two main parties had often been virulent during the years since 1945. The serious nature of the country's plight, however, was apparent to all. Butler later said that he and his officials foresaw a greater crisis than that of 1931, the worst year of the great Depression. The Treasury believed that the country was 'heading for early bankruptcy unless immediate remedies were employed'.[26]

Butler was very lucky, however, in his civil service team. The Permanent Secretary, Sir Edward Bridges,[27] was a tower of strength for the four years during which Butler held the most difficult of all ministerial appointments save that of Prime Minister. It was inescapable that the first measures to be taken would be to reduce public expenditure, and the postponement of all social schemes promised in the Conservative manifesto. In addition, Butler raised the Bank Rate from 2 per cent to $2\frac{1}{2}$ per cent: this was a severe shock to Conservatives who, as so often in the past as well as in the future, expected sunlight and success to attend the mere arrival of a Conservative government. Butler had, in fact, wanted to administer the even more severe shock of raising the bank rate to 4 per cent. He did not take this draconian – as it was considered in those days – measure until the 1952 Budget. Further, acting under the powers which a Chancellor enjoys between Budgets, he cut overseas expenditure by £350 million. Further still, the overseas travel allowance – a hangover from the war – was cut in half to £50 per person per annum.

It was not appreciated in the 1950s, and was not appreciated until the 1980s, how long it takes such fiscal measures to work through into the economy.[28] Butler himself was, according to his biographer,[29] 'dispirited' in his first months at the Treasury. Nonetheless, he determined to pursue the policy of austerity which he considered to be the best available to him. Adding to his woes was the fact that, though the Prime Minister agreed with him in principle about the nature of the challenge that the government faced, Churchill nonetheless insisted that one new spending programme was sacrosanct. This was the undertaking to build 300,000 houses a year which had arisen as a consequence of an almost unique incident in the history of the Conservative Party – at the 1950 Party Conference a motion from the floor was carried against the wishes of the leadership. It sought to bind the leadership when and if the Conservatives returned to power to build 300,000 publicly-funded houses a year. The high figure was, of course, not due solely to a population explosion, though the population was steadily rising, but to the consequences of war damage. Under impulsive pressure from Macmillan, the Party Chairman, Lord Woolton, instantly rose and accepted the motion. The following year, after Churchill's General Election victory, he sent for Macmillan and in offering him the post of Minister of Housing gave him the task of fulfilling the commitment. The two men had been close allies in Churchill's pre-war campaign against appeasement. Subsequently he served in North Africa as a Minister with Cabinet rank and, essentially, as Liaison Officer between the various allied forces assembled in that theatre. Here he won golden opinions and made a deep impression on Churchill. When asked what help he would require with the housing programme, apart from money, Macmillan requested only his old friend, Sir Percy Mills, the chairman of a large and highly successful building company, as his assistant at the Department. Before Churchill retired Macmillan had achieved his target.[30]

The strange, and in many ways sad, thing about Butler as Chancellor of the Exchequer was that he knew that the problems which he faced were imponderable. In his inner mind he knew, also, that he was the man to solve them. But, from the beginning to the end of his political career, from being a Parliamentary Under Secretary at the India Office, to being Chancellor of the Exchequer, and thrice – in 1954,[31] 1957 and 1963 candidate for the Leadership of the Conservative Party – he lacked that aggression, whether subtle like Macmillan in 1957 or open like Mrs Thatcher in 1974, which is required to provide a real leader. Butler regretted, in later years, that he had not had the conviction nor the courage to float the pound in 1952.[32] The fact of the matter, in my judgement, is that Butler was a supreme technician of government, with a kind heart and a clean soul, an enormous capacity for work but no compelling ambition.

In his first speech to the House after the General Election the Prime Minister laid the grim facts before the members:

> In overseas payments we are in a deficit crisis worse than 1949, and in many ways worse than even 1947.[33] Confidence in sterling is impaired. In the present half-year, we are running into external deficit at the rate of 700m. a year, compared with an annual rate of surplus of about 350m. in the same period a year ago. That means a deterioration of more than 1000m. a year. The latest estimates show that in 1952, on present trends and policies and without making any allowance for further speculative losses, the United Kingdom would have a deficit on its general balance of overseas payments of between 500m. and 600m., and the loss to the central gold and dollar reserves in the transactions of the sterling area as a whole with the rest of the world might be appreciably more.[34]

Of course, in later years, Britain became, if not happy with, at least accustomed to, much greater deficits than Churchill had to tackle in 1951. Moreover, it is important to remember that inflation was a negligible part of economic activity in 1951. It was not until public spending got increasingly out of hand from the late 1950s onwards that the national economy got into as dangerous a situation as that of the immediate post-war years. Churchill's difficulties were compounded by the existence of the sterling area. In simple essence, the sterling area consisted of the Empire and the Commonwealth. Even if a Commonwealth country – like Canada, for example – had a denominated currency of its own, its value was fixed, by agreement with the Bank of England, in terms of sterling. This system did not work too badly as long as the United Kingdom was dealing with the stable economies of the old Empire, such as Canada, Australia and New Zealand. It was to go seriously awry as African and Asian colonies gained their independence, printed their own currencies and still had to be sustained by the Bank of England. The system was finally brought to end by the Heath government in 1971.

Easier though the burden of the sterling area was in 1951 compared to later, it was nonetheless a not insignificant addition to Churchill's problems. For a time Butler contemplated the dissolution of the area by floating the pound. In general it can be said that a floating currency relieves a central bank, such as the Bank of England, of responsibility. Until 1971 the British government of the day was obliged – albeit with certain qualifications – to shore up other currencies, however irresponsible the governments of the area were, at the ultimate expense of the British taxpayer. When a currency is floated its value is determined by the market. Thus, a multitude of transactions take place. It is true that a central bank may from time to time find it desirable to support the value of its own currency, which it does by buying it in. This, of course, has to be done by using another currency, which must be, in the parlance of the banking world, 'hard'. The distinction between a 'hard' currency and a 'soft' currency is that the former is acceptable in trade worldwide, while the latter is not. The best known example, today, of a hard currency is the German mark, and the best known example of a soft currency is the Russian rouble. The mark is acceptable everywhere, the rouble now only in the former Soviet Union. It follows that countries with a soft currency are desperate to acquire hard currencies. They do this either by a barter system or through tourism.[35]

Butler's temptation to float the pound, though he did not yield to it, was nonetheless indicative of one of the policies most central to the government's thinking. Envious eyes were being cast at the Federal Republic of Germany, where the finance minister, Dr Ludwig Erhard, had dismantled most of the economic controls imposed by the Allied Powers at the end of the war and had produced a remarkable economic boom. The theory of free-market economics dictates that the fewer centrally-imposed controls there are on an economy and the lower personal taxation is, the more quickly an economy can grow. Thus it was that the Attlee government had already begun to dismantle the system of controls set up during the war: its most famous, and most welcome, decision was to abolish most food rationing. The Churchill government took this whole process much farther. Indeed, of all post-war governments, that of 1951–55 took in taxation the smallest percentage of Gross National Income. The boom that ran from 1951 to 1960, with a hiccup between 1954 and 1956, was directly attributable to the decisions taken by Churchill.[36]

However, there was a corollary to the freeing of the market and the lowering of taxation, which was to sow dragon's teeth which were harvested in the 1960s and the 1970s. The Churchill government continued the Attlee policy of according to the trade union movement a privileged position in the British economy. Churchill himself had a somewhat romantic view of trade unionists, fostered by the close relationship he had developed from 1940 with Ernest Bevin. (It is also worth remembering that, in alliance with David Lloyd George, Churchill set up the first system of unemployment benefit in 1912.) Butler was later to recall his extreme irritation and concern with Churchill's propensity to settle trade union disputes without reference to the Chancellor which, of course, frequently disrupted the even tenor of Butler's economic policy.[37]

Having eschewed the more daring economic measures available to him, Butler became a cheese-paring Chancellor. It might be more accurate, however, to refer to another metaphor he liked to deploy. This was his self-description as a 'candle-end' Chancellor, which was a reference to Edward Goschen, who was Gladstone's Chancellor in the nineteenth century. Goschen once said that if people saved all their candle ends and melted them down they could make new candles from them. This homely metaphor illustrated a Treasury policy which was governed not by grand initiatives, but by good housekeeping.[38]

According to his biographer,[39] Butler was the most 'circumscribed' of Chancellors. In whichever direction he chose to move he met opposition from Cabinet colleagues, which opposition gained the support of the Prime Minister. To take what might seem to be a trivial issue, which was nonetheless indicative, the Cabinet vetoed his proposal to reduce the sweet ration from six to four ounces a week. The 1952 Budget, of necessity, had to be a harsh one. Just before it was presented Butler delivered a radio broadcast in which he repeated, and embellished, the metaphor he had used before. 'We really are up against it,' he said, 'our life-blood is draining away, and we have to stop it.' Butler was always a master of prestidigitation and, in the midst of his troubles, he fell upon a proposal by Sir George Bolton, a director of the Bank of England. Bolton's plan had two parts.[40] The first was to float the pound, the second was to render overseas deposits held in sterling fully convertible, up to 90 per cent of their value, into dollars. The plan – codeword 'Operation Robot', because it was supposed to relieve the Treasury of the responsibility of manipulating the value of the pound virtually day by day – excited the hostility of most of the Cabinet. One can only speculate about the precise reasoning of Cabinet members, notably Churchill and Crookshank, but my own belief is that what influenced opposition to the Chancellor was the feeling on the part of older Cabinet members, from the Prime Minister down, that dependence on the dollar represented an unacceptable humiliation for the United Kingdom and the British Empire. We must return again[41] to the matter of the age and experience of the Cabinet. At forty-eight in 1951, Butler was its youngest member. The average age of the Cabinet was sixty-two: the Prime Minister was seventy-eight years of age. Butler's Cabinet colleagues had, therefore, an experience of life very different from his own. They had been brought up in, trained in, and led to believe in, the absolute solidity of British power, and the unshakeable strength of sterling. It was hard indeed for them to accept that sterling had to be valued not on its own merits but in terms of the American dollar. It is ironic that all of these men were emotionally – perhaps sentimentally – pro-American; but they did not want their national currency to be valued in American terms. This was the tragic period in which the government of the United Kingdom quite simply failed to come to terms with the country's reduced status in the world. There is a plangent note to the debates and discussions of the time. One has, reading the memoirs of the period, a consciousness of men who could not recognise that their time had passed.

Butler arrived at his conclusions about sterling, and about Britain's place in the world by a different route. His childhood and youth in India[42] led him to sympathise deeply with the desire of the people of the subcontinent for independence: this was not a sympathy readily shared by his older Cabinet colleagues. The sympathy he had with the Indian people led him, in later years, to a similar feeling for the peoples of Britain's African colonies. Between 1951 and 1955 the fact that he had no particular regard for an empire in which Britain was dominant led him to conclude that there was nothing wrong with sterling becoming dependent upon the dollar. What to colleagues was an unbearable subjugation, to Butler was a simple necessity of life. Except in the most generalised and ameliorative of ways Butler had no political philosophy. What he had – and what proved invaluable to the 1951 government – was his immense capacity for detailed work. Butler's difficulties were essentially those of personality. He was able to get George Bolton's plans for convertibility through the Cabinet, but unable to implement the first part which involved floating the pound. Greatly to Bolton's disgruntlement, he did not even fight for the float – he gave way as soon as he saw that the opposition to the plan was substantial, even if intellectually inchoate. At no point in his career did Butler ever seem to realise how much power he had, and how much support he commanded. 'That Butler is mystifying, complex and sometimes hard to approach I would concede', Iain Macleod wrote in the *Spectator* on 18 February 1964, 'but, on the other hand, he has the priceless quality of being able to do any job better than you think he will, and of attracting to himself wide understanding support from many people outside the Tory Party.' The thing that Butler's supporters invariably found frustrating was his unwillingness to fight either for a cause or, more basely, for himself. That he was a superb administrator is beyond doubt. He could not have achieved the turn-around in the British economy between 1951 and 1954 shortly to be described without the superb skills of management with which he was endowed. Writing of the period when Butler, still Chancellor of the Exchequer, was also looking after the Prime Minister's Office, the Foreign Office and various other matters, Enoch Powell wrote:

> In the end he was a horse for all work, and one of immense pulling-power. I have put on record before, that, such was his capacity for the sheer dispatch of business, that once during a brief indisposition, when David Kilmuir replaced him in the chair of the key Home Affairs Committee of the Cabinet, it felt just as if the clock of government itself had stopped. It was this quality of incomparable competence which convinces Cosgrave now, as in 1963 it convinced not only Macleod and me but others who did not put their judgement to the touch, that, if he had become Prime Minister then, he would have won the 1964 election for the Conservative Party and given it new life afterwards.[43]

Butler, for all that he was hemmed in by domestic spending demands, had at least one advantage: the Prime Minister had decided to devote most of his still very considerable energy to matters of defence and foreign policy. As the life of the 1951 government unfolded, however, Churchill's powers began to fail, and his interventions on economic matters became less frequent. As the time for a General Election approached, knowing that he could not conceive of leading the party again, he concentrated every ounce of his energy on securing the agreement of Stalin and President Eisenhower to hold a summit conference with disarmament as its main subject. He was much attracted by the idea that he, the great war leader, should crown his political life with a striking act of peace. At the Bermuda Conference with the Americans and the French in December 1953, Churchill pressed his case hard, but both Eisenhower and, thousands of miles away, Stalin were suspicious of one another. Churchill had suffered a stroke the previous June – the third in a series – and in 1954 his physical strength having greatly declined, he decided privately to abandon his great hope of *détente* and retire the following year.

The great years of Butler's economic achievement were those between 1951 and 1954. The struggle to turn the economy round after the 1951

General Election was certainly a serious one. At the end of January 1952, Butler made a statement to the House which expressed both fears about the future and his own personal apprehension at the possibility that the British economy was in terminal decline. However, the favourable response to his first Budget in 1952 – one which combined further cuts in public expenditure with a lightening of the burden of direct taxation, both on individuals and, more importantly, on business – suggested that a corner had been turned. Almost immediately the drain on the reserves (essentially money held by the Bank of England) stopped. There was little doubt that Butler's calm, his honesty about the situation, and his steadfastness in the face of pressure contributed greatly to public confidence. At the Conservative Party Conference in Scarborough in 1952 he made it clear that there would be no relaxation of the tight policy he had adopted. 'We have got to keep up the pressure,' he said, 'we cannot relax.' This, for all its gloom, was probably the most successful speech Butler ever made to a Tory Party Conference. He was fortunate in that his patient exposition of the nature of the difficulties which lay ahead was fully understood by an audience willing, like the public at large, to accept that austerity was the necessary order of the day. But one should also understand the quality of Butler's achievement in compounding his policies. In later years a view became widespread that he was no communicator: indeed, one of the reasons Macmillan gave for opposing Butler's succession to himself in 1963 was the conviction that Butler could not get through to the electorate in what had to be an imminent General Election. The years following 1951 demonstrated that the British public could understand and accept even the driest and most technical of economic arguments provided they were expressed with honesty and elegance.

By the end of 1952 all the economic indicators were improving. The balance of payments was reasonably healthy. Incomes were rising, slowly but in real terms. Productivity was going up, and opinion cautiously came to hold that the British economy was well on the road to recovery. It was still to be a difficult road, for the patient was convalescent but not recovered and convalescence is always uncertain.

As time wore on from Butler's cautious Budget of 1952 there loomed over the political scene the question of when Churchill would retire. The two dominant politicians of the time were Eden and Butler. It had been assumed for quite some time that Eden would succeed Churchill. There were, however, those who believed that Butler was the better man, and, although an outsider, it was not impossible that he could be chosen under the arcane system prevailing at the time by which Leaders of the

Conservative Party 'emerged'.[44] The doubts about Eden centred around both his inexperience and his temperament. The contrast between the two men was intelligently expressed by Lord Moran in his diary entry for 8 August 1953:

> Lunched at Chequers. Rab Butler and Salisbury there. Butler, like an Asquith, is rather too impatient with pedestrian folk. He has more staying power than Anthony, but at present he lacks what people call the 'common touch'. They complain, too, that he will back a horse both ways. He seems none the worse for the grind while the P.M. and Anthony were away ill. He does not get worked up like Anthony. Of course, he is aware of the danger of racing the engine, but he says he has 'a normal family life and does not feel the strain'.[45]

For Eden, when Churchill decided to retire, there was the fact that he was glamorous. For Butler was the fact that he was immensely efficient. Against Eden was the fact that he was inclined to fits of temper, particularly on subjects which he knew little about. Against Butler was the fact that, as Moran says, he seemed unable to develop a 'common touch'. It is fair to say that, while Butler could have mounted a challenge to Eden in 1955, Eden remained the favourite. Apart from the fact that he was married to Churchill's niece, he had other claims to the succession to the great war leader. He had stoutly opposed the appeasement policy of Neville Chamberlain before the war. He had been, at 36, the youngest Foreign Office Minister of Cabinet rank that the country had ever known. Though theoretically subordinate to the Foreign Secretary, Sir John Simon, Eden had a reasonably free hand in his particular area of responsibility, relations with the League of Nations. When, in 1935, Simon was moved to the Home Office, Eden had every expectation of succeeding him. However, the post of Foreign Secretary went to Sir Samuel Hoare, Eden being mollified by being given full Cabinet rank. Hoare did not, however, last long. Mussolini having invaded Abyssinia, France and Britain decided to impose oil sanctions on Italy. But Hoare and the French Foreign Minister, Pierre Laval, without the approval of either government, entered into a pact, which, in essence, gave Mussolini all he wanted. Indignation in Britain was so great that Hoare was forced to resign and Eden succeeded him. However, in 1938, finding himself increasingly disenchanted with the policy of appeasement of Germany and the new Prime Minister, Neville Chamberlain's, increasing arrogation of authority over foreign policy to himself, Eden resigned, and thus became a hero to a substantial section of the Conservative Party.

During the war itself, he had first served as Secretary for War and, subsequently, as Foreign Secretary.

Butler, on the other hand, in Churchill's eyes, and in the eyes of most of the senior members of the Conservative Party, was suspect. His instinctive sympathy with pre-war moves for Indian independence was a cause to which Churchill, in the pre-war years, was implacably opposed: he resigned from the Conservative front bench in 1932 because Stanley Baldwin accepted the inevitability of independence for the subcontinent. Butler had been a junior minister in the Foreign Office during the years of appeasement and in 1939 engaged in somewhat indiscreet talks with the Swedish Ambassador to London in order to try to make a peaceful settlement with Nazi Germany. This did not endear him to Churchill.[46] However, Churchill took the view when he became Prime Minister that a sponge should be passed over the blackboard of those who were, in the pre-war years, weak in their attitude to Germany. In 1941 Churchill, engaged in a ministerial reshuffle, had expected Butler to ask for a job either at the Ministry of War or the Foreign Office and seemed surprised when Butler accepted with enthusiasm the Presidency – as it was then called – of the Board of Education.[47] Having come from an academic family, Butler was particularly fascinated by the task of reforming British schools along the lines recommended by the 1942 Post-War Reconstruction Committee.

Eden became increasingly frustrated at Churchill's unwillingness to retire. But Churchill was not happy with Eden either. He took the view – and events proved him to be correct – that Eden had a somewhat unstable personality. It is perfectly true to say that Churchill was determined to cling on to power as long as he possibly could, and Lord Moran goes into considerable detail about the various manoeuvres he made to postpone his retirement a for as long as possible.[48] Then again, from 1953 onwards Churchill's powers were steadily failing. Harry Crookshank recorded on 22 March 1954 that the Prime Minister was 'ga-ga'.[49] However, the Prime Minister enjoyed playing games with his potential successors. He would frequently promise to set a date for his retirement and then fail to fulfil the promise. On 19 March 1954, realising the tremendous pressure within the party and the government for him to resign, he was amused by the fact that no colleague had the face to tell him that it was time to leave. He told Moran, 'I'm going to resign at the end of June. They have all been so nice. That's what gets me. If they had attacked me, I could have snarled back.'[50] On 26 March 1954, in another conversation with Moran, he said: '. . . I don't know when I shall retire. I have to think of other people. It may sound egotistical, but I don't know what the boys will do when I go.'[51] More than a year later, not least as a result of representations by Harold Macmillan, he decided, on 5 April 1955, to abandon the post which he had sought so long and held so successfully. On that evening he gave his final dinner party at Number Ten, Downing Street. His guests were the Queen and Prince Philip. The following morning the Prince wrote to Clementine Churchill:

Dear Lady Churchill,

This is a most inadequate note of thanks for the perfectly delightful dinner.

It was such a friendly and happy occasion that I find it hard to realise that it must have been a rather sad moment for you both.

Yours sincerely,

Philip.

However, something else lay behind the conviviality of Churchill's farewell dinner and is best expressed in a moment which mixes comedy and first class political judgement. Churchill's devoted Private Secretary for many years, John (later Sir John) Colville, had been present at the dinner. When the Queen and the Prince departed, Colville records that he went up with Churchill to his bedroom;

He sat on his bed, still wearing his Garter, Order of Merit and knee breeches. For several minutes he did not speak and I, imagining that he was sadly contemplating that this was his last night in Downing Street, was silent. Then suddenly he stared at me and said with vehemence 'I don't believe Anthony can do it.'[52]

Eden had waited a long time for the succession, and Churchill had teased him unmercifully about his prospects though, in the event, when consulted by the Queen about who the successor should be, he gave only Eden's name. However, his reservations about the Foreign Secretary were made even more explicit to Charles Moran than they were to Colville. Moran records him as saying on 15 June 1954, when he was contemplating resignation in September of that year:

'It is not' – and his voice rose – 'as if I were making way for a strong young man. Anthony seems to be very tired. I detect strain in his telegrams. Sometimes he sends three thousand words in one day – and there is nothing in them.[53] . . . The Foreign Office keeps on splitting hairs. There is no-one to say: "Bloody well go and do it."[54]

Whatever Eden's weaknesses, however, there can be no doubt that indecision about Churchill's future bedevilled the government, possibly from late 1953, and certainly from early 1954 onwards. Quite apart from major questions of international relations, economic policy was allowed to drift. Moreover, as he strove to emerge from Churchill's shadow, Eden betrayed a very serious lack of self-confidence. But he was determined to prove himself. Thus, he was insistent on acquiring a parliamentary majority in his own right. This was not, strictly speaking, necessary. The Conservative majority was small but secure on account of divisions within the Labour Party – particularly because an ageing Attlee clung to the leadership solely in order to keep out his shadow Foreign Secretary, Herbert Morrison, and to encourage the ambitions of the young Hugh Gaitskell.

Eden's first letter to Churchill after he succeeded came from 10 Downing Street on 8 April. In it he told his predecessor and patron of his intention to call a general election on 26 May.[55] As well as wanting a majority in his own right, the financial position of the nation was again dangerous and, as he told Churchill, that was 'the disagreeable reality which pushes us towards a May election'. He won a majority of 58 over all other parties, and a plurality of 67 over Labour.

The new Prime Minister scarcely realised how dangerous things were; and what, in the nature of tragedy, lay ahead of him as he entered upon an inheritance that for so long had seemed to him so glittering, but was to end in personal and political disaster.

CHAPTER THREE

The First Break in the Consensus
(1955–1960)

The inheritance upon which Anthony Eden entered was, however, not a glittering one. He had prepared long and sedulously for his succession to Churchill. But, as already mentioned,[1] his experience in domestic affairs was negligible. The one great strength he was presumed to possess was his knowledge of, and his deftness in, the handling of foreign and defence policy. It was, therefore, the most remarkable aspect of a political career which ended in both personal and national tragedy that his downfall came about as a result of his ineptitude in the handling of a crisis in foreign affairs – the Suez War of 1956.

There were other factors involved in the downfall of Anthony Eden after so brief a period as Prime Minister. Not least among them was ill-health: he had several operations between 1951 and 1955, one of which was disastrously unsuccessful, due to a crucial mistake by the surgeon.[2] Constant physical pain aggravated a propensity to nervous excitement which Eden had, with a supreme effort of will, concealed throughout his time as Foreign Secretary. When the great crisis following Colonel Nasser's nationalisation of the Suez Canal fell upon him, his self-control cracked. He had neither the energy to satisfy himself that British forces were in place for a speedy attack on Egypt, nor the concentration to do what he had hitherto been best at – ensuring the maintenance of happy Anglo-American relations. In the event, it was the United States of America which foreclosed on the Suez War. Foreclosed is the precise word here, for it was the deliberate American creation of a run on the pound that made it impossible for the United Kingdom to sustain the financial burden of a war that would, of necessity, be protracted.

However, the dramatic nature of the circumstances attending Eden's fall, concerned as it was with a matter of foreign policy, had drawn attention away from the course on which he set British domestic – and specifically economic – policy during his brief administration.

Butler's success in steering the economy in 1954 concealed a fundamental structural weakness. Initially, after the 1955 General Election, Butler was retained as Chancellor, though Macmillan tells us that Eden had offered him the job.[3] Butler found that it was necessary, because of a balance of payments crisis, to introduce an emergency budget in the autumn of 1955. This was repugnant to the Prime Minister who, like Macmillan, was inclined invariably to react to economic crises by expansion of credit. The prudent Butler, who believed in the husbanding of resources, and the restriction of expansionary schemes which depended on borrowing, was now out of tune with the Prime Minister.

The early months of the Eden administration were not a happy period for Butler. Despite his success in economic management, the British economy had – though this was not generally recognised – entered into what later became known as the 'stop-go' cycle. He knew that Eden wanted to get rid of him, and he no longer found much satisfaction in his job. 'If I had been less scrupulous about the economy,' he wrote in his memoirs, 'I would have retired in May [of 1955].'[4] Eden finally made the change on 20 December 1955, having agreed to Macmillan's terms: that he should be in undisputed charge of all domestic policy, and therefore not in an inferior position to Butler, and that Butler should not enjoy the title of Deputy Prime Minister.[5]

There were several reasons for Eden's belief that Macmillan would suit him better as Chancellor than did Butler. The first was Macmillan's record as Minister of Housing in the 1951 government. In April 1955 Eden had sent Macmillan to the Foreign Office. His reasoning appears to have been that the North African experience had shown Macmillan to be highly skilled at the technical business of negotiation. At first, Eden had been tempted to remain Foreign Secretary when he became Prime Minister. The new Prime Minister concluded, however, that the task of running both the government and the Foreign Office was too great. But in Macmillan he had a man who was already a close ally – again, their relationship dated back to the pre-war period and their opposition to Neville Chamberlain. Eden believed, of course, that he would continue to control the strategy of foreign policy, which Macmillan would execute.

However, as the spring and summer wore on, his mind turned more to what Macmillan had achieved at the Ministry of Housing. He had never cared for Butler, who had gone uncomplainingly along with the policy of seeking peace with Germany on almost any terms.[6] While Churchill had always followed the doctrine of magnanimity which is inscribed on the opening page of each of the six volumes of his *History of the Second World War*, those, like Eden and Macmillan, who had been his lieutenants in preparing for that war did not have an equivalent generosity of mind. Churchill in 1940 was prepared to forgive and forget. He appointed appeasers to the coalition government on the grounds that national unity was more important than settling old scores. Eden did not feel the same way in 1955.

In his final speech as Chancellor, presenting the Autumn Budget of 1955, Butler had this to say:

> Do those who say that government expenditure could be drastically reduced propose a reversal of policy in education, or a cut in the cost of pensions? Or are we to hold up work on the roads? Perhaps I can answer by saying that in each of these spheres we have to do all we can to meet imperative needs – in the case of education, of a rising school population, in the case of the old, of an increased number of retired persons, and in the case of the roads, with a programme which I cannot increase but which is already insufficient to deal with the needs of the country.[7]

The trouble for Butler was, however, that his luck had run out and the darkening economic clouds hovered above his head. Moreover, while his technical skill was such that he could usually combine prudent management with generous spending, he was not in Macmillan's class as a politician who was prepared to risk inflation as a consequence of exceptionally high expenditure. It is always possible to use an expansion of credit to finance prosperity for a short period.[8] The Autumn Budget managed to offend almost everybody. Purchase tax, profit tax, and a cutback in local authority building all gave offence to middle-of-the-road and left-wing Conservatives – and, of course, the Labour Party was outraged. A central characteristic of Butler, however, was that he was never afraid to increase taxation when he judged it to be necessary to prevent overheating in the economy. Macmillan had no such scruples, as he was to demonstrate most dramatically in 1960, when as Prime Minister he accepted the resignation of all three Treasury Ministers after an argument over inflationary public spending. So far as Eden was concerned, however, Macmillan was, at the end of 1955, the ideal Chancellor. The new man was ever willing to spend his way out of trouble, and he did preside over an undreamt-of increase in national prosperity. What was not realised, except by a small group of economists of the persuasion nowadays dubbed 'monetarist', was that Macmillan had set in train policies that would lead, ultimately, to the massive inflation that beset

Britain from the 1960s onwards. Butler also gave offence to the early monetarists by his continued maintenance – exemplified in the quotation above – of high social spending. At the end of 1955, therefore, he had very few friends.

What Eden was looking for was rapid expansion, and he believed that Macmillan could give it to him, as indeed he did in his first budget in 1956. Although, of course, Eden had long left office by the time the consequences of his appointment of Macmillan were realised, he did, in his later years in retirement, seem to grasp the damage he had inflicted by his selection of the new Chancellor in 1955.[9]

The most extraordinary thing about Eden's brief period as Prime Minister, however, is not that he made mistakes in domestic policy – and domestic political appointments – but that he failed in foreign policy. A recurring theme of this book is the difficulty that the United Kingdom had in coming to terms with the close of its imperial history. Nonetheless, the management of that post-war and post-imperial period could, it seemed in 1955, be in no better hands than those of Sir Anthony Eden. After all, besides being the crown prince of the Conservative Party, Eden was a renowned specialist in foreign policy. Yet, in 1956, he plunged the government which he headed, and the nation, into the most disastrous foreign involvement since the war.

The Allied Powers had watched with mounting anxiety rapidly developing relations between the USSR and Egypt. On 26 July 1956 President Nasser of Egypt nationalised the Suez Canal Company. The Canal was an international waterway, mainly staffed by British and French technicians, and the Egyptian move, it was thought, would enable an ally of the Soviet Union to impose a stranglehold on world trade. After much prevarication, dithering and international negotiation an Anglo-French force sailed for Egypt to retake the Canal. France and Britain concluded a secret agreement with Israel, herself already worried by growing Egyptian power. Israel attacked her old enemy and Britain and France, under a hypocritical fig-leaf, claimed that their subsequent intervention, on 31 October 1956, was a means of separating the combatants rather than, as was Eden's intention, to bring down Nasser and repossess the Canal.

One of the reasons for the nationalisation of the Canal was an American decision, taken at the instigation of the Secretary of State, John Foster Dulles, to withdraw promised funds for a grandiose Egyptian project to irrigate Egyptian farmland by the building of the Aswan High Dam. Though the Americans therefore precipitated nationalisation they immediately denounced Britain and France in virulent terms. Because Britain's economic relations with the United States were very close and because sterling was a reserve currency, the United Kingdom was especially vulnerable to American hostility. (This did not apply to France, because the franc was not a reserve currency.) The Americans withdrew dollar credits and there was a potentially catastrophic run on the pound, as foreign investors from all over the world decided to sell sterling short, and the value of the pound plummeted.

Britain was deeply divided on the desirability of military action. Hugh Gaitskell, now leader of the Opposition, having initially supported the use of force, under severe pressure from his Party, which was determined not to countenance an attack on a Third World country, completely changed tack and launched an increasingly bitter series of denunciations of the government.[10] Macmillan had been an enthusiastic supporter of an assault on Egypt but, as he viewed the mounting economic crisis, he decided to insist on withdrawal. Butler, to mention a fact that was to have an important influence on the rest of his career, was sceptical throughout and did not conceal his scepticism. Withdrawal was agreed upon, somewhat to the chagrin of the French. Eden suffered a combined nervous and physical collapse.[11] Leaving Butler in charge of the government, he left for Jamaica to recuperate. Upon his return to London it was clear that, quite apart from his widespread unpopularity, he could not continue, and he resigned.

It was not until 1965 that a system of election of Conservative leader was devised. On this occasion, the Lord Chancellor, Lord Dilhorne, and a senior Conservative Minister, Lord Salisbury, who was much revered in the Party, undertook informal consultations both with MPs and with members of the House of Lords.[12] Eden was consulted by the Queen on the choice of his successor and, although the point has never been finally settled, it is generally believed that he recommended Macmillan. In any event, on 9 January 1957 Macmillan became Prime Minister. Peter Thorneycroft, the President of the Board of Trade, replaced him as Chancellor. Thorneycroft's junior Ministers were Nigel Birch and Enoch Powell. Throughout most of his career in senior office Macmillan showed himself to be a good picker of men, that is to say, he chose able Ministers who agreed with him. In the case of the Treasury trio, however, he blundered badly in this respect. The new Prime Minister was above all determined to keep control over the strategy and the details of economic policy himself, and to pursue the expansionary and inflationary policy which he had introduced in April 1956. His last important act as Chancellor was, on 11 December 1956, to organise through the Bank of England stand-by credit to shore up the pound. The principal source of credit was the United States. Of his two major tasks on taking office, the other being to repair the divisions within the Conservative Party, the restoration of good relations with Washington was a vital priority. In this initially difficult task Macmillan was greatly helped by the fact that he and President Eisenhower had become close friends in North Africa during the war, and the President, who had been re-elected with an overwhelming majority the previous October, and who was delighted with the ending of the Suez adventure, was only too pleased to help out the new British government.

When British troops withdrew from Egypt, Eden's authority was virtually non-existent and Gaitskell's extraordinarily high. Macmillan realised that, apart from anything else, it was necessary to instil a sense of well-being in the nation. The essential tool for creating the required mood was a popular economic policy. At cabinet level, of course, Macmillan had considerable difficulties. He decided to keep the Foreign Secretary who had served under Eden, Selwyn Lloyd, and persuaded Butler to serve as Home Secretary. He was fortunate in that both men were governmental workhorses. Lloyd had been deeply bruised by the experience of Suez, when he had served the Prime Minister with exceptional loyalty over a policy the merits of which he doubted.[13]

The new Chancellor of the Exchequer, Peter Thorneycroft, was, in due course, to reveal himself as an economist of rigour. For the moment, however, he accepted the overall requirements that Macmillan laid down – reconciliation with the United States, unity in the Tory Party, and the generation of prosperity. Macmillan had believed, from the period of economic depression in the thirties, in that combination of public expenditure and moderate taxation which I have described above.[14] Such a policy, of course, required increasing central control of general economic policy. He was determined, in essence, to be his own Chancellor of the Exchequer. Labouring under the belief, however, that the trade union movement had to be conciliated, rather than legislated against, he sought agreement between all the relevant corporate institutions of the state. To this end he set up on 12 August 1957, a Council on Prices Productivity and Incomes. This conciliatory body had almost no effect and was abolished by Macmillan in 1961. Thorneycroft was not averse to conciliation. He was not, further, averse to economic policies which might produce restraint on wage demands, if restraint could be procured.

However, the economic situation continued to deteriorate. On 19 September 1957 it was found necessary to raise Bank Rate to 7 per cent. The reason for this was a massive outflow of capital from the United Kingdom to foreign countries, which had prompted a sharp decline in the value of sterling.

During the following year the currency continued to decline in value. Further rises in Bank Rate had to be contemplated, but at the Treasury the view was that any measures ought to be taken if they were such as to stabilise the value of sterling. Macmillan nonetheless insisted that expanding public expenditure was necessary to produce economic recovery, both for social reasons and in order to win the forthcoming General Election. Thorneycroft and Nigel Birch, aided and abetted by the junior Treasury Minister, Enoch Powell, insisted that any and all measures to prevent fluctuations in the value of the currency should be taken. The Prime Minister had resisted for some time the plan to raise Bank Rate: in his memoirs he confessed regret for his resistance.[15] His main ambition was to go to the country in 1959, and he was utterly determined that anything that needed to be done to create even the illusion of prosperity should be done.

When the House rose on 2 August 1957 it was revealed that gold and dollar reserves had fallen by $14 million in the previous month. During August sustaining the value of sterling was to cost the Bank of England $400 million.[16]

The most critical period for budgetary policy begins when the House of Commons rises at Christmas and concludes when the Budget is prepared for delivery in March or April the following year. During this period spending departments negotiate with the Treasury on what their overall budget will be for the following year. By virtue of the laws of human nature, spending Ministers always want more than the Treasury is willing to allow them.[17] So far as Thorneycroft, Birch and Powell were concerned there were two ways of keeping the currency stable. One was to borrow on the international exchanges. To this idea they were resolutely opposed because they foresaw that the burden of debt over coming years would be intolerable. They therefore resorted to their preferred policy. This was to reduce public expenditure and, if necessary, to increase taxation. Neither a reduction of public expenditure nor an increase in taxation appealed to the Prime Minister. Reducing expenditure would lead to electoral unpopularity. Reducing taxation was almost an article of faith with Macmillan.[18] Even the Treasury Ministers did not seriously propose to increase personal taxation, which had been steadily declining since 1951. They opted, therefore, for reductions in public expenditure.

Between August 1957 and the beginning of 1958 the tussle between the Treasury and the spending Departments became increasingly tense, with the Prime Minister generally siding with the spending Departments. The Treasury Ministers, however, were convinced that a pro-

gramme of austerity was the only option open to the government – that is
to say they wanted substantially to cut public expenditure. Birch said as
much to his constituency on 5 October. Three days later Thorneycroft
repeated the message in a speech at the Mansion House. On 10 October,
at the Tory Party Conference in Brighton, Powell said it all again. For
the positive part of his message he emphasised all the reductions in
taxation which had been made since 1951. For the pessimistic part he
emphasised the necessity of reducing public expenditure.[19] This line of
argument was popular neither with the Prime Minister nor with the
Party Conference.

Arguments about expenditure continued, in full Cabinet, throughout
the winter months. Thorneycroft and Birch[20] argued the case for austerity. Eventually the difference between what the spending Departments
wanted and what the Treasury would concede came to a notional figure
of £50 million though, in fact, given contingency allowances, the sum,
though it cannot be estimated exactly, was probably very much greater.
The penultimate act was played at an emergency meeting of the Cabinet
on Sunday, 5 January 1958. The meeting convened at 9 a.m. It finished
at 10.30 a.m. Thorneycroft immediately told the Prime Minister that he
proposed to resign. Birch followed suit. The two men went back to the
Treasury, where Powell was waiting. Thorneycroft made it clear that he
did not expect either of his Ministers to resign with him. Indeed, he was
anxious that, for the sake of their careers, they should not do so. They
insisted that they were determined to go with him. The three men spent
the rest of the day composing and comparing their letters of resignation.
These were delivered at 10.30 a.m. on Monday. Half an hour later
Macmillan announced that he had appointed the Minister of Agriculture,
Derick Heathcoat Amory, as Chancellor. On Tuesday morning Macmillan embarked on a six-week tour of the Commonwealth. A cluster of
journalists awaited him at the airport on his departure. To them he said
that the resignation of his entire Treasury team was 'a little local
difficulty'.

Macmillan's observation was taken to be an example of his famous
unflappability. Nobody could believe that the resignation of all three
Treasury Ministers would not do other than shake to its foundations a
government still not recovered from the trauma of Suez. However,
Macmillan was tactically right. With just under two years to go before his
favoured election date of October 1959, and unburdened of a difficult
and, as it seemed to him, penny-pinching trio, Macmillan could get on
with the business of expanding public spending. In fact, the resignations
did him no harm whatsoever, particularly as all three men observed a

self-denying ordinance not to attack government economic policy. Their departure, in truth, did far less harm than the refusal of Powell and Iain Macleod to serve under Alec Douglas-Home in 1963. Given the narrowness of the 1964 General Election result, it is reasonable to attribute Home's defeat to his loss of two of the most powerful politicians of that time. Moreover, Amory truly was Macmillan's creature, and the Prime Minister's economic policy went ahead without any troublesome criticism in Cabinet.

Economic expansion now went ahead at great speed. The standard rate of income tax remained steady at eight shillings and sixpence in the pound; the wholesale price index remained steady between 1958 and 1959 at 111; the retail price index rose only one point between 1958 and 1959; and annual purchasing power also remained steady. All industrial production figures either rose or remained steady with the exception of coal, production of which declined from 206 million tons a year to 194 million tons a year, and this drop had no significant effect on the economy. Throughout election year Bank Rate was held at 4 per cent.

At the same time industrial investment was increasing rapidly, very much helped by substantial government subsidies. There was a dramatic increase in private sector housing, from 149,900 in 1958 to 166,000 in 1959. There was a drop in the number of houses built by local authorities from 113,100 to 99,500, but, in conditions of an expanding economy and growing prosperity, this decline had little or no political effect. Expenditure on health, social services and education was increased, and the Conservative Party, at this stage, was beginning to regard Macmillan as a miracle worker or, in the words of a caption to a famous Vicky cartoon of the time, which depicted the Prime Minister flying through the air wearing a Superman outfit, as Supermac.

All this offered the Labour Party a dismal prospect, all the more dismaying because, after Eden's resignation, they were in a triumphal mood, certain beyond a peradventure that they would trounce the Conservatives, whenever the next General Election came. Hugh Gaitskell, who had been a prudent Chancellor of the Exchequer in the last year of the Attlee government,[21] was forced to try to outbid Macmillan on public expenditure. This invited and received a sustained Conservative riposte demanding to know by exactly how much the leader of the Opposition proposed to increase taxation in general and income tax in particular to pay for policies which the Tories denounced as extravagant. Aware of the intense unpopularity of rises in income tax, Gaitskell denied that he had any proposals for increases. The government retorted that, if that was the case, the Opposition's promises were meaningless.

The government had another advantage. Macmillan proved to be a superb campaigner. Gaitskell, though he was capable on occasion of making powerful speeches in the House of Commons or at a Labour Party Conference, was at best awkward, and at worst dull, on a public platform, and on television. He had been an academic, and he never lost the pedantry which had entered into his soul at Oxford. Bevan's description of him as 'a desiccated calculating machine' was on every Tory's lips during the campaign leading up to the election in October 1959. Although his gloom increased as the campaign progressed[22] nevertheless Gaitskell had hopes of at the very least doing in 1959 what Churchill had done in 1950 – making large inroads on the government's majority, destabilising the parliamentary situation and winning a subsequent General Election. Public opinion polls were in their infancy at the time and few politicians paid any attention to them. Thus, the seriousness of their situation was not brought home to the Labour Party. Their depression was profound when, after a very peaceful campaign, the result announced on 8 October gave the Conservatives 365 seats to Labour's 258. There were also six Liberals and one Independent.[23] Macmillan was now a hero to his followers, and regarded with increasing respect and affection by the people.

The election victory was, however, to be the highest point of Macmillan's career. Nemesis had begun to stalk him. His fiscal irresponsibility between January 1958 and October 1959 was to be his undoing. Difficulties in foreign affairs and in the field of defence mounted, not least on the question of Britain's nuclear missile, Blue Streak, which had so many teething problems that it had to be cancelled and an American replacement sought. When that too was cancelled by the United States for similar reasons the United Kingdom was humiliated. The failure of Blue Streak demonstrated that Britain could no longer fund a nuclear deterrent of its own, given the government's commitment to social expenditure.

Moreover, from 1960 to 1963 the government was beset by a series of espionage scandals. There was the nuclear scandal, when Klaus Fuchs (a German who worked on nuclear weapons in the United States and Britain after the war) and Alan Nunn May were discovered to have been passing atomic secrets to the Russians. A senior diplomat, Donald Maclean, accompanied by a drunken and homosexual former junior diplomat, Guy Burgess, defected to Russia hours before arrest. They had clearly been tipped off, and a hunt began for a third man. Suspicion fell heavily on H. A. R. ('Kim') Philby, who was high in the ranks of MI6. He was suspended from duty until cleared by Harold Macmillan, in the House of Commons. Shortly afterwards, however, Philby was named in the House by a Labour backbencher, Colonel Marcus Lipton, and, though insufficient evidence to charge him was found, he was forced to resign. After a spell as a journalist in Beirut he too subsequently defected to Moscow. An Admiralty civil servant, John Vassall, who was in the Private Office of a Civil Lord of the Admiralty, Tam Galbraith, and who had the task of bringing Galbraith's despatch boxes to him in the country each weekend, was also found to be a Russian spy.[24] Unpleasant innuendoes suggesting that the Minister had been having an affair with Vassall deeply distressed Galbraith and Macmillan, and Galbraith resigned. Finally, in 1963, the Secretary of State for War, John Profumo, was accused by the *Daily Express* of consorting with a prostitute, Christine Keeler. Profumo denied his association with the girl and Macmillan believed him. Profumo then made a statement to the House of Commons further denying the business. Only days later it was revealed that he had lied. What was now widely believed was that the government was incompetent, and the Prime Minister gullible beyond belief.

The air of insouciance which Macmillan demonstrated on his departure on his Commonwealth tour after the Treasury resignations was not affected, but he did not fully understand the consequences of measures he had already taken. While he was away, however, the chickens started to come home to roost. At the end of 1959 evidence had been produced of a substantial and dangerous fall in Britain's currency reserves. The boom he had engineered, moreover, had produced extremely low unemployment figures. This, while electorally popular, had certain undesirable consequences. Because of greater prosperity and industrial expansion wage claims began to rise. For the first time, further, inflation began to become a serious problem for a British government. True, it was nothing, in percentage terms, compared to what happened in the 1970s. But 5 to 6 per cent was judged to be a catastrophic figure in 1960.

So far as the trade unions were concerned the railwaymen led the field. They had had a settlement in 1958, but one of its terms was that there should be a Committee of Enquiry into their pay structure. Before this Committee reported the British Transport Commission (the predecessor of British Rail) unilaterally offered 4 per cent. Macmillan telegraphed from South Africa (where he had made his famous 'Winds of Change' speech) instructing the Cabinet to meet the railways unions' demand for 5 per cent. Other unions followed the railway unions' demands, and by the end of February 1960 public expenditure had reached £340 million over and above what the Treasury thought wise. Amory was so worried at the prospects that, on the advice of his civil servants, he wrote to Macmillan on 19 January 1960 pointing out, having listed the danger signals, that:

> None of the foregoing factors *taken by itself* would . . . point to the necessity for immediate action. But, taken together, they reveal conclusively to my mind a situation and still more, perhaps, a trend in which an early warning signal is most certainly called for . . . psychologically it seems to me of great importance to make such a warning signal early rather than late.[25]

Macmillan promptly agreed, from Africa, to an increase in Bank Rate to 5 per cent.

As Peter Thorneycroft and Enoch Powell were to point out for years to come, the government, particularly by virtue of excessive wage settlements in the nationalised industries, was living beyond its means. The bubble had to burst. As Thorneycroft never ceased to repeat, had expenditure been reined in while he was Chancellor to the tune of £50 to £60 million, a sense of discipline would have been instilled into the guardians of the public purse. But the 1958–1960 economic boom instilled in the British people a belief that prosperity had come to stay. They thus went on what Macmillan called a 'refrigerator buying spree'. Credit was more readily available than it had ever been before. As a result, inflation continued to climb and many citizens, not to mention businesses, got themselves into serious trouble through hire purchase schemes and the nascent credit card network.[26] The ready availability of credit, moreover, meant an alarming increase in imports: by the end of 1960 British exports had increased by only 4 per cent, while imports had increased by 10 per cent.

When Macmillan returned from his tour, consulted Ministers and advisers and examined the figures, he became alarmed. But it is questionable whether his alarm was proportionate to the situation.[27] The theory by which he operated was that a certain amount of inflation was tolerable, since it provided the cash and credit to fuel the expansion of the economy.[28] The difficulty a country with a large, publicly-owned sector, and with the privately-owned industrial sector in decline faces is that if it resorts to subsidisation the demand can become endless. A perfect example of this, albeit on a small scale, was the decision of the Wilson government of 1966–70, in the person of the Secretary of State for Industry, Tony Benn, to bail out the Meriden motorcycle manufacturing company. Millions of pounds were spent and the company went under anyway, because it could not face Japanese competition. A much more dramatic example of this process, and on a much larger scale, was the constant subvention of British Leyland until it was broken up and privatised by the Thatcher government in the 1980s. But the process of throwing good money after bad had started with Harold Macmillan.

What became increasingly worrying after 1960 was that the process of expanding credit to finance expansion was clearly not working. The United Kingdom began to experience a new economic phenomenon to which Iain Macleod gave the title 'stagflation' – a combination of stagnation and inflation. The sad fact of the matter, however, was that no post-war government until that elected in 1979 was willing to go to the root of the problem by reducing public spending, resisting excessive wage claims in the public sector and declining to bail out employers who granted wage rises in excess of any profits they could hope for. There were several reasons for this sorry state of affairs. One was excessive trade union power. In the case of British Leyland, in particular, concession after concession was made to militant trade unionists and British Leyland's share of the car market fell again and again, until its South African-born Chairman, Michael Edwardes, appointed by Harold Wilson but fully backed only by Margaret Thatcher, applied his ruthless mind to the business of sorting out the company.[29] Another factor was the British conviction that a great country required a substantial manufacturing, and particularly industrial manufacturing, sector: the slang phrase for the kind of industry that was thought most desirable was 'metal-bashing'. Despite the decline of Britain's international economic position after the war, successive governments, Conservative and Labour alike, made massive and unsustainable efforts to save from decline such, as they saw them, symbols of greatness as steel and volume car manufacturing. This form of national vanity was particularly marked in Harold Macmillan's case. Particularly when he decided to wind up the Empire by granting independence to the African colonies, he sought to persuade his fellow countrymen that the United Kingdom was still a great, perhaps even a super, power. He himself had no illusions about the extent to which British influence in the world had declined with the rise of the Soviet Union and the United States, but, by what amounted to prestidigitation, he sought to persuade the people otherwise. It was, of course, true that Britain could still play a useful marginal role in international diplomacy, as he demonstrated when he brought Russia and the United States to agree on a Nuclear Test Ban Treaty. But, in domestic affairs, first propping up and then developing heavy industry was at the heart of his concerns, not least because of the unemployment that would result from serious decline.

71

The troubles that greeted him on his return from overseas were such as to persuade his colleagues that serious retrenchment was necessary. Macmillan fought them fiercely and managed to hold his favoured line for the moment. Amory was unmanned by the horrors he could now see coming in the near future. He had always seemed willing to do Macmillan's bidding, but the Prime Minister had come reluctantly to the view that he was neither sufficiently in command of economic matters nor sufficiently skilful in the House of Commons to warrant continuance in what was becoming an increasingly difficult job. He decided, therefore, to reshuffle the Cabinet, and to replace Amory with the equally pliable Selwyn Lloyd.[30] In his most dramatic appointment, Macmillan made Lord Home Foreign Secretary. Again, Butler's hope of the Foreign Office was dashed. Butler remained at the Home Office and he twice declined to take the post of Commonwealth Secretary.[31] Edward Heath moved from being Minister of Labour to being Home's number two, with the brief of supervising negotiations with the EEC. Enoch Powell (who had refused an earlier offer of office because he would not return until Thorneycroft was invited) became Minister of Health, and Thorneycroft himself became Minister of Aviation (Nigel Birch's sight was failing, and he was not up to handling a department).

Lloyd's appointment meant that, in essence, Macmillan remained his own Chancellor. Lloyd was reluctant to take the job on, for, like Amory, he had no experience of economics and doubted his ability to perform successfully. He was, however, very close to Macmillan. One slightly unusual aspect of that closeness was the fact that Lloyd, being a *divorcé* with one child in his custody, was grateful for Macmillan's offer of a grace and favour flat at Chequers. Lloyd was right in foreseeing trouble. July and August 1960 saw a strike by power-workers and a longer one by the seamen, which, of course, disrupted international trade. These were both settled by inflationary wage increases and another railwaymen's strike was averted by the same means. September saw a strike by tally-clerks, which crippled the London docks, and partly as a consequence of which the balance of payments deficit rose from £76 million in September to £122 million in October. In November, Ford USA made a bid for Ford UK, which was then an independent company. This created great disaffection in the motor trade trade unions, beginning the long cycle of industrial disruption of the motor manufacturing industry, which lasted until the privatisation of British Leyland. Early in the New Year the Post Office workers went on strike and were followed in the spring by another dockers' strike, led by the Communist General Secretary of the Dockers' Union, Jack Dash.

Whatever the problems, however, Macmillan was determined to hold to his belief in economic expansion, fuelled by increased public expenditure and lower taxation. This view he held to in spite of all advice to the contrary. Alistair Horne[32] illustrates Macmillan's attitude graphically when he recounts a visit to No. 10 Downing Street just before the 1961 budget by Sir Roy Harrod. Harrod was a personal friend of long standing. He had been a pupil of Keynes and, indeed, his biographer.[33] That such a man should enjoin upon the Prime Minister a policy of retrenchment and drastic reduction in public expenditure was remarkable. In his diary, Macmillan rather scornfully described Harrod as a 'prophet of woe' and went on 'he says the £ will crash in the summer. We *must* restrict imports. Treasury and Board of Trade say the opposite. What is a poor Prime Minister to do?'[34]

Harrod was right. Balance of payments figures, which were published just before the Budget, were very nearly disastrous. A run on the pound began, and the contradictions in Macmillan's economic policy were about to become apparent. They were dramatically illustrated by Enoch Powell's decision to double prescription charges, which happened at the same moment as Selwyn Lloyd raised the upper earnings limit on which surtax was payable from £2,000 a year to £5,000. The technique of 'fine-tuning' was now, for the first time, introduced. The Budget gave the Chancellor a number of regulatory powers whereby he could vary excise duty on tobacco, alcohol, petrol and television advertising, without recourse to Parliament. This was a typically cynical Macmillan manoeuvre. The Prime Minister was a curiously complicated blend of idealist and cynic. There is no doubt that his attitude to economic policy was fundamentally based on a desire to improve the lot of the people, nor that poverty deeply distressed him. On the other hand, he was ever willing to resort to the most blatant manipulation of colleagues and the electorate. For all that he resisted the advice of such as Roy Harrod, and most of his colleagues, to relent on his determination to reduce income tax and continue with high levels of public expenditure, he did see that the summer of 1961 would be a very difficult one.

However, the regulatory powers given to the Chancellor in the April Budget could be used even in the absence of Parliament. If the House was in recess, this, of course, made it impossible for the Opposition to mount an attack from the floor of the House, with the attendant publicity that such an attack would generate, on anything in the economic sphere which the Government felt impelled to do. What Macmillan feared was that if inflation continued to rise, and the balance of payments continued to deteriorate during the summer recess, he might be forced, under the law as it applied before the 1961 Budget, to recall Parliament. What he hoped was that any measures which needed to be taken during the summer recess could be taken by the use of these new powers. Had he been forced to recall Parliament a sense of national crisis would have been engendered, greatly to the detriment both of the Government's reputation and the stability of the pound. He was determined, therefore, to avoid a recall.

Always a consummate tactician, Macmillan had acted in a wily fashion. The balance of payments continued to deteriorate, and the pound continued to fall. At the end of July, Lloyd raised Bank Rate to the then undreamt of figure of 7 per cent.[35] He raised duties on tobacco, alcohol and petrol. The major difficulty, as Lloyd had told the House before the recess, was that, whereas productivity over the previous year had risen by only 3 per cent, wages had risen by 8 per cent. Macmillan and Lloyd therefore sought to introduce a 'pay pause'. This was the forerunner of the prices and incomes policies which, at various times, were used by all subsequent governments until the Thatcher government of 1979.[36]

The Lloyd measures steadied the pound during the month of August, but Prime Minister and Chancellor alike were convinced of the need for some sort of organisation which brought politicians, industrialists and trade unionists together on a regular basis for consultation about economic policy. It was believed by the two men that once the leaders of the trade unions understood the facts of economic policy they would be more responsible in their negotiations on wages. Other members of the Government, and perhaps most notably Enoch Powell, were highly suspicious of a central organisation of this kind, but the combination of a Prime Minister and a Chancellor, acting in full agreement with one another, is always certain to overcome Cabinet resistance. Thus, despite the misgivings of their colleagues, Macmillan and Lloyd were able to preside over the birth of the National Economic Development Council (familiarly known as 'Neddy') on 21 September 1961.

In later years Selwyn Lloyd was to say that he believed the creation of the NEDC was his greatest achievement in government. In truth, however, the organization was always ineffective and, though it remained in existence into the 1990s, it was increasingly disregarded by government. Indeed, its ineffectiveness was demonstrated almost immediately after its creation when, in September 1961, the Electrical Trades Union secured a wage increase 10 per cent above the rate of inflation. Macmillan and Lloyd had hoped, as I have already mentioned, that the NEDC would provide a forum in which trade union leaders would, by learning more about the facts of economic life, be persuaded to moderate wage demands. It was not to be so. But that this belief was held by these two men illustrates, to my mind in a rather poignant fashion, two important facts about the psychology of British politics in this period, underlining not only the essential nature of the Macmillan years but the character of British politics until 1979.

The first fact was the character of Macmillan himself. He was a master of illusion, able to persuade colleagues and rivals alike that he had a particular gift for resolving national problems. Harold Wilson, for example, though he faced Macmillan only in the final months of the Prime Minister's stewardship of the nation, always professed the most profound admiration for his rival's ability and, indeed, carried on government along much the same lines as Macmillan did.[37] (Wilson's essential appeal in 1964 was that he would run affairs more efficiently than the Conservative Party.) The second characteristic of the political psychology of those who governed Britain after 1945 was their folk memory of the Second World War. After the fall of France in 1940 the United Kingdom, though sustained by the Empire and Commonwealth, and buttressed by friendship with the United States, faced a grim future. But Churchill's appeal to national unity did not fall on deaf ears. From 11 May 1940, when he became Prime Minister, Churchill set in hand a massive reorganisation of the war effort. Certainly, politicians and the fighting forces, as well as the nation, depended to a great extent on his capacity to inspire. But he was also diligent in matters of administration. A vast number of boards and offices were set up to handle the day-to-day work of the war. Men and women, Conservatives as well as Socialists, became accustomed to believing in the proposition that collective effort, organised by bureaucracies, was essential to governmental efficiency. This belief carried over into the post-war years. It was universally acknowledged, moreover, that the period of peace would be a critical one for the country. It seemed natural, therefore, to organise for peace in the same way that the nation had organised for victorious war. This, of course, was a quite unforced view for the Labour Party to hold, because of the ideology to which they cleaved. It was not natural for Conservatives; but it was natural for Harold Macmillan because of the doctrines he had developed in pre-war years.[38]

However, in 1961, even Macmillan could not forever conceal from himself and the country the parlous nature of Britain's economic situation. It was necessary both to administer more efficiently the industries which the Attlee government had nationalised, and to find substantial savings in government expenditure. In the first area Macmillan was as brilliant in an appointment as he had been when he brought Sir Percy Mills to the Ministry of Housing. He persuaded the Shadow Foreign Secretary, Alf Robens, to leave politics and become Chairman of the National Coal Board.[39] Robens ran the coal industry for ten years, during which time there was considerably increased productivity and no industrial disputes. (It has to be remembered, of course, that the industry continued to receive substantial subsidies from the taxpayer, but these, in real terms, were considerably reduced under Robens's stewardship.)

Then there was the vital matter of reducing public expenditure. It was personally unpalatable to Macmillan, and would have been politically vastly unpopular, to reduce expenditure on the National Health Service or in the social services generally. Defence, particularly in view of the threat posed by the might of the USSR, was sacrosanct. Macmillan was prompted by the Minister for Transport, Ernest Marples, to turn a beady eye on the railway system. Marples recruited Dr Richard Beeching, the Technical Director of ICI, to conduct an enquiry into how savings could be made on the railways. There had been two earlier enquiries, which had yielded nothing in the way of improvement. His own investigation scarcely begun, it seemed reasonable both to government and Beeching alike that he should become Chairman of the Railway Board, so that he could not merely recommend reforms but implement them. It was September 1962 – by which time the Railway Board deficit had risen to £159 million – before Beeching was ready with proposals which immediately caused a strike by the National Union of Railwaymen. Beeching's plans, eventually implemented with very little change, were to close half the railway stations of the country, abandon one-third of the total route mileage, severely cut back the number of goods depots, introduce a fast inter-city service at considerably greater cost to the passenger and bring in trains which could carry container goods which could easily be transferred to road transport. In agreement with Marples, Beeching further proposed a vast extension of the motorway system. The consequence of the Beeching Plan was a cut of 70,000 jobs on the railways. It was this which provoked the NUR to strike. The strike, which lasted three weeks, was ended by a package which provided increased pay for those remaining in work, allowed for substantial redundancy payments to those who wished to leave, and which ordained that natural wastage should account for a large proportion of the job losses.

In retrospect, Martin Redmayne, who became Conservative Chief Whip in 1960, told Macmillan's biographer [40] that Macmillan had reached the top of the hill by the end of that year: from then on the path led downward. The Prime Minister's own mood was curiously variable, but, then, he had always been prey to switches from elation to depression. Despite his very considerable parliamentary majority, he was plunged into the depths of gloom by the loss of a by-election at Paisley on 10 May 1961. He was even upset by a mischievous suggestion in the 'Crossbencher' column in the *Sunday Express* on 22 May 1961 that Butler was planning to revolt, break up the Conservative Party and lead something to be called the Country Party. Nothing, of course, would be more uncharacteristic of Butler than so daring a ploy. But, by this stage, Macmillan was becoming increasingly paranoid, and he had a deep feeling that the government he led had lost its sense of direction. The period leading up to his retirement was not without its successes. He developed a warm relationship with John F. Kennedy after Kennedy was elected President of the United States in 1960. There was his programme, then judged highly successful though considered with a more jaundiced eye in later years, of decolonisation in Africa. There was the Test Ban Treaty. And there was, of course, a general perception by the people that their living standards had improved. All this, however, seemed to be doing the government no political good. Macmillan – like Harold Wilson later on – was an obsessive student of opinion polls, and they looked increasingly unfavourable throughout the second half of 1961 and the whole of 1962. The Conservatives continued to do badly in by-elections, but the real shock did not come until March 1962 when, at Orpington, the Liberal candidate, Eric Lubbock (now Lord Avebury), turned a Conservative majority of 15,000 into a Liberal majority of 8,000. The Orpington result was particularly distressing for Macmillan because the constituency adjoined his own, that of Bromley.[41]

From the moment he became Prime Minister Macmillan watched, with a certain amount of anxiety, the rapid development of the European Economic Community. The United Kingdom had, after the War, declined to join the European Coal and Steel Community, which was the precursor of the EEC. Churchill, it is true, had advocated European unity but, as present-day British advocates of closer European union too readily forget, he meant unity for the continental powers. In 1959 Britain played the essential role in creating the European Free Trade Association, not so much as a rival to the EEC but as a different kind of organisation. EFTA was primarily founded on the idea of free trade between sovereign nations, whereas the Community aspired, in however cloudy a way, towards political unity and the control of national economies from a centre. Reginald Maudling (later to be Chancellor of the Exchequer) was President of the Board of Trade when the EFTA Treaty was negotiated, and he carried the burden of the exchanges which led to the setting up of the organisation. He was, at that time, an outright opponent of Britain seeking to join the EEC. However, Maudling was never a man of very firm convictions and, when he became Chancellor of the Exchequer in 1962, he went happily along with what was to become both the most momentous decision of Macmillan's time as Prime Minister and his most monumental blunder.

CHAPTER FOUR

Consensus at Home
(1960–1964)

The question of British membership of the European Economic Community was to prove to be a vital issue between the Conservative and Labour parties over the years in which Macmillan was Prime Minister. Crucial though the matter was, discussion of it tended to obscure the extent to which the two major parties were in agreement on matters of domestic policy. The Conservative government until 1964 leant towards lower public expenditure and lower individual taxation. The Labour opposition leant towards higher welfare spending and more centralised control of the economy. But there was no major ideological difference between the two: both parties made their claim to the electorate on the basis of how efficiently they could administer the settlement of national affairs instituted by the Attlee government.

Macmillan had, personally, always been, albeit mildly, in favour of the United Kingdom joining the EEC. By the time of the summer reshuffle of 1960 he had decided to make an application for membership and appointed, to supervise the negotiations for entry, the then Minister of Labour, Edward Heath, who became Lord Privy Seal. He knew that Heath's commitment to the ideal of membership was total. The Foreign Secretary, Lord Home, was far more sceptical but he was willing to consent to the new European policy being run in tandem between the Prime Minister and the Lord Privy Seal.[1]

Heath and Macmillan alike, and there were other British politicians of a similar attitude of mind, were idealistic in their approach to the Community. The difficulties Macmillan faced at home with regard to the EEC negotiations were three. He had to persuade a largely hostile British public of the economic benefits of membership. He had to try to infuse that same public with something of his own enthusiasm for the project and he had to outface an extremely angry Commonwealth. The foreign policy of the United Kingdom after the war had been, in Anthony Eden's formulation, based on a tripod consisting of the Commonwealth, the United States and the European continental powers.[2] The idea was that each of the legs of the tripod should be of equal concern and benefit to Britain. Eden was adamant in his hostility to any idea of the United Kingdom joining the EEC, and remained so until the end of his life. To this day, it remains uncertain when Macmillan made up his own mind about lodging an application to join. When the House of Commons rose for the summer recess in 1960 the question of Common Market membership was being much discussed in political circles and in the press. Alarm bells were already ringing in the capitals of the old (that is to say, white) Commonwealth countries. Of the three white Dominions, Canada, Australia and New Zealand, the worry was greatest in New Zealand. All three countries had preferential trading arrangements with the United Kingdom, and these arrangements, it was believed – rightly – would have to be repealed if the United Kingdom joined the EEC, but the economy of New Zealand was the most vulnerable in the event of the British application succeeding.[3]

There was another problem for Macmillan. Not only was the white Commonwealth deeply, and sometimes bitterly, opposed to Britain's membership of the EEC, but within the ranks of the Conservative Party there were many who believed that closer Commonwealth links were infinitely preferable to membership of a European grouping, the structure of which would, ultimately, they believed, draw the United Kingdom into a federalist system. Over and above such practical calculations there existed in the early sixties in Britain a powerful sentimental feeling for the Commonwealth. All these things Macmillan had to consider very carefully. However, in the early months of 1961 he persuaded his Cabinet colleagues that membership of the EEC, if the arguments were properly presented, would both give a fillip to the government's flagging popularity and, ultimately, restore the country's economic fortunes. On 10 August 1961, therefore, the United Kingdom applied for Common Market membership.

It was not, however, until April 1962 that Macmillan began his campaign to convince the electorate of his wisdom in changing completely the direction of British foreign and economic policy. He had the difficult task both of assuaging fear and of arousing conviction. He decided that the keynote speech would be made during the course of a by-election campaign in his pre-war constituency of Stockton-on-Tees. It was there that the spectre of unemployment caused him to formulate the ideas expressed in *The Middle Way*.[4] So appropriate did he feel Stockton to be as the venue of his European crusade that he took the then unprecedented step for a Prime Minister of intervening in a by-election campaign.

Determined though he was in his own mind, however, he was, as was not infrequently the case with him, undecided how to express himself. The draft of his speech was seen by George Hutchinson, his press adviser, over lunch in the train on the way North. Hutchinson found it 'weak on Europe, not sufficiently clear-cut or decisive'. He gave his honest opinion to the Prime Minister, turned over his menu card and wrote:

> Of course it has its risks, its pitfalls: all great transactions have. What I can now do is to hold out to you the Government's hope of success. Success in securing our Commonwealth interests. Success in securing the interests of our manufacturers and farmers. Success – at the end – in achieving an ever more dynamic influence in the affairs and the future of Western Europe and the Western world. These are high stakes – as high as any that Britain ever contemplated. High stakes – and the prospect of high reward, of peace and security, of rising prosperity and happiness for the British people: all the people, the people in the great centres of industry like Tees-side, the people in the farming belts like those nearby.
>
> The Common Market presents us with a tremendous challenge – and a gigantic opportunity. The Government accepts that challenge. It has seized that opportunity. But, of course, we have set about our negotiations with care as well as confidence, with responsibility as well as resource. This is not child's play. This is high policy – and we know what we are doing.[5]

Not for the first, nor the last, time did Macmillan have cause to congratulate Oliver (now Lord) Poole, the Joint Chairman of the Conservative Party, on advising him to appoint as his press adviser a journalist of the skill and political insight of George Hutchinson, who had moved to Conservative Central Office from the political editorship of the London *Evening Standard*.

In spite of his best efforts, however, Macmillan's European adventure achieved none of its objectives. In Edward Heath he had a negotiator of exceptional diligence and competence in the handling of detail, but all too ready to immerse himself in that detail.[6] Unfortunately for his cause, Macmillan never grasped the strength of General de Gaulle's opposition to British membership of the Community. Throughout 1962 the fact that

Heath was so ready to go into the most intricate detail in his discussions gave the French exactly the opportunity they wanted to drag out the talks and to put all manner of obstacles in the Lord Privy Seal's way. On 1 December 1962 Macmillan wrote in his diary, apropos of a report from Heath, 'The *French* are opposing us by every means, fair and foul. They are absolutely ruthless. For some reason they *terrify* the Six by their intellectual superiority, spiritual arrogance and shameful disregard of truth and honour . . .'[7]

Macmillan, urged on by President Kennedy, believed, however, that he personally could persuade de Gaulle at least to modify his hostility to Britain. On 15 September 1962 the Prime Minister flew to Rambouillet for a summit meeting with the French President. The two-day meeting opened with a pheasant shoot, and Macmillan was disconcerted to find that he had to pay for his own cartridges (because of his poor eyesight, the President did not shoot, but he accompanied the guns and felt free to make rude remarks when one of his guests missed). The two men conversed throughout in French, in which Macmillan was fluent. The conversation ranged over many subjects other than Britain's application to join the Common Market. De Gaulle was particularly concerned about the United Kingdom's closeness to the United States and the fact that she was becoming ever more dependent on the Americans for her nuclear armament. (Kennedy had, in fact, offered France, anxious to create a nuclear capacity of her own, exactly the same kind of agreement that was in place between Britain and the United States, but de Gaulle turned him down, being determined to create the *force de frappe* entirely out of French resources.) It seems clear that the liking of both Prime Minister and President for speaking in elevated and impressionistic tones about large matters of policy, and their fondness for the elliptical, meant that neither fully understood the other. Macmillan, though he found de Gaulle difficult, came away from Rambouillet convinced that he had set de Gaulle's mind at rest about the Anglo-American alliance. The French officials, on the other hand, were satisfied that their President's most devout wish was that Britain should withdraw her application, and that he had made this clear to the Prime Minister. Macmillan, then, was worried, but still very hopeful of a successful outcome to Heath's work.

On 14 January 1963 de Gaulle held his regular monthly press conference at the Elysée Palace. Among other things he said:

Sentiments, as favourable as they might be and as they are, cannot be put forward in opposition to the real facts of the problem . . . England is insular . . . in short, the nature and structure and economic context of England differ profoundly from those of the other states of the continent . . . in the end there would appear a colossal Atlantic community under American dependence and leadership which would soon swallow up the European Community.

It was clear immediately that the President had vetoed the application. Heath and Macmillan, however, continued to hope against hope, until the *coup de grâce* was delivered by the French Foreign Minister, Maurice Couve de Murville, at Brussels fifteen days later. He told the negotiating teams of the Six and Britain: 'The facts are that Britain, at present, is not in a state to accept the discipline of the Rome Treaty, notably of carrying out the Community's common agricultural policy.' He was, at least, less condescending than his President, who had deeply offended Macmillan personally by saying at his press conference:

. . . it is highly possible that Great Britain's own evolution and the evolution of the world would lead Britain to the Continent, whatever may be the delays before complete realisation. For my part, this is what I am inclined to believe, and that is why, in my opinion, it will be in any case a great honour for the British Prime Minister, for my friend Harold Macmillan, and for his Government, to have perceived this so early, to have had enough political courage to proclaim it and to have had their country take the first steps along the path that, one day perhaps, will bring it to make fast to the Continent.[8]

But at Brussels the party was over.

However, the government, believing that the only real – if, for the moment, immovable – obstacle to British entry into the Community was the President of France, determined to develop better relations with the continental countries with a view to renewing the application when times were more propitious. Every EEC member except France wanted Britain in. Professor Walter Hallstein, President of the EEC Commission, observed: 'There can be no doubt the chance of success was great enough to justify the continuation of negotiations.' Later, he issued a declaration on behalf of the Commission which opened: 'The manner in which one member government took and communicated its decision to interrupt the negotiations is not in harmony with the duties imposed by the Community.'[9] On 29 January 1963, Edward Heath defined what was to be the future policy of the British government towards the EEC:

> We in Britain are not going to turn our backs on the mainland of Europe or on the countries of the Community. We are part of Europe by geography, tradition, history, culture and civilisation. We shall continue to work with our friends in Europe for the true unity and strength of this continent.

In my own opinion the French veto was the tocsin that tolled the knell for the Macmillan government. Macmillan was to soldier on until the following October, and then to retire on grounds of ill-health. Further, he agonised constantly over whether or not he should lead his party for the second time in a General Election. His colleagues, several of whom he consulted, were dismayed by the frequency of his changes of mind.[10] Of the members of the Cabinet only Iain Macleod consistently held that a General Election, which could not be postponed beyond October 1964, was most likely to be won under Macmillan himself. 'I was, I think, at the end perhaps the only member of Macmillan's Cabinet to hold steadily to the view that the Tory Party would do better under Macmillan's leadership at the polls than they would under any of the possible alternatives', he wrote in the *Spectator*.[11]

The shattering thing about the French veto was not merely that the nation and the Prime Minister had been humiliated in the eyes of the world. In the sphere of international relations, even apart from the EEC, things had been going badly for Macmillan.[12] The application to join the EEC represented Macmillan's only hope of breaking out of a cycle of decline at home.

Throughout 1962 unemployment was rising, inflation was rising, the balance of payments and industrial relations were worsening and public satisfaction with the government was diving steeply. Selwyn Lloyd's budget was profoundly disappointing to commentators and politicians alike. Reluctantly, Macmillan had given way on his ambition for an expansionist budget, for he saw that the situation was too dangerous to take any further risks. The only measure which Lloyd took which could be considered expansionist was a reduction in Bank Rate from 7 per cent to 4.5 per cent. A 15 per cent tax was slapped on sweets and soft drinks and there were minor adjustments to purchase tax rates. Even these minor adjustments caused public irritation, for while tax was increased on clothing and furniture it was reduced on cosmetics. However, Lloyd did introduce one new tax. This was the Capital Gains Tax which, again, managed to create offence right across the political spectrum. Those who favoured austerity as an answer to economic problems were people who favoured the free market as a means of expansion and it was widely

believed that the tax would reduce investment. Those on the left, however, who were genuine supporters of the principle of taxation on capital
held that Lloyd's imposition was too low and his exemptions too many.
It seemed that the Macmillan government could no longer please anybody, and the Prime Minister's thoughts began to move towards the idea
of finding himself another new Chancellor.

Macmillan's problems were compounded at the beginning of May by a
pay settlement of 9 per cent for dockers: the government's voluntary
incomes policy had advised no more than 2.5 per cent. This was yet
another heavy blow to Macmillan's prestige. Macmillan was in Washington later in the month, and on his return was dismayed to find that
the Treasury had produced no new ideas for handling the economic
situation, and that the party in the House of Commons was in great
distress and urgently in need of firm direction.[13] Throughout June the
Prime Minister pondered the situation and held a number of consultations with the Chief Whip, Martin Redmayne, and with Butler. He
was, further, under constant pressure from Iain Macleod, who was then
Party Chairman, to undertake radical changes in the administration. The
cry everywhere was for new blood, and Macmillan had at least two jobs
on offer – for the Lord Chancellor, Lord Kilmuir, and the Minister of
Power, Lord Mills (Macmillan's old adviser at the Ministry of Housing)
both indicated that, on grounds of age and exhaustion, they would like to
retire. Two further Ministers had personal reasons for their willingness
to depart: the Secretary for Scotland, John Maclay, was deeply concerned about his wife's health, while the Minister for Defence, Harold
Watkinson, was anxious to return to his business career. The intimations
of all these men to the effect that they would like to leave government
certainly gave Macmillan some room for manoeuvre.

But the trouble was that their posts were not strategic, and Macmillan
wanted to make strategic changes. At the end of the first week of July,
however, he had made only one major decision: he was going to fire
Selwyn Lloyd. He decided to do this at a meeting he was due to have
with Lloyd on 12 July. There then entered nemesis in the form of
Butler.[14] On 11 July Butler lunched with the proprietor of the *Daily
Mail*, Lord Rothermere, and the paper's chief political correspondent,
Walter Terry. Butler was notorious for his indiscretions, called 'Butler-
isms'. He had been consulted by Macmillan about replacing Lloyd and
Macmillan had asked him whether he himself would like to return to the
Treasury, a suggestion which did not appeal to Butler. There had been
the usual crop of rumours about a reshuffle, for reporters and politicians
alike had taken note of the fact that the Cabinet was ageing. Terry,

naturally, quizzed Butler on this and was able, as a result, on the morning of 12 July, to produce a front page story under a banner headline saying that Lloyd was to be dismissed. This hardly made pleasant reading for Lloyd on the morning of his meeting with the Prime Minister. The meeting lasted two and a half hours, and Lloyd was shattered to discover that he was to lose, not only the Treasury, but his place in government. He refused a peerage (though he was to accept the later offer of a Companionship of Honour). In later years Lloyd was to say, at every opportunity, that this had been the very worst moment of his life.

Until this moment Macmillan had had the reputation of dealing with his colleagues with great tact and subtlety. Now something seemed to snap inside him. For all that their meeting was a long one, he appears to have been brusque throughout, as he was to other Ministers whom he dismissed. The four men mentioned above presented no problems. The upshot of his moves over the next few days meant the departure of a third of the Cabinet. He decided that Butler could not continue to be Home Secretary as well as handling intricate negotiations in Central Africa.[15] He did, however, give him the sop of a new title, First Secretary of State, implying that he would be Deputy Prime Minister. Henry Brooke became Home Secretary; this was widely held, and proved to be, a disastrous decision. Brooke's heavy handedness was in marked contrast to Butler's subtlety and he was to get the government into all sorts of trouble. Iain Macleod became Leader of the House, in addition to being Chairman of the Party. This was another decision widely condemned. A Party Chairman has, of necessity, to be a combative figure and adept at the rough and tumble of politics. A Leader of the House, on the other hand, is required to be able to gain the respect of the opposition as well as his own party. He should show himself to be even-handed and considerate towards Members, senior and junior alike. But Macleod was all pugnacity. This made him a good man to have at Conservative Central Office, where he could concentrate on banging the drum and leave the administrative work to his Deputy, Oliver Poole. Unfortunately, pugnacity carried over into his work in the House of Commons, and for all his brilliance he was the reverse of successful as Leader.

David Eccles, the Minister for Education, had made some mistakes in the running of his Department which had irritated Macmillan. Eccles wanted above all things to be Chancellor of the Exchequer, for he had been a highly successful businessman, building up a substantial fortune having started with nothing.[16] The post was not available and he, too, was sent to the backbenches. Charles Hill, the Minister for Housing, had an immensely popular public image because of his work as the Radio

Doctor on the BBC during the war. Macmillan summarily dismissed him in the course of a cocktail party.

Although he had been perfectly willing to go, the Lord Chancellor, Lord Kilmuir, was deeply distressed by the abrupt manner in which Macmillan gave him the news. His replacement was the Attorney-General, Sir Reginald Manningham-Buller (once dubbed by Bernard Levin, with poetic accuracy, 'Sir Reginald Bullying-Manner'), who took the title, Lord Dilhorne. This also was a disastrous appointment. First of all, Dilhorne was not a very good lawyer, and the Lord Chancellor's main duties consist in legal business connected with the appointment of judges and maintaining good diplomatic relations with the legal professions. In the discharge of these duties Dilhorne was at best incompetent and at worst offensive. The Lord Chancellor is also required to take the chair at debates in the House of Lords. Unlike the House of Commons, the House of Lords has no Standing Rules of debate or behaviour. It is a self-disciplining Chamber, and over the years has become a sort of well-mannered collective. However high passions may run on a given subject in the Lower House, the same subject will be discussed in the Upper House in a climate of civility. The Lord Chancellor's duties in the Chamber are minimal, although he is allowed to intervene in debate, unlike the Speaker in the Commons. Dilhorne sought both to extend his powers and to intervene in a highly combative way in debates.

Only three new appointments met with universal approval, that of Reginald Maudling to the Treasury, of Sir Edward Boyle to the Ministry of Education, and Sir Keith Joseph, who replaced Charles Hill, at Housing. Various other changes were made, particularly at the level of Minister of State, but the most interesting appointment was a new one. Effectively this was the creation of a Ministry of Information, with a seat in the Cabinet. This job, with the title of Minister without Portfolio, went to a backbencher who was also a distinguished journalist, William (now Lord) Deedes.[17]

The purpose of a reshuffle, particularly one as drastic as this, is to give new life and a new image to a government. In time, the more popular of Macmillan's appointments were seen to have strengthened the government, while the more unpopular clearly weakened it. Above all, the Prime Minister, because of the way in which he handled the whole business, completely lost his reputation for smooth and urbane management – what was called his 'unflappability'. It was quite clear to the press, and through the press to the public, that Macmillan had got himself into a panic. When he became Prime Minister he had caused to be pinned to the back of the door of the Cabinet room a card bearing words transcribed from Trollope. It read, 'Cool, calm deliberation unravels every knot'. He certainly did not attend to the maxim in June and July 1962.

Hostile reaction was immediate. Nigel Birch wrote a caustic letter to *The Times*:

Sir,

For the second time the Prime Minister has got rid of a Chancellor of the Exchequer who tried to get expenditure under control.

Once is more than enough.

Yours truly,

NIGEL BIRCH

On the Tuesday following the reshuffle, when Lloyd entered the Chamber of the House of Commons he was cheered to the echo from all quarters of the House. Shortly thereafter the Prime Minister came in to answer questions. He was jeered by the Labour Party; and the mass Tory ranks remained mute. No Prime Minister had had such a reception from his followers since Neville Chamberlain after the Norwegian débâcle in 1940, which led to his resignation. There was even a widespread rumour that between 40 and 50 Conservative backbenchers would abstain on a motion of censure which the Labour Party was planning to lay down. This massive abstention, which would certainly have forced Macmillan's resignation, did not materialise, but the fact that it was seriously discussed demonstrated how enfeebled the Prime Minister's position had become. Perhaps the cruellest remark was made during Question Time by Jeremy Thorpe, the Leader of the Liberal Party. 'Greater love', Thorpe said, 'hath no man than this that he lays down his friends for his life.' The whole House roared its appreciation, for Thorpe's inverted quotation expressed exactly the general judgement on what Macmillan had done.

Of the four Chancellors – Thorneycroft, Heathcoat Amory, Lloyd and Maudling – who served under Macmillan, Maudling was the one most genuinely in tune with the Prime Minister's attitudes to economic management. He genuinely believed, and with a great deal more intellectual rigour than Macmillan could ever muster, that steady expansion could be achieved, and a solid economic base constructed, through a combination of increased public expenditure, lower taxation, and control of incomes.

Moreover, he was genuinely unflappable, whereas Macmillan had adopted unflappability as a pose, for which reason his sharper critics dubbed him 'the last of the actor-managers'.

Nonetheless, Maudling could not immediately apply the policies which he favoured. The evident embarrassment of the government was such that the currency seemed to be in danger of a plunge on international markets, something which, in the days before floating exchange rates, invariably happened when a Conservative government was in trouble, or when the Conservative Party lost a General Election.[18] Macmillan and Maudling decided, therefore, to issue a statement to the press to the effect that economic policy, as laid down in the Lloyd budget of 1962 would continue unchanged. That is to say, the indirect taxes in place would continue; there would be no early reduction in direct taxation; and public expenditure would be held at its present levels. The market steadied. Nonetheless, Maudling began immediately to prepare what was to be the expansionary budget of 1963. Ultimately the 1963 budget was to have a devastating effect on the British economy and, in its long-term consequences, compares very unfavourably with the supposedly dull and boring Finance Bill of Selwyn Lloyd. While Maudling's statement reassured the City it did nothing for the Prime Minister's standing with the public. A Gallup poll on 11 July 1962 showed 47 per cent of those polled satisfied with his performance, 39 per cent dissatisfied and 12 per cent who had no opinion. On 20 July, the reshuffle having been completed, Gallup did another poll. There were still 12 per cent who had no opinion, but 52 per cent were dissatisfied and 36 per cent were satisfied. It is worth recalling that exactly two years previously he had enjoyed a satisfaction rating in the Gallup poll of 79 per cent.

Nonetheless, Maudling's calm and skilful management soon began to have its effect and in a matter of weeks expansionary economic policies were again set in train.

Macmillan himself, at last happy with a Chancellor, made a remarkable personal recovery from the fit of nerves that had inflicted him during and immediately after the reshuffle. Labour tabled its motion of censure on 26 July. All rumours of Conservative rebellions or abstentions proved unfounded. In a vintage debating performance Macmillan destroyed Gaitskell, whom he described as 'more of a lecturer than an orator'. The Conservative majority at the end of the debate was 98. There was not a single abstention. It was thought, not least by a number of senior Labour Party figures,[19] that Gaitskell had been unwise to table a censure motion at this time. It is possible to bring down a government by use of such a motion, but not when that government has so large a majority as Macmillan enjoyed, particularly given the propensity of the Tory Party to rally behind decisive leadership in time of stress. The only successful use of a censure motion this century was that by the Tories under Mrs Thatcher on 28 March 1979, and then the Tories overthrew a minority government with the aid of the smaller parties.[20]

The summer recess of 1962 began, largely because of Macmillan's triumph in the censure debate, with the Conservative Party in a mood of optimism that could not have been imagined in the four days following 12 July. Macmillan, partly because he needed a rest, and partly in order to try to re-establish his reputation for imperturbable command, spent the whole of August visiting various country houses for shooting parties. Upon his return, Maudling presented him, in advance of the Party Conference at Llandudno, with a series of expansionist economic proposals. Purchase tax was lowered; Bank Rate was reduced from 4.5 per cent to 4 per cent; and, *mirabile dictu*, inflation stood at only 1.9 per cent. In the circumstances, and given the travails of the middle of the year, Macmillan and Maudling surely deserved their rapturous ovations. Even Butler, for so long, with his liberal and humanitarian views, a figure usually disliked and sometimes hated by Conservative Party activists, was cheered to the echo. It was the only truly successful Party Conference speech he ever made.

It was significant that Macmillan devoted most of his winding-up speech to the Conference to the prospects of joining the EEC, and the tremendous economic benefits that he believed would follow from membership. It is now clear that he and Maudling both believed that they could take certain risks with economic policy – such as the measures described above – because they were both convinced that membership of the Community was assured and would provide, not least because of its popularity in the City, the fillip which they needed to restore the government's position in national esteem. The optimism which was evident both in Parliament and in the party in the country when Parliament resumed after the Party Conference deeply depressed Hugh Gaitskell, who could not make up his own mind about the EEC, and was eventually to come down against membership.[21] It is because this new mood of confidence was so strong in October 1962, and because both the fortunes and the optimism of the government declined so sharply after the French veto of Britain's membership of the EEC in January 1963, that I believe, as I said above,[22] that the veto was the death-blow to Macmillan's premiership.

Mr Anthony Howard, however, believes that it was the absence of Butler, so frequently abroad in Central Africa from the central management of domestic affairs which so damaged the government. He does, however, quote Butler observing on two occasions that it was the veto that really mattered. To Tony Benn on 20 February 1963 he said, 'You know, the Common Market breakdown was a much bigger shock for us than you chaps realised.' In his private papers, moreover, Butler recorded his agreement with an article by James Margach, political editor of the *Sunday Times*, that 'the engine had fallen out of the entire government strategy'.[23]

But, even before the approaching veto, the economic situation had begun to deteriorate throughout the winter of 1962–3, and Maudling's bright start at the Treasury looked increasingly fragile. At one level, one could say, the Macmillan Government had simply run out of luck, and luck is a crucial ingredient in successful government. The winter was a particularly harsh one and the electricians' union was threatening a power strike. Even without the strike, inclement conditions had brought the construction industry virtually to a standstill and power cuts – one of which blacked out Chequers during a Cabinet meeting – were found to be necessary. Partly, but not solely, because of the weather unemployment rose in the winter months to 4 per cent, a figure which Government and public alike regarded as alarming.

Macmillan's energy was by now fitful. Although he had dismissed, or seen retire, some of his oldest associates, he nonetheless felt their absence keenly, for he had always felt that he benefited greatly from lengthy and informal conversations on policy with men he had known for most of his political life. He had also, at 69, begun to feel his age. At this time John F. Kennedy was attracting the eyes of the world because of his youth, his energy and his charm. Moreover, in January 1963, after Hugh Gaitskell's sudden and untimely death, the Labour Party chose Harold Wilson as his successor. Wilson was 46, of an age with Kennedy.

As Maudling prepared his first Budget he had both good and bad news from NEDC. The Council believed (wrongly, as it turned out) that a growth rate of 4 per cent per annum could be achieved over the period to 1966. That was the good news. It would have been unimaginable during the stagflation of 1961–2. However, the bad news was that the Council went on to say that, because of what had happened in 1961–2, it would be necessary to procure a growth rate of 5 per cent in 1963–4. Maudling's problems were compounded by his own and Macmillan's propensity both for increasing public expenditure and embarking on dramatic initiatives that were, in effect, little more than meaningless public relations gimmicks. One such initiative was the appointment on 5 January of Lord Hailsham, then Minister of Science, to take on responsibility for reviving the depressed North-East. Hailsham went North, ostentatiously wearing a cloth cap, which excited derision rather than appreciation. It is not insignificant that, in his diary for 2 April 1963, Macmillan praised Maudling by calling him 'an ingenious accomplice'.[24]

The Budget which emerged in April reflected both the constraints imposed by circumstances on the Prime Minister and the Chancellor and their common belief in expansion. Income tax was reduced by raising personal allowances from £140 to £200 for a single person and from £240 to £320 for a married taxpayer. Child allowances were raised by £15. Various other reliefs were improved. Stamp duties were reduced. Investment allowances were improved and various measures were taken to benefit industries in development districts. Macmillan was immensely pleased with what he believed to be a satisfactorily expansionist Budget, but it seemed to do him no good with the public. Opinion polls from March 1963 onwards suggested that 62 per cent of the electorate believed he should resign.[25]

Macmillan, as the months wore on, had little time in which to proclaim the merits of the budget. This was because his great ambition from January onwards was to negotiate an agreed ban on the testing of nuclear weapons. To achieve his ambition in this regard he needed to persuade the United States and the Soviet Union that they could safely halt further nuclear development without weakening the existing system of deterrence. He succeeded after protracted personal diplomacy. Britain and the USSR signed the Nuclear Test Ban Treaty on 24 July 1963. At this stage Kennedy only initialled the Treaty, since he required a two-thirds majority in Congress to sign any Treaty. That majority was not achieved until September.

Maudling was an indifferent publicist and did not have the talent convincingly to stump the country in support of his reforms. In this respect he had much in common with Butler. Both men were at home and impressive in the House of Commons, but wretchedly inferior on public platforms and on television: being able to impress a television audience was increasingly becoming a requirement for prominent politicians.

The modest measures of reflation taken by Maudling were to sustain the economy for a time. However, the perennial problem of using public expenditure and reduced taxation to induce economic development remained. There was another difficulty. Alastair Horne[26] recounts, in an affecting way, Macmillan's physical and mental decline throughout 1963. He told Horne that in 1963 he had begun 'to get very tired . . . to lose grip'. Quite apart from the question of whether the kind of economic policy he favoured could be made to work there was the fact that his powers were failing. There is no doubt that the Profumo scandal hit him very hard. And, in spite of the successful negotiation of the Nuclear Test Ban Treaty, a multitude of problems confronted him. We can detect here the symptoms of declining health, indicating the onset of the problem of an inflamed prostate gland, which led to his retirement in October 1963.

From the French veto in January to the Tory Party Conference in October Macmillan was evidently losing command. Even though it is fair to say that he was the guiding hand behind the Test Ban Treaty negotiations, he left the work to Home and to Hailsham.[27] Thus it was that the magisterial hand which had first slipped during the reshuffle of July 1962 had fallen quite away in 1963. There was almost no guidance from No. 11, Downing Street (where the Macmillans had been living for nearly three years while No. 10 was being reconstructed) on the conduct of economic affairs. It must be remembered that, although Maudling was an assured Chancellor, he was a newcomer to the front rank of politics and needed the guidance of a Prime Minister possessed of the manipulative skill that Macmillan showed in his heyday. So far as domestic affairs were concerned, Macmillan seems to have spent the better part of his time discussing, with various confidants, the question of whether or not he should stay on and fight the forthcoming General Election, or resign.

Macmillan was a complex man and it is difficult to form a definite opinion about the reason for many of his decisions. Alistair Horne believes that he was too embarrassed to confess to his doctor, Sir John Richardson, his increasing urinary discomfort. In any event, on the night of 7 October he found himself in severe pain. Sir John Richardson being on holiday he consulted Richardson's locum, Dr King-Lewis, who gave him temporary relief. The following morning Macmillan chaired his last Cabinet. He had resolved, by then, to announce his retirement at the Conservative Party Conference the following week.[28] At the Cabinet meeting he seemed to his colleagues to be distracted, and sipped constantly from a glass containing the medicine which King-Lewis had prescribed for him. That evening he was in pain again and was admitted to King Edward VII Hospital for Officers, where he was operated on two days later.

At the time, it was generally accepted that Macmillan's state of health was the reason for his resignation. This is, at the very least, questionable. Within a week, while requiring a period of convalescence, he was fit again. My own conviction is that the operation was an excuse for a man who had, quite simply, lost heart. The French veto and the Profumo affair, not to mention the various espionage scandals,[29] had sickened him of office. (It is worth mentioning that in January 1964 General de Gaulle was operated on for exactly the same prostate condition that had afflicted Macmillan and was back at his desk ten days later.) What, I believe, was important for Macmillan was not to be seen to be driven from office by an accumulation of economic problems and scandals. His prostate provided a convenient excuse.

Home was President of the National Union of Conservative and Unionist Associations, and was to preside over the final day of the Party Conference. To him, therefore, Macmillan consigned his letter of resignation as Leader of the Party.[30] When Home read the letter out to the Conference, near chaos ensued as rival factions immediately began to campaign for their favourite candidates. However, Macmillan had organised the succession to himself.[31] Supposedly ill, he nonetheless managed to so arrange matters that Butler would not succeed him. He cast around for other possible candidates and considered, at various times during his stay in hospital, Iain Macleod, Reginald Maudling and Quintin Hailsham, all of whom, for one reason or another, he judged to be unacceptable to the Party, either in Parliament or in the country. He therefore settled on the Foreign Secretary, Lord Home.

The operation by which he procured the succession of Lord Home was marked by chicanery. Home was willing to be Prime Minister; he did not realise that he was merely the object of Macmillan's determination to block Butler. In a slender book, published in January 1964, *The Fight for the Tory Leadership*, Randolph Churchill argued that 'Macmillan did all he could during his seven years as Prime Minister to advance the fortunes of Butler.' As Iain Macleod pointed out in the *Spectator* on 17 January:

> Almost anything can no doubt be argued, but no one close to politics or to Harold Macmillan could seriously support this suggestion for a moment. The truth is that at all times, from the first day of his premiership to the last, Macmillan was determined that Butler, although incomparably the best qualified of the contenders, should not succeed him. Once this is accepted, all Macmillan's actions become at least explicable.

Thus, when the Queen visited Macmillan in hospital, he gave her his view that Home had the overwhelming support, not only of Parliament, but of the Cabinet.[32] On 25 October 1963, the Chief Whip, Martin Redmayne, made a speech at Bournemouth, timed to coincide with the by-election at Kinross and West Perthshire at which Home was seeking to return to the House of Commons. He argued that Macmillan was right in this respect. On 18 October five members of the Cabinet met for lunch. All five were for Butler. Butler himself, Hailsham and Boyle were not present. We know, however, that Boyle was for Butler, Butler for himself and Hailsham likewise for himself. That left six Cabinet members, one of whom was Home, who, obviously, was for himself. Even if one were to suppose that all of them were for Home it is ludicrous to contend that he had the overwhelming support of the majority.

The immediate difficulties that Lord Home faced were political, though, in the longer term, the state of the economy was to present him with most of his problems, and in that area he proved in the brief period that he was to hold office creative in a very different way from Macmillan and Maudling. His immediate political problems, however, were two. He had to disclaim his peerage and find a seat in the House of Commons. He was determined that the House should not begin the business of the session in his absence. He therefore instructed the new Leader of the House, Selwyn Lloyd, to use the Conservative majority to prorogue Parliament until he became, again, an MP. A month later he won the seat of Kinross and West Perthshire.[33] His second major political problem was the refusal of Iain Macleod and Enoch Powell to serve in his administration, having nailed their colours so firmly to the mast of Butler, thus depriving Home of the services on the front bench of two of the most effective debaters in the House of Commons. The action of the two men was judged to be quixotic – after all, Butler himself joined the new Cabinet as Foreign Secretary. Macleod, however, had a particular argument. When Lord Hailsham succeeded to his title in 1950 he tried to persuade Churchill and Attlee to introduce the same kind of legislation which was eventually introduced by Macmillan, to enable him to disclaim the title and remain in the House of Commons. In Macleod's view, therefore, Hailsham was acting naturally in taking advantage of the Peerage Act of 1963 and would have been an acceptable candidate for the leadership. Macleod later wrote:

Unlike Hailsham, he [Home] was not a reluctant peer, and we were now proposing to admit that after twelve years of Tory government no one amongst the 363 members of the party in the House of Commons was acceptable as Prime Minister. I felt it more straightforward to put these views to him tonight [17 October] rather than perhaps have to put them in other circumstances tomorrow.

I did not hear what Powell said to Lord Home, but I believe that he spoke to him on similar lines.[34]

Sir Alec Douglas-Home, as he then became, made more than one surprising appointment. He gratified a wish that Butler had had for many years and made him Secretary of State for Foreign and Commonwealth Affairs. He brought Selwyn Lloyd back from the wilderness to be Leader of the House of Commons, and he moved Edward Heath from the Foreign Office to become Secretary of State for Trade and Industry, with particular responsibility for regional development.

Sir William Haley, then the Editor of *The Times*, had written a leading article suggesting that the Conservative Party should skip a generation and choose Heath as their Leader because of his relative youth and commitment to radical economic policy. On the evening of 13 October 1963 Heath had written to Home – his senior at the Foreign Office – to say that he would in no circumstances be a contender for the leadership of the party. Douglas-Home had been impressed by Heath's grasp of economic and industrial affairs, as demonstrated in a series of reports from the Brussels negotiations. Douglas-Home was no economist but he, instinctively, took the view that the United Kingdom would be most effectively revived by ending controls on retail prices. One hangover from wartime controls was the Retail Price Maintenance Act of 1940. This Act, by controlling prices, ensured that small shops and firms were protected from the breeze of competition from the burgeoning supermarket chains. Edward Heath, drawing on his experience in negotiations with the EEC, had come to the conclusion that Retail Price Maintenance should be abolished, and a Bill to that effect was introduced in the House of Commons on 14 April 1964. Heath attempted to justify the terms of the Bill to the 1922 Committee[35] just after its printing. He met a wave of hostility, for Conservative backbenchers, many of whose constituents were small shopkeepers who feared the advent of the supermarket age, enjoyed the comfort of a government which provided for security of prices. For a few days it seemed as though Heath's Bill would never pass through Parliament. Douglas-Home, however, believed in competition rather than control. Against the advice of Maudling, he reconvened the 1922 Committee and persuaded them that healthy competition being the prerequisite for the development of a strong economy they should support Heath's bill. His easy authority within the party was such that, despite misgivings, the Bill passed through the House and became law on 16 July 1964.

It is worth emphasising that the abolition of RPM prefigured not only the policy of the Heath Government of 1970 and that of the Thatcher Governments of 1979 onwards, but that it was, though unrecognised as such at the time, the beginning of the break with the post-war consensus

Clement Attlee, Leader of the victorious Labour Party
at the 1945 General Election.

Winston Churchill
speaking at the annual Conservative Party Conference.

A small admirer presenting Winston Churchill with some flowers
after he recorded his vote at St. Stephen's Hall, South Kensington for the 1950 Election.

Ernest Bevin, the formidable Foreign Secretary in the first post-war Labour administration.

Aneurin Bevan in 1951.

Hugh Dalton, Chancellor of the Exchequer
in the first post-war Labour administration, photographed with the famous Budget Box.

Sir Anthony Eden at the time of the Suez Crisis,
October 1956.

Hugh Gaitskell, Leader of the Labour Party.

R. A. Butler leaving his home in Smith Square
with the Budget Box, 1955.

and Keynesian economics. There were many crises to come; but the abolition of RPM marked the beginning of a new economic order.

Nonetheless, the fact that the Prime Minister had to come to the rescue of the Secretary of State for Trade and Industry and persuade Conservative backbenchers – not to mention supporters of the party in the country – to back the necessary legislation indicates how difficult economic reform can be in Britain. The unpopularity of the measures to abolish RPM did not prevent Heath becoming Leader of the Party in 1965, but it certainly damaged Douglas-Home's election prospects. Heath's success in 1965 had a number of causes which we will examine later, but it is a particularly good illustration of the rule that unpopular action in the economic sphere excites initial outrage but, once the electorate adjusts to the new order of things, it is generally prepared to accept it.

Douglas-Home's difficulty was that he had so little time. There was no question that the government of which he took charge in October was in trouble. Racked by scandal and by the intra-party quarrelling that had followed Macmillan's retirement, it also faced a highly uncertain economic situation. There was the further problem that speculation about the date of the General Election had become intense. Douglas-Home immediately acted by issuing a statement saying that he would not hold an election before the last possible date, October 1964. While this had the useful effect of calming the money market and generally making the political waters more still, it also, to the detriment of Douglas-Home's ambitions, deprived the government of any opportunity to spring an electoral surprise.

In planning the election campaign, Douglas-Home decided that the retention of an independent nuclear deterrent for Britain would be a key issue and that economic policy, vital though it was, would not necessarily tell in favour of the Labour Party.[36] Quite apart from the fact that Douglas-Home felt strongly about defence matters, there was the advantage that Conservative defence policy was sharply distinct from that of Labour. In deference to the left wing of his party, Wilson had undertaken to absorb Britain's nuclear forces into an Atlantic Nuclear Force.[37] So far as the economy was concerned, the question posed to voters was which side could manage affairs better. Labour, it is true, had promised to nationalise the steel industry, but that was the only major economic difference between the parties as the election approached. Unfortunately for Douglas-Home he, as a landed aristocrat, was far less convincing in his enunciation of economic policy than was Wilson, and even the considerable skills of Maudling were insufficient to overcome the perceived gap in capacity between the two leaders. Nonetheless, it is important to remember and to emphasise the fact that, while in October 1963 Labour enjoyed a 15 per cent lead in the opinion polls, the swing to the opposition a year later was only 3 per cent. Instead of his expected majority of more than 50, Wilson had a majority of only three in the House of Commons, and this was insufficient to enable him to go ahead with the nationalisation of steel, since two Labour backbenchers, Woodrow Wyatt and Desmond Donnelly, had made plain their intention of voting against any measures of nationalisation. Alec Douglas-Home, for all that he went down to defeat, had served his party well. As Iain Macleod said of R. A. Butler, Douglas-Home always performed better in any job he was given than he was expected to.

CHAPTER FIVE

The Promise of White Heat
(1964–1966)

When he became Prime Minister Harold Wilson had a distinct advantage in that he had served as Leader of the Opposition for only a brief period. Initially, when Hugh Gaitskell's untimely death caused Wilson's elevation, with a General Election imminent, Wilson's situation was widely thought to be disadvantageous, for he was pitted against one of the most remarkable, and most skilful, politicians of modern times – Harold Macmillan. Iain Macleod, indeed, to the end of his life, believed that Macmillan would have beaten Wilson in a General Election.[1] In the event, however, he was confronted by a man widely seen to be incompetent in matters domestic and a Conservative Party seriously divided and weakened by the refusal of Macleod and Enoch Powell to serve under their Party Leader.

As already mentioned, Lord Home had announced almost immediately upon becoming Prime Minister that he would not seek a dissolution until the last possible moment – that is to say, October 1964. In consequence, the Labour Party could husband its financial resources without being kept constantly in dread of a snap General Election. At the same time, it gave Wilson, free from the cares of fund-raising and administration, a golden opportunity to exploit his undoubted superiority to the Prime Minister in the House of Commons and on public platforms. Wilson's verbal dexterity and, it is not unfair to add, his unscrupulousness with words regularly caught Home at a disadvantage. In addition the pace of events from February 1963 was so fast that the superficiality of the Labour Party's planning for government did not become evident. Once in power Wilson used his slender majority – of three – to justify his failure to deliver on any of his major promises: he enjoyed, in addition, the advantage which any incoming government enjoys for some time, of being able to blame its own problems on the failures of its predecessor.

Wilson exploited this advantage with what can only be described as brilliance. It was not until 1966, when the country responded to his plea for a decent majority by giving him one of almost 100, that the threadbare nature of his policies and of his competence began to become apparent.

Wilson's savagery in political debate became legendary within a few weeks of his succession to Gaitskell. However, the public image belied the private man. He used his oratory to convey the impression of a man who, while possessed of ideals, was also ruthless in action. He was an essentially kindly man, among whose major weaknesses was a chronic reluctance to dismiss from government old friends and supporters whose inadequacies were glaringly apparent to the public.

Wilson was also intensely patriotic. His patriotism took forms, one at least of them foolish, but nonetheless representative of most of the politicians of the time. The first was the retention of a British military presence of considerable size in the Far East. The second was the retention of a similar presence in the Middle East in Aden and the area now known as Yemen. It is fair to say that he was fully supported in these objectives by the Cabinet which he headed, and by no Minister more enthusiastically than the Secretary of State for Defence, Denis Healey. Given that, under the NATO Treaty, the United Kingdom had substantial responsibilities in Western Europe, these burdens were beyond the capacity of a fragile economy. To Wilson, however, retaining a world-wide military presence was an essential part of his concept of his country's role in the world.

Given these burdens, combined with domestic economic problems, the most important error of the first Wilson administration was its determination to preserve the fixed exchange rate of sterling. I have already noted[2] that the fact that sterling was a reserve currency imposed burdens on the British economy which were eventually to prove intolerable. Nonetheless, the Prime Minister and the Chancellor of the Exchequer, James Callaghan, fought to the bitter end to preserve the value of the pound as against all other currencies. Since the world did not share their conviction as to its value there were constant attacks by international financiers on the pound and, ultimately, the Wilson government was forced, in 1967, to devalue. So much time had been lost in holding to a fixed exchange rate, however, that it was virtually impossible for the government to organise an economic recovery.[3]

When Wilson took office the balance of payments deficit was expected to reach £400 million by the end of 1964. (The figure for the year turned out to be £385 million, but it is important to remember in the 1990s how enormous those figures seemed at the time.) Wilson's first act, once he had appointed a Cabinet, was to impose a surcharge of 15 per cent on all imported goods. This created uproar among the members of the European Free Trade Association, because it was against the rules to which Britain had agreed on joining EFTA on 20 November 1959. The new Government's action particularly excited annoyance on the part of Reginald Maudling: Maudling, who was sceptical in the extreme about the desirability of the United Kingdom joining the EEC, was a particularly strong supporter of EFTA, and indeed could fairly claim that EFTA was his brainchild. The surcharge, however, was more of a gesture designed to emphasise, during a period when the Government was, from day to day, unsure of its parliamentary majority and fearful of by-elections, the supposedly dreadful legacy that it had inherited. The impost was reduced to 10 per cent in April 1965 and abolished in November 1966. The balance of payments deficit did fall, during 1965, to £45 million. In the election year of 1966 there was a surplus of £109 million, though that had turned into a deficit of £294 million by the end of 1967.

By far Wilson's most striking innovation, however, was one based on a blueprint prepared for him by two Cambridge economists, Nicholas Kaldor and Thomas Balogh (both later to receive peerages). The idea was to create a Department of Economic Affairs, which through the operation of what Wilson called 'creative tension' would compete with the Treasury.[4] This Ministry Wilson gave to his Deputy Leader, George Brown. Brown was a fervent believer in the policy of economic expansion through high public expenditure and state regulation of industry. He was the creator of a whole series of National Plans. At the Treasury, however, Wilson installed a far more prudent figure in the shape of James Callaghan, who was, largely through his inability to understand economics, to preside over a disastrous collapse of sterling three years later. The difficulty facing Brown was that he had no real power to engage in anything other than exhortation. The spending Ministries preferred to negotiate direct with the Treasury, as they had done from time immemorial. In August 1966 Wilson was to move Brown to the Foreign Office and replace him with the then Foreign Secretary, Michael Stewart, whose brief it was to run the Department down.[5]

The first Wilson Cabinet was gravely inhibited by the fact that it enjoyed only a tiny majority. Moreover, it suffered a severe blow on election day itself, when the Foreign Secretary-designate, Patrick Gordon Walker, lost his seat at Smethwick. The Prime Minister went ahead and made Gordon Walker Foreign Secretary anyway. This was, however, a situation that could not be long sustained. A seat had to be found for him and the member for Leyton, Reg Sorenson, very much against his will, was prevailed upon to stand down.[6] Unfortunately for the Government, but the cause of much hilarity for the Opposition, Gordon Walker lost Leyton, hitherto a safe Labour seat. Wilson was therefore obliged to find a new Foreign Secretary, which to general amazement turned out to be Michael Stewart.

Wilson's other major innovation, by which he set much store, was the creation of the Ministry of Technology. Like so many of Wilson's initiatives, the creation of this new Ministry had more style than substance. It grew out of the slogan about technology which so influenced his short time as Leader of the Opposition. Wilson admired Winston Churchill's conduct of a wartime government and, convinced that the country faced a monumental crisis, thought it wise to bring into the Cabinet a senior trade union leader. The appointment of Frank Cousins, General Secretary of the Transport and General Workers Union, as Minister for Technology, was done in imitation of Churchill's appointment of Ernest Bevin as Minister for Labour in 1940. Churchill's view was that Bevin, as the most important trade unionist of his time, could ensure that there was no disruption of labour during a war: Bevin did that job with great efficiency.

Wilson's view was that the trades unions could be brought to accept radical changes in their patterns of work and in their attitudes to wage negotiation if they were confronted across the negotiating table by one of their own; and Cousins seemed to him to be the perfect man. Wilson was particularly influenced by his desire to save the British computer industry and, during the evening after his General Election triumph, he asked Cousins to accept a Labour nomination to a seat in the House of Commons, and to take, among many other things, the computer industry under his wing.[7] Wilson was, at least notionally, clever in doing this. The advent of the computer age was bound to, as he saw it, reduce the demand for labour at a time when British industry was labour-intensive. Of all unions, the TGWU was most insistent on keeping its members in jobs. Wilson, therefore, thought that by co-opting its General Secretary into government he would turn Frank Cousins from poacher into gamekeeper. It was the role of Cousins to persuade the trade union movement to accept large-scale redundancies rather than to keep his members, as well as members of other trade unions, in work.

However, Wilson failed to distinguish between a country at war and a country at peace. Though Bevin was unable to prevent a brief strike by the National Union of Mineworkers in 1941,[8] by and large he was able to keep the labour force happy during the protracted and bloody war against Germany. Cousins was both unable and unwilling to do the same job for Harold Wilson in peacetime. Wilson did not delude himself, however, with the idea that Cousins understood the developing requirements of either the computer industry in particular or the demands of modern industry in general. The Prime Minister had, himself, been deeply impressed by a lecture delivered by C. P. Snow in 1963. Snow had been a physicist who had taken to writing novels, and was a close friend of a brilliant Labour backbencher, Maurice Edelman.[9] His most famous work, consisting of eleven novels, was the 'Strangers and Brothers' sequence, the final volume of which, *Corridors of Power*, came out in July 1964. This novel was concerned particularly with political manoeuvres in the Civil Service. Snow's lecture, which was published in 1963, was called *The Two Cultures*. Its thesis was that modern man needed to have a serious knowledge of science, as well as a serious knowledge of literature and that 'culture' should be defined in both dimensions. The most quoted passage of the lecture, delivered to the Royal Academy of Science, laid down that knowledge and understanding of the Second Law of Thermodynamics was an essential part of the equipment of any civilised human being.[10]

This was the sort of flashing phrase that appealed to the new Prime Minister. He approached Snow, and asked him to take on the job of Parliamentary Under Secretary at the Ministry of Technology, dangling before the novelist the inducement of a peerage. Despite some misgivings, Snow accepted. The misgivings were based on the quite justified belief that, having been a novelist since 1946, he was quite out of date with scientific developments and could not perform the task which the Prime Minister had laid down for him. He was soon to find, however, that he could not get on with Frank Cousins and he told the Prime Minister before the General Election of April 1966 that he intended to resign as soon as the campaign was over. His resignation was delayed only because he did not wish to embarrass his patron. The creation of the Ministry of Technology, like the creation of the Department of Economic Affairs, was an example of Wilson's belief that the dramatic gesture constituted substantive policy. It is intriguing to reflect on the fact that Harold Macmillan and Harold Wilson had more than their Christian names in common. Both men tended to react to problems and crises by creating new institutions.

The situation in which Harold Wilson found himself between October 1964 and March 1966 was one in which he had very little power, and his liking for office was such as to enable him to indulge the tactical cunning which was so marked a feature of his character. From the moment of his

victory over Douglas-Home Wilson's eye was firmly fixed on the next
General Election, and his appeal to the electorate was based almost
wholly on the proposition that, without a proper mandate, he could not
fulfil the glittering promises of the Labour election manifesto of 1964.
The Government that took office in 1964, therefore, devoted itself almost
entirely to short-term stratagems. The electorate, however, came to
believe that Wilson did deserve a decent mandate, and returned him to
power in March 1966 with a majority of 110 over the Conservative Party:
there were also 12 Liberals and two Nationalist Members. The Wilson
government had won an unchallengeable majority. By then, however, it
was too late for achievement. The various measures that the first Wilson
Cabinet introduced in 1964 were such as to promote inflation, unemployment and a run on sterling. So adroit was the Prime Minister as a
political performer, however, that he was able to postpone the day of
reckoning until 18 November 1967 when, the currency having collapsed,
the Chancellor of the Exchequer, James Callaghan, had to devalue the
pound. The Chancellor immediately proffered his resignation, but Wilson persuaded him to move to the Home Office. The then Home Secretary, Roy Jenkins, replaced Callaghan at the Treasury.

The rhetoric of the Labour Opposition between 1963 and the General
Election of 1964 suggested that a Labour government would act in a
radical fashion to restore the health of the British economy. However,
the Leader of the Opposition himself, and his various colleagues, gave
some important hostages to fortune. One statement by Wilson covered a
whole series of proposals and promises. In his October 1964 election
address Wilson said 'Labour plans to get our economy on the move
again, so that we can have steady industrial growth all the time.' A
month earlier he had promised that the whole Labour programme could
be carried through without any increase in taxation. George Brown
undertook, on 27 September 1964, to stop the rise in the cost of living.
Brown also said that mortgage rates would be 'of the order of 3 per cent'.
The Labour election manifesto further promised to reduce the average
number of pupils in school classes from 50 to 30. There was also a
commitment in the manifesto to a massive expansion of university education. At the same time Wilson promised to expand the Navy and not, as
some left-wing Labour Members had suggested should be done, to
cancel TSR 2.[11] Finally, there was a Labour commitment substantially to
increase overseas aid as a percentage of Gross National Product.

It is a melancholy part of the record of the Wilson government of 1964
that it proved impossible to keep any of these promises. Personal and
business taxation doubled between 1964 and 1966. The cost of living rose

by 25 per cent. Mortgage interest rose to 8.5 per cent. School classes, far from declining to an average of 30 pupils to a class, remained at the average of 50. The percentage of Gross National Product devoted to overseas aid declined within a year of Wilson's victory from 0.53 in 1964 to 0.42 in 1966.

Throughout 1963 and 1964 the Conservative government had constantly asked how the Labour Party proposed to pay for all its schemes. The answer, invariably, was that a Labour Government would substantially increase economic growth, though the methods which they would employ were nebulous in the extreme. It is a matter of record that, Wilson having promised a growth rate of between 5 per cent and 6 per cent, saw that rate decline from just under 3 per cent at the time of the General Election to just under 2 per cent by 1966.

The first Wilson government was faced with a serious dilemma. Its ambitious schemes, it seemed from the beginning, could be paid for only by dramatic increases in national productivity. But the required growth was not forthcoming. A decision was therefore taken to control prices and incomes, the belief being that if these costs were held down the economy would enter a boom period, thus making the increased expenditure to which the Government was committed possible.[12]

One of the tactical advantages which Wilson enjoyed, and which drew attention away from his difficulties, was the turmoil in the Tory Party after the October 1964 defeat. For all that he had come so close to victory, it was clear that Sir Alec Douglas-Home would have to introduce a new and more open system of leadership choice. It was no longer acceptable to the Party either in the House of Commons or in the country that a Leader should emerge: some form of election had to be adopted. Wilson affected to be amused by the Opposition's troubles, and affected further to treat the Liberals, with their handful of seats, as being as worthy of consideration as the Conservatives: he emphasised this attitude by making the Liberal Leader, Jeremy Thorpe, a member of the Privy Council, the first time this had been done since the decline of the Liberal Party in the 1930s. The period of Conservative turmoil was most aptly summarised by Wilson in a sentence he was to repeat again and again whenever he was asked to comment on Conservative affairs: 'I never intrude on private grief'.

Alec Douglas-Home was more than willing to change the system by which his Party chose a Leader, and he set up a committee to consider alternative methods. Two early decisions were taken. The first was that Conservative Members of the House of Lords would have no vote in a leadership election. The second was that the National Union of

Conservative and Unionist Associations – supposedly the voice of the Party in the country – would have no vote either. Conservative Members of Parliament were, therefore, sovereign. To the distress of his many friends and supporters, Home made it clear that he would not stand in any election.[13] Of the conceivable candidates Iain Macleod saw, sensibly, that his role in the decolonisation of Africa had gained him so many enemies that he had no prospects of success. The star of Quintin Hogg had long been in decline, and he also decided not to stand. Under the new system a victorious candidate would require a majority over all the other candidates of the votes cast. If no candidate acquired such a majority there would be a second ballot which only the first two – assuming there were more than two – candidates would contest. The winner in the second ballot would then become Leader.[14]

In the event three candidates – Edward Heath, Reginald Maudling and Enoch Powell – came forward. Heath did not gain a sufficiency of votes for outright victory in the first ballot, but Maudling and Powell immediately withdrew from the contest and thus, on 2 August 1965, Edward Heath became Leader of the Conservative Party.

Although before 1965 there had been no formal system of choosing a Conservative Leader, nonetheless there had frequently been competition. The striking thing about the election of 1965 was that all three candidates came from more or less the same background. Powell's parents were teachers; Maudling's father was a minor civil servant; and Heath's father a small builder. Heath's two successors, Margaret Thatcher and John Major, likewise came from humble backgrounds. In the leadership battle in 1975 only one candidate, William Whitelaw, came from a moneyed county background: 1965 thus marked the moment when the aristocratic or landowning gentry lost their hitherto dominant position in the Party.[15]

Edward Heath privately believed what Harold Wilson proclaimed in public – that the Conservative government had been tired and out of tune with the times in 1964. He realised both that a General Election could not be delayed for long given the government's slender majority and, further, that he was unlikely to win it. He therefore saw no reason to delay his elaborate plans for reformulating party policy root and branch. Unfortunately for him, however, the internal turmoil in the Conservative Party delayed the development of a tactically effective opposition. More-over, it quickly emerged that Heath was a wretched performer in the House, while Wilson showed himself to be always adroit and often brilliant. The travails of the government, many and great though they were, did not appear to damage the administration. Wilson actually went into the 1970 General Election campaign as a strong favourite, and it was a very great shock when he lost.

Wilson was a great admirer of President Kennedy, many of whose mannerisms he aped, and whose most famous phrase he adopted as his own.[16] This was the promise of 'a hundred days of dynamic action'.[17] The hundred days were scheduled to begin the day after the October 1964 General Election. Like most of Wilson's promises, this one turned out to be glittering rather than substantial.

Wilson had persuaded the country – and probably himself – that his economic legacy was a horrendous one, and it is certainly true that by a vital yardstick of the times, the balance of payments figures, the Conservative government had left behind it serious difficulties for the newcomers. Everything that the Wilson government did up to the General Election of April 1966 showed a clear determination to prove that government could run the economy through a series of controls more efficiently than could business. There was one qualification to this idea of control from Westminster and Whitehall, and that was the notion that government must proceed in collaboration with the trade unions. This was not an idea exclusive to the Labour Party, for the Churchill government of 1951 had believed in it as well.[18] The difference between Wilson and Churchill was that, while Churchill proceeded *ad hoc* in individual trade disputes, Wilson was prepared to enshrine trade union privilege in statute.

In 1965 the Trade Disputes Act was passed, giving more power to trade unions to establish closed shops. This immediately followed a successful action brought by a man against a trade union and his employer who had insisted that he join the union against his will. The Act made further legal actions of this kind impossible, thereby providing immunity for trade unions against actions in civil law. In addition it greatly strengthened and indeed enshrined the power of trade unions to enforce closed shops. Further – and this principle was not reversed until Mrs Thatcher became Prime Minister – it prevented employers from suing unions on the grounds of vexatious industrial action. Moreover, it established the right of unions to undertake secondary picketing. Thus, if there was industrial action in one factory there was nothing to prevent workers in another factory who may not even have belonged to the same union, from coming out in support of that industrial action. Wilson was later bitterly to regret the passage of this legislation and, in 1969, he sought to reverse it. But, despite the valiant efforts of the Secretary of State for Employment, Mrs Barbara Castle, he failed.[19]

Again, in 1965, the government imposed upon employers much more stringent conditions of employment, including much more generous terms for redundancy payments to their employees. This was, of course, yet another sop to the unions. The Wilson government, however, appreciating that the state of the economy was delicate, took further measures which, it was hoped, would provide breathing space for their grandiose plans to work. A surcharge of 15 per cent was imposed on all imports. Exchange controls, limiting the amount of money an individual could take abroad, were tightened. A Monopolies and Mergers Act imposed further controls on private, but not state-owned industry. A National Plan was announced – though without legislative backing – by which the Department of Economic Affairs would exhort, cajole and bully industry into setting targets approved of by the government. Finally, a Prices and Incomes Board was established, again without legislative support, to persuade the unions to limit wage demands and employers to restrict prices under the minatory influence of the government.

All of these measures proved futile. They were not, nonetheless – with the exception of the import surcharge – abandoned. As the sixties proceeded, the government increasingly resorted to legislation to enforce its wishes.

Just as Edward Heath assumed, in 1965, that there would be an early General Election which he would lose, Harold Wilson assumed that he would be able to call an early General Election, which he would win. Both men were right. The parliamentary situation for the first Wilson administration was so parlous that the Prime Minister could be forgiven for thinking that it was necessary to preserve his and his party's position rather than to embark upon the fundamental changes in the structure of the British economy which he had promised from 1963 onwards. Nonetheless, the fact was that time was lost between the narrow Wilson victory of 1964 and the substantial victory of 1966. The bright dreams with which the Labour Party came to power in 1964 were put aside for the nonce. Everything done by the government between October 1964 and April 1966 had more about it of showmanship than of substance. The harvest of powerlessness, and of display, was to be reaped only in 1967, when sterling was devalued.

It cannot be emphasised too often how the fate of British politics at the time depended upon Harold Wilson's failure to act on matters fundamental to the future of the country until he was forced to. The creation of a new ministry, the DEA, semi-official boards, and the endless succession of Royal Commissions were no substitutes for decisions on vital matters, of which there were two. The first was the value of sterling in relation to other currencies. The second was the question of trade union privilege: the rights, powers and influence of trade unions were to bedevil every government of whichever party from the mid-1960s until the mid 1980s.

The history of British politics since 1945 can be seen entirely in terms of imperial and economic policy. As the United Kingdom withdrew from Empire, she became more concerned with ideas of prosperity and economic management. Macmillan, Wilson and, afterwards, Edward Heath were the victims of a view of how to handle the economy which came directly from the period between the First and Second World Wars. But it had a deeper historical pedigree. From the Reform Act of 1832 – which gave the vote to all property-owning male householders – there was an ineluctable movement towards the making of decisions on behalf of the whole nation by central government. In our own century the most formidable proponent of this policy of centralisation was David Lloyd George. In 1911, with Winston Churchill, Lloyd George set up the first scheme for unemployment benefit and National Health Insurance. After the First World War, the Liberal Party having split between the followers of H. H. Asquith and Lloyd George, and the Liberal-Conservative coalition having broken up, Lloyd George, under the influence of Keynes, put forward a policy of the public financing of industry as well as welfare, which was accepted for many years thereafter as the only method of preserving and maintaining the prosperity which Britain had enjoyed when she was an imperial power. The essence of public policy from the 1930s until 1981 was the expansion of state power and state financing.[20]

'All politicians', said Keynes, 'are the slaves of some defunct economist.'[21] Strongly though he held to his view of how national policy should be conducted, Keynes was, at least, prepared to be self-critical, as the quotation illustrates. His general views, however, permeated British politics from 1918 onwards. It is a singular fact that those views were bred into the tone not only of naturally collectivist parties like Liberal or Labour, but into the ranks of Conservatives. There is no question but that many Conservatives believed that it was the duty of those who sought to govern the nation to improve the condition of the people, but there is also no question that, in an era of universal suffrage, the Conservatives felt themselves to be in crude electoral competition with other parties who made a more obvious, albeit superficial, appeal to the people. Various attempts to present a more radical Tory view of what needed to be done were made in the late 1960s and throughout the 1970s. But the continuing popularity of an essentially Keynesian view can be seen over nearly twenty years by reference to two books by exceptionally intelligent Conservative politicians, Timothy Raison and Chris Patten.[22] The major reply to Keynesianism was produced to virtually uniform ridicule by F. A. Hayek in 1944.[23] Hayek's belief was that, in a democratic age, there were collectivists in all parties, whatever their title. These were people who were convinced that good could be achieved only by centralised action and, in Hayek's mind, were essentially socialist. In his great attempt to persuade such people of the error of their ways, Hayek dedicated his masterwork 'To The Socialists of All Parties'. By the time Harold Wilson came to office in 1964, however, it was the ideas of Keynes rather than those of Friedrich Hayek which were triumphant.

Wilson was, of course, constrained by his tiny parliamentary majority, and by the sheer lack of experience of a Labour government. Ever afterwards Wilson believed that it was his vestigial majority which deprived him of the opportunity of enforcing radical measures between 1964 and 1966. He claimed that he wanted a mandate for radical reforms, 'in the event, we were denied that mandate; once again, a Labour Government was prevented from building on the foundations which it had laid'. (This excuse could not, of course, be given for the years of Labour government from 1966 to 1970, when Wilson enjoyed a majority of nearly 100). However, it is fair to say that the 1964 Government was inhibited by its inability to command a secure majority day by day in the House of Commons.

There is no evidence, however, that Wilson would have adopted any policies different from those he put forward between October 1964 and April 1966 than he did, in fact, propose. He was, throughout his first period in office, the victim of the collectivist notions outlined above.[24]

The Labour Party, of course, was born of ideology. It was also born of what can only be called sectarianism. The party was created by trade unions for trade unions, and it was therefore understandable that even as late as the period after the Second World War the major unions believed that a Labour government was *their* government, and that the Conservative Party represented only the employing classes. The Conservative Party never understood the deep resentment with which trade unionists greeted the economic proposals of a Labour government, particularly when such a government appeared to them be on the side of a Conservative front bench. The depth of feeling of the Labour Party, as stated again and again in speeches at party conferences, exemplified a resentment that was so powerful as to bring to defeat the administrations headed by Harold Wilson. The origins of this feeling about what made up the Labour Party were visceral and it seemed impossible to trade unionists that a Labour Government should act against the interests of the unions, as the unions saw them.[25] The essence of the Conservative appeal to the electorate throughout the century, but particularly after 1945, was and is the assumption that they are more competent in government, and particularly more competent at handling the economy. Another Conservative advantage is the widespread belief that Tory politicians are more patriotic, and more vigorous in pursuit of Britain's defence interests, than are their Labour counterparts: one of the issues which most helped Douglas-Home in the 1964 General Election campaign was his emphasis on the necessity of retaining Britain's nuclear deterrent, while Wilson proposed to submerge it in an Atlantic Nuclear Force. In times of international trouble the Conservative Party invariably is at an electoral advantage. It is believed, by myself among many others, that Douglas-Home would have won the General Election of 1964 had Nikita Kruschev been deposed twenty-four hours before, rather than twenty-four hours after the British General Election. The Labour appeal has almost always been to idealism rather than to efficiency. Wilson decided to alter that appeal and to argue that, in the modern age, the Conservatives were outmoded, and that he and his generation could provide the technocratic thrust that would make Labour, to use his own phrase 'the natural Party of Government'.[26]

Harold Wilson was an exceptionally adroit politician. He had no rival for cunning in the Labour Party, and his only rival as a political tactician was Harold Macmillan. It would be unfair, both to Wilson and to Macmillan, to say that they had no principles, but each man believed that his possession of office formed a perfect equation with the national good. This is not an uncommon characteristic of politicians. Indeed, the longer a politician holds office the more likely he is to see his continuance in office as a cause in itself. We need here, however, to distinguish between office and power. Power means doing things, probably of a radical nature. Holding office, on the other hand, increasingly becomes a matter of self-gratification.

It was necessary, of course, for Wilson to choose his moment for going to the country accurately. In February 1966 there was a by-election in the constituency of Hull South-East. The press believed that the Conservatives would retain the seat. The fact, however, that Mrs Barbara Castle, the Minister for Transport, was able to find funds for a new Humber Bridge did not do the prospects of the governing party any harm. Mr Kevin MacNamara, at the time of writing adorning the Labour front bench as Shadow Secretary of State for Northern Ireland, won the seat from the Conservatives by a majority of 7,500. This gave the green light to the Prime Minister to call a general election for 31 March. While the Conservative Party drew 11,418,433 voters to their cause, Labour attracted 13,064,951. Nonetheless, Labour emerged with 363 seats as against 253 Conservative seats. The Liberals returned 12 Members and other minor parties two. Wilson at last had the majority which he craved.

CHAPTER SIX

The Failure of a Majority
(1966–1970)

The belief that a government which has no fears of defeat in the House of Commons will be able readily to implement its programme has surfaced again and again throughout British political history. However, it is a melancholy fact about the nature of politics that a substantial majority can, of itself, achieve nothing unless the political leadership of the day is both decisive and competent. The second Wilson administration merely extended the politics of central planning in a way prefigured in the aspirations expressed between 1964 and 1966. Ministers failed to see two things. The first was that the international weakness of sterling would lead to economic crisis. The second was that the growing power of the trade union movement would prove to be incompatible with reform of the economic structure of the nation.

It seems increasingly clear that, having won his great majority in 1966, Wilson was more than content to lie back on the comfortable cushion of his oft-repeated assertion that Labour was by now the natural governing Party of the United Kingdom. This assertion was reinforced by his genuine contempt for the abilities of Edward Heath. His view, expressed in the preface to his memoirs, that Labour was in 1970 denied a mandate to continue down a path of radical and rejuvenating reform is self-serving: the fact of the matter is that the years from 1966 to 1970 were wasted, partly because most of the decisions taken were wrong; and partly because nearly all of them were incompetently administered.

For all that I have said about Harold Wilson in particular and the Labour government in general, the truth is that their aspirations for the country were generous. The plan, for example, to phase out grammar schools and introduce a wholly comprehensive system in the state sector may well be judged to have been misconceived – but that is to make a judgement in retrospect. The object of achieving a uniformly excellent

113

education for all children attending public sector schools was a worthy one. The aim of achieving full employment[1] was likewise worthy. Regarding the National Health Service, the government did not appreciate how great the fundamental problems were. These were accentuated by increasingly rapid advances in medical science and by the consequent rise in life expectancy of the population. But, then, the Labour Party having created the NHS, they regarded it with particular pride and joy, and were unwilling even to contemplate reforms in its basic structure.

From the General Election of April 1966 onwards Nemesis began to stalk the Wilson government. The contradictions inherent in what that government hoped to do became increasingly apparent. Further, the electorate was irritated by relatively trivial measures such as the announcement of the adoption of decimal currency in May 1966. More important was the fact that there was yet another sterling crisis in the middle of the year: this was caused by the conviction, yet again, of foreign investors that the United Kingdom was not a safe country in which to place their money. The Autumn Budget of 1966 saw, not only a sterling crisis, but an increase in credit restraints and, most important of all, the enactment of prices and incomes control by statute. The idea that prices and incomes could be controlled by government was a part of the centralising tendency which had become increasingly pronounced by 1966. Unfortunately for the Labour Party the trade unions were no longer reliable in the matter of controlling public expenditure. That the trade union movement was increasingly disenchanted with a Labour government was demonstrated by the highly successful merchant shipping strike at the end of 1966. This did serious damage to both exports and imports, and showed the inability of government to manage the economy on a day-to-day basis. The unions were particularly irritated by the idea that wage bargaining should be controlled by Whitehall, and by law. The union conviction was that *their* government was failing them. It is hard to recapture the emotional feelings of more than a quarter of a century ago. The conviction of most commentators, as well as of most politicians, that centralising economic decision-making was the way to success, led to the belief that there was something inherently wrong about the attitude of the British worker. Hence, blame for economic failure tended, in the early stages of the second Wilson administration, to be attributed to the people rather than the government. The connection was not made between the Wilson administration's ambitions and the fact that they were certain to be frustrated by the power of the trade unions. It followed that intelligent and informed commentators concluded that there was something fundamentally wrong in the body politic rather than in the government. In my own view the inability of the administration elected in 1966 to take early and harsh decisions was crucial to the steady decline both of the Labour Party and of the nation.[2]

A year after his General Election triumph of 1966 Harold Wilson found himself and the government which he headed in an exceptionally difficult position. He decided on two dramatic reversals of policy. In May 1967 he finally made up his mind to renew the application to join the EEC, initially made by Harold Macmillan in 1961. Much to his dismay, President de Gaulle renewed his veto on British membership in November. By this stage sterling was in a dangerous situation: very few foreign investors wanted to buy the currency, and those who held it wanted to sell.

In spite of repeated and emphatic assurances that he would not devalue the currency, Wilson nonetheless decided to do just that. This decision was arrived at sometime between October and November 1967. James (now Lord) Callaghan, the Chancellor of the Exchequer, having had little confidence in his own economic perceptions, and feeling himself guilty of poor stewardship of the national economy, promptly tendered his resignation.

Initially, Wilson tried to persuade the Chancellor to stay on, and to preside over the mechanics, as well as the tactics, of devaluation. This Callaghan could not bear to do.[3] Indeed, he wished to leave the government altogether. Nonetheless, with that adroit touch which never betrayed him in the handling of party politics, Wilson persuaded Callaghan to move to the Home Office while presenting the Home Secretary, Roy Jenkins, with the poisoned chalice of the Treasury. He himself took upon his shoulders the task of justifying the new policy to the nation. On 19 November 1967 he announced a drastic devaluation of the pound from $2.80 to $2.40, accompanied by a rise in Bank Rate to 8 per cent. A major credit squeeze was thus introduced, but however nimble Wilson's handling of devaluation was in party terms it did not go down well with the public, and the Prime Minister's televised statement, which included the unfortunate – and inaccurate – sentence 'the pound in your pocket will not be devalued', gave the Tory Party much propaganda fodder in the years to come.

Callaghan[4] gives us an account of a Cabinet meeting in July at which the question of devaluation was discussed. In the view both of Prime Minister and Chancellor there was an alternative. Hire purchase controls could be tightened; there could be a 10 per cent increase in duties on drink, tobacco, petrol and purchase tax; there could be a 10 per cent surcharge on surtax, and a cut of £100 million pounds on overseas military and civil expenditure. Finally, the Prime Minister proposed that all prices, wages and salaries should be frozen for a six-month period. With the exception of the last proposal, the measures that Wilson favoured were very similar to the central doctrine of what later became known as monetarism: the principal idea was that the government should not spend more than it raised in revenue. In other words, the budget should be balanced. However, the Cabinet could not agree to this package, and George Brown, as Secretary of State for Economic Affairs, maintained a sulky silence throughout the debate.

Using hindsight is always a risky business. But, in my judgement, Wilson would have been wiser to have devalued the pound immediately after his General Election victory in 1964, when he could have blamed the necessity for this drastic action on the economic legacy of the Conservative government which, he had convinced the public, was a disastrous one. As a second best choice, he could have devalued after his victory in April 1966. The difficulty Wilson faced until he was forced to take action in November 1967 was his emotional commitment to maintaining sterling at the international parity which he inherited: as a supreme party political propagandist, moreover, he was acutely conscious of the fact that, in the post-war past, only a Labour government had, in 1949, devalued the currency. He was certain that the Conservative opposition would make a great issue of a second Labour devaluation, particularly as the very word 'devaluation' implied to the public at large not merely a technical economic adjustment, but a moral defeat.

It is salutary at this point to remind ourselves of the comparative records of the Conservative governments whose thirteen years in power ended in 1964 and that of the Labour government which ruled from 1964 to 1970. This requires a survey of the general economic indicators of the whole period from the end of the Second World War. Over the thirteen years of Conservative rule from 1951 the average standard of living went up by 50 per cent. That is more than in the whole of the previous half century. Prices rose half as fast as they did while Clement Attlee was in power. The top rate of purchase tax came down from 100 per cent to 25 per cent. The Conservatives ended rationing and, in the dying months of the Douglas-Home government, government controls on retail prices were abolished. Personal savings, encouraged by tax incentives, totalled £2,000 million in 1964, as opposed to just under £200 million in 1951. These figures are adjusted to allow for inflation.[5]

Why, then, was it deemed necessary by a Labour government to devalue the currency in 1967? The problems Labour faced at the point of devaluation were several. The trading deficit was a third larger than in

1964. Growth, which in 1964 was 3 per cent, had fallen to less than 2 per cent, which rapidly increased the erosion of confidence by investors, both domestic and foreign, in British industry. An unquantifiable foreign debt had been incurred: it certainly ran to hundreds of millions of pounds.

There were two Labour answers to this economic conundrum. The first was that favoured by George Brown and constituted the reason for his opposition to devaluation. This was that insufficient funds had been provided for the subsidisation of British industry. The second was that favoured by the left wing of the Labour Party, then strident but weak, though later to become powerful: it was for more stringent bureaucratic controls over private industry. Labour's tragedy lay in the fact that the government vacillated between these two strategic choices, and was unable, because of its visceral beliefs, to consider a third option – relaxation of controls and ending of subsidies paid for by the taxpayer. The first two Wilson administrations failed, at a very simple level, to deliver anything they promised to the people. Between 1964 and 1967 (the same held true of the following three years) there was no increase whatsoever in the standard of living of the average family.

Lest this stark account of the Labour record in the second half of the sixties be deemed unduly critical, it should be said that the Conservative governments between 1959 and 1964 had sustained themselves on the basis of a credit boom which was artificial. The belief was that by extending consumer credit the temporary problems of inflation would be overcome by the greater productivity excited by the desire of manufacturers and importers to appeal to the cupidity of consumers. It can thus fairly be said that governments of both parties failed to address themselves, until in both cases it was too late, to the underlying problems of the British economy. Each time a crisis arose which suggested that fundamental reforms had to be undertaken a cosmetic solution was propounded. The most prominent of these cosmetic solutions was membership of the European Economic Community; the most insubstantial was the National Plan propounded by George Brown in 1965. Between 1959 and 1970 governments of both parties were driven from pillar to post by their incapacity to do anything other than resort to expedients, when what was required was a cold and hard scrutiny of the structure of the economy itself. The truth was that both the Labour and the Conservative Parties – not to mention the Liberal Party – were working on the assumption that the United Kingdom could sustain both a welfare state and a manufacturing base which were heavily subsidised. This was because both Conservative and Labour governments believed

117

that subsidies from the taxpayer through the Treasury to manufacturing industry would be temporary. Bitter experience was to prove them wrong.

The 1967 devaluation was the moment when Wilson began to face up to the fact that the grand pretensions, both domestic and international, of British politicians could not be fulfilled. Wilson, in his memoirs[6], gives an affecting but, in my view, unconvincing account of his preparation for his announcement, on 19 November 1967, of devaluation. In the broadcast he said:

> I've said that imports will cost more, and this means higher prices over a period of time for some of our imports, including some of our basic foods. And it's vital that price rises are limited to those cases where increased import costs make this unavoidable.[7]

From 19 November 'politics were', as Wilson writes 'totally dominated by devaluation'.[8] In his memoirs Wilson defends his decision to devalue sterling as a solution to Britain's economic problems, but, as became rapidly clear, it was insufficient. The broadcast statement, however, presaged a further development of centralised control of the economy by its reference to limitations on price rises. Once the first move was made in this direction a universal control of price and wage levels by government was inevitable. It is fair to add that the movement towards controls undertaken by Wilson in 1967 was followed up by the Conservative government led by Edward Heath in 1972.

By November 1967 Wilson had still managed to avoid one of his major difficulties. This was the exceptional power which trade unions enjoyed to enforce wage rises, by means of industrial action, irrespective of the profitability of the companies involved.[9] Throughout 1968 more and more technical measures were adopted to reduce inflation. Major cuts were made in public expenditure. There was a strike by engineers, and the new Chancellor, Roy (now Lord) Jenkins, was obliged to arrange special financial provisions with the International Monetary Fund, which provisions enabled Britain to borrow more from the IMF.

Both the Chancellor and the Secretary of State for Employment, Barbara (now Lady) Castle, agreed that legislation to restrict trade union privilege was now necessary. In his budget statement on 15 April 1969 Jenkins agreed to abandon all measures to curb price and income increases, but insisted that the government would legislate to limit trade union powers. He said:

> We need to facilitate the smooth working of the process of collective bargaining in industry and to help to prevent the occurrence of

unnecessary and damaging disputes of which we have seen all too much recently, and which are totally incompatible with our economic objectives.

Thus the Chancellor acknowledged that the government of which he was a member had no power to go forward with the achievement of its aims as long as the unions enjoyed as much power as they then did.

This speech also revealed a serious division of opinion in the higher ranks of the Labour Party, and between the leadership of that party and the trade union movement. While the speech brought division to a head, the origins of the Labour government's problems were exemplified by the publication in 1969 of a White Paper prepared by Barbara Castle.

Confident in the support of Roy Jenkins and Barbara Castle, Wilson gave his authority for Mrs Castle to put her proposals for the reform of trade union law to the House of Commons, in a White Paper entitled *In Place of Strife*. This became the Industrial Relations Bill of 1969, which was debated in the House of Commons on 3 March 1969. Had this Bill been enacted it would have included provisions sketched out in the Chancellor's budget speech. The right of any individual worker to belong to a trade union would be enshrined in law. When an employer refused to acknowledge a trade union, that union would have the right to appeal to an industrial tribunal. Where more than one union was represented in a given industry a system of arbitration would ordain how matters were to be organised.

All this seemed agreeable to the trade union movement. What, however, was disagreeable to the unions was the provision, in Mrs Castle's Bill, that the government of the day would have the power to stop strikes by the imposition of a twenty-eight day ban on any industrial action. Even though unemployment benefit would be available to striking workers, the proposal to prohibit industrial action and the proposal, further, to impose financial penalties on trade unions supporting striking workers proved to be unacceptable to the majority of the Labour Party.

In the drama which rapidly unfolded there were certain key players. The first was the Prime Minister himself. There was the Chancellor of the Exchequer; the Secretary of State for Employment; the General Secretary of the Transport and General Workers Union, Jack Jones; the General Secretary of the General and Municipal Workers' Union, Hugh (now Lord) Scanlon, and the Chairman of the Parliamentary Labour Party, Douglas (now Lord) Houghton.[10] There was one other player in the game who was to prove to be of immense importance: he was James Callaghan, the Home Secretary.

On 7 May 1969 Douglas Houghton made a speech to the Party in which he said:

> The Government and the Party are one, and the sooner we become indivisible the better. Ministers must not fall into the error of believing that their determination and their resolve to force things through the Party and the House is either necessary or possible. It can only be done with us. It cannot be done without us. We must all strive to prevent 'Government by disintegration of the Labour Party' . . . No good that any contentious Bill of this kind can do to industrial relations or to the economy will redeem the harm we can do to our Government by disintegration or defeat of the Labour Party. Our unity and our political purpose matter more to the country than the marginal damage of unconstitutional strikes.

Houghton's speech represented a turning point in British politics. The fundamental problem that the Prime Minister faced was that he could certainly not rely on the support of the trade unions for Mrs Castle's policy and he might, even, not be able to rely on the support of his party in the House of Commons. He made a minatory speech to his back-benchers in which he threatened to seek a dissolution of Parliament in the event of their refusal to support Mrs Castle's Bill. Houghton consulted the Palace and came away with the conclusion that a dissolution would not necessarily be granted if the Labour Party could find an alternative Leader. The alternative Leader would have been James Callaghan, who made it clear to his friends – and there were many – among leading trade unionists that he was available.

The TUC General Council was utterly opposed to the proposals in the Castle Bill which would restrict their freedom of action, and on 7 January 1969 resolved that:

> To impose financial penalties on a union, on the grounds that in a Minister's opinion an (interunion) dispute may cause economic damage, would militate against finding a genuine solution for this problem . . . The General Council regard as completely misguided and quite unacceptable the Government's proposal to take discretionary powers to require a union to conduct a ballot (on an official strike) which, in a Minister's opinion, threatens economic damage . . . The General Council do not accept that it accords with democratic procedures to give a Minister unfettered discretion to invoke powers to fine workpeople solely on the grounds that in his opinion the results of

a(n unconstitutional) strike are likely to be serious, using such criteria as he may think appropriate . . . The General Council do not accept that there is any justification whatever for the Government to pursue (compulsory trade union registration) unless and until it can produce evidence that the General Council's own plans are not going to produce a satisfactory result.

As the year wore on it became increasingly apparent that the Prime Minister could not be certain of a majority in the House of Commons for his proposals to reform trade union law. This was a crucial period in the history of post-war British politics. If – and this was the way the matter was put in the press and on the broadcast media – a Labour government could not control the trade union movement, nobody could.

Given that the government had a majority of around 100, and could reasonably expect some Conservative votes, it was astonishing that the vote was won, with the help of the minority parties, by only 5 votes. One hundred Labour MPs either voted against Mrs Castle's Bill, or abstained. Harold Wilson's authority was undermined by the fact that the government had issued a three-line whip requiring the support of all Labour backbenchers. Still the Prime Minister did not see how much in danger he was. Mrs Castle saw the economic necessity of bringing the trade unions into line, but Wilson did not. The Prime Minister was confident that, faced with the economic difficulties of the nation, the most important trade union leaders, and the Labour Party, in the country as well as in Parliament, would support him. He was mistaken. Wilson and – in his wake – Jenkins and Mrs Castle retreated reluctantly. 'But the question at issue', Wilson told the TUC on 19 April 1969, 'really is whether the Labour government can continue. When I addressed the Parliamentary Labour Party and when I informed them of our intention to meet [with the TUC], I said "I have to tell you that the passage of this Bill is essential to the continuance of this Government in office".'

At this juncture the Conservative Party, in the person of the Shadow Secretary of State for Employment, Robert (now Lord) Carr, announced that the Conservative Party would support the proposed legislation. It now seemed clear that Wilson and Mrs Castle would have a majority in the House of Commons, but very possibly not a majority in the Labour Party. There now entered another player on the scene. This was Victor Feather, the General Secretary of the TUC. In a letter to Wilson he said that 'there was no chance of the Government carrying in the Commons a strike curb Bill containing any penal clauses . . . Not even if the

Commons were kept sitting well into August would there be any chance of the Bill getting through.'[11]

Feather was wrong since Wilson could certainly have carried the legislation through the House of Commons at Second Reading, but he could have been sure of doing so only with the support of the Conservative Party. This was bitterly unpalatable to him and would perhaps have undermined the government altogether. On 18 June, therefore, the Prime Minister and Mrs Castle met the TUC General Council and agreed that, in return for withdrawing the proposed legislation they would accept the promise of the trade union movement of 'a solemn and binding undertaking'[12] that the unions would attend to the national interest as defined by Ministers. In procuring this agreement the Prime Minister believed that he could rely on the leaders of the two biggest trade unions, Jack Jones and Hugh Scanlon (both, by virtue of the size of their unions, members of the TUC General Council), to keep in line not only their own members but the smaller unions as well. Therefore, although Victor Feather was the mediator who agreed the terms with the Prime Minister, the people who had, or were believed to have, the muscle to enforce it were Jack Jones and Hugh Scanlon.[13]

It was, of course, only a matter of four months before the agreement broke down. A rash of unofficial strikes broke out in the car industry; and Joe (now Lord) Gormley, the General Secretary of the National Union of Mineworkers, led his men out on an official strike. Jones and Scanlon either could not or would not use their influence to stop these industrial actions. The government quietly acquiesced in the proposition that the trade union movement was now virtually all-powerful. Mrs Castle was humiliated, but the Prime Minister survived. Mrs Castle, however, was consoled by the introduction of another piece of legislation on which she had set her heart. This was the Equal Pay Act, enshrining in statute equal payment for men and women doing jobs of equal value. The Equal Opportunities Commission was set up to police this Act. This represented a further growth in government power.

Giving Mrs Castle her way on equal opportunities for women was not, however, *just* a consolation prize for the failure of the Prime Minister to support her, but an adroit outmanoeuvring of the Conservative opposition. Robert Carr, the Shadow Secretary of State for Employment, immediately welcomed Mrs Castle's Bill and, against the advice he received from the Conservative Research Department, decided not to oppose the Bill on second reading, and to confine himself to marginal amendments during the Standing Committee Stage. The Equal Pay Bill, had, therefore, an easy passage through the House: it was popular throughout the country, and most particularly in the press and on radio and television.

Whatever its merits, the Equal Pay Act simply avoided the serious problems that British industry faced. A statistical comparison is in order here. It would be tedious to go into this comparison year by year, but it is instructive to note that while in 1946, days lost at work numbered 2,156,000 days lost at work in 1969 numbered 6,772,000. At this latter stage unemployment was approaching 600,000. One has to remember that, over the whole post-war period, local strikes had become a feature of the British industrial environment, and the number of strikes reflected not just the loss of control by governments of whichever Party over industry, but also a loss of control by the leadership of the major trade unions over their members. To illustrate: there were 2,191 strikes in 1946 and 3,021 in 1969. The dream of full employment and economic success with which Labour entered office in 1945 was therefore proved, by hard, and cold, statistics, to be unfulfilled by 1969. A further statistical comparison is apposite. Between 1963 and 1967 the United Kingdom lost 184 days of work per 1,000 employees, due to stoppages in the mining, manufacturing, construction and transport industries. Norway, on the other hand, lost 74 days. West Germany lost 34 days. The United States, Britain's only serious competitor in this slippage, lost 934. The Netherlands lost 16 days. To be fair, very large and very small economies can sustain losses of working days better than those of medium size. The population of the United Kingdom in 1969 was about 46 million, whereas that of the United States was rather over 300 million. Thus, the relative loss in productivity to a country striving to maintain its share of world markets was enormous. A striking comparison is with Japan, becoming increasingly a main competitor to Britain and the United States: the Japanese lost 200 working days in 1969, but the majority of these were in service, rather than manufacturing industries, and that figure was to come down very rapidly in the following years. Since Britain and Japan competed in many of the same markets the significant disparity between the United Kingdom figures and the Japanese figures meant, as we know by now, that the Japanese would enjoy an advantage in all markets where the two countries were in competition. Again it has to be said that British assumptions about the country's ordained right to a preferential share of world markets were to be shown to be unrealistic.

It was not merely the relative decline in British industrial productivity in relation to her competitors, but the inability of the Labour government to discipline the trade union movement which caused national

123

anxiety. When Harold Wilson decided to call a General Election in 1970, therefore, the new proposals for reform of the economy propounded by Edward Heath found a welcoming national ear.

However, Wilson did not appreciate how weak his electoral position was. He was a man of essentially sunny temperament, and, knowing his powers as a campaigner, could not bring himself to believe that he faced any formidable threat in Edward Heath. Moreover, he had himself secured the resignation of R. A. Butler and, in January 1970, Sir Edward Boyle, who, being unhappy both with Heath as Leader and with the direction of economic policy which he favoured, decided to accept an offer to become Vice-Chancellor of Leeds University. Heath made strenuous efforts to dissuade Boyle, and these became known. He made these efforts because he believed, as did the Prime Minister and most political commentators, that Boyle's appeal to the centre ground – and particularly educated, middle class, floating voters – was immense.[14] A further reason for Wilson's optimism was that, by April 1970, for reasons discussed below, the opinion polls, in which he had an almost religious faith, suggested a sharp upturn in the fortunes of the government.

But, the single most important buttress for Wilson's conviction that Heath could not win an election had in fact occurred two years earlier, following a speech by Enoch Powell on immigration on 20 April 1968. This procured Powell's dismissal from the Shadow Cabinet the following day.

The dismissal of Powell was, from Heath's point of view, necessary, for several Shadow Cabinet Ministers, including Edward Boyle and Quintin Hogg (now Lord Hailsham), had said they would resign if Powell retained his post. However, there was an angry national chorus of approval for Powell's stand. This made Heath's position more and more difficult. The crucial passage from the speech is this:

> That tragic and intractable phenomenon which we watch with horror on the other side of the Atlantic but which there is interwoven with the history and existence of the States itself, is coming upon us here by our own volition and our own neglect. Indeed, it has all but come. In numerical terms, it will be of American proportions long before the end of the century. Only resolute and urgent action will avert it even now. Whether there will be the public will to demand and obtain that action, I do not know. All I know is that to see, and not to speak, would be the great betrayal.

In general, Powell received more than ordinarily unfavourable press coverage for the speech. However, he also enjoyed demonstrable approval from the public: London dockworkers – natural Labour voters – marched to the House of Commons to demonstrate their support for him; and he received more than 40,000 letters of support from the general public. This, of course, worried Heath and cheered Wilson. The Labour Party, in keeping with its intense belief in egalitarianism and antiracialism, was virulent in its opposition to Powell. But no one could deny his popular support. We know now that Wilson believed that Powell would embark on a consistent programme of seeking to destroy Heath.[15]

It is interesting to observe that, for the next six years, while opinion polls recorded often dramatic fluctuations in the popularity of Harold Wilson and Edward Heath, Powell's public approval rating remained rock steady at 41 per cent. My own opinion is that between 1968 and February 1974 Enoch Powell was the most influential politician in the country in the sense that he could persuade important numbers of voters to give their support to whichever major party he favoured. During the 1970 General Election campaign Harold Wilson was prepared to contemplate, with pleasure, the spectacle of a Conservative Party divided against itself. In the campaign of February 1974, however, Wilson took the greatest care to synchronise his own speeches with those of Powell, for he had sound reasons to believe that, on this occasion, Powell, who had stood down as a Conservative candidate, would advocate a vote for Labour.[16]

The quarrel between Heath and Powell in 1968 was dramatic, but it did not interrupt the steady preparation by the Leader of the Opposition for a General Election. The most radical proposals adopted by Heath were to eschew altogether restraint of incomes by government fiat and thoroughly to reform trade union law, taking away from the unions privileges that they had enjoyed since 1905 and which were enhanced by the 1966 government.[17]

While it is an obligation enforced on British governments to hold a General Election after five years in office, the more normal post-war pattern has been to go to the country after four years. The assumption is that a Prime Minister can seek a dissolution of Parliament from the sovereign at any time he or she wishes, and have his or her wish granted. From 1966 onwards Harold Wilson's eyes were fixed on the next occasion on which he would seek a renewed mandate. His contempt for – and dislike of – the Leader of the Conservative Party was such that, once public opinion polls showed an improvement in the government's position, Wilson began to think of going to the country once again. He was convinced that the difficulties he had been experiencing in government were less relevant to his concern with holding on to power than were the problems of the economy.

Those difficulties in the economy were serious. The trade unions were far less pliable that Wilson supposed them to be. In 1969 both the car workers at British Leyland and the miners struck for increased pay. At the beginning of 1970 the dockers and local authority workers, and the miners again, struck. As, it seemed, the almost perennial cuts in public expenditure under a Labour government were made, this time to the tune of £330 million, the economic prognosis was serious to the point of being disastrous. Wilson, nonetheless, concluded that he had another General Election victory in his hands. He decided, therefore, to appeal to the electorate in June 1970.

His campaign lacked the zest of his initial battle in 1964. His self-confidence was such that he felt it unnecessary to present a detailed manifesto, nor to make any major speeches laying down what a new Wilson government would do. The General Election was to be on Thursday, June 18.

It is invariably the case in British elections that the government – of whichever party – gains support during an election campaign. When, in the middle of the 1970 campaign Wilson was seen to be between 11 per cent and 13 per cent ahead of Heath it seemed certain that the Prime Minister and his Party would be returned. For two days Edward Heath seemed to lose all confidence in himself and his party's chances of victory.[18] Wilson grew ever more confident.

Heath was sustained, however, by the absolute certainty of the then Chairman of the Conservative Party, Anthony (now Lord) Barber, that the Tories were going to win. Barber had been devoted in his cultivation of local Conservative Associations, and could not find anywhere the lack of support for the party which would justify Wilson's faith in a victory he thought was inevitable. Barber detected an underlying swell of opinion in favour of the policies which Heath was offering, and he put his judgement, day by day, not only to his Leader, but to the morning press conferences, which are a necessary part of any British General Election campaign. He was more often than not greeted by the press with derision.

Barber had made his survey. In addition, on 16 June, two days before the General Election, Enoch Powell made his final electoral speech. To Wilson's horror, and Heath's amazement, he said:

On Thursday let none delude you that you are choosing between individuals, or that the questions you decide will come up again in the same form, the same circumstances, a few years ahead, should you dislike the outcome now. On Thursday your vote is about a Britain that, with all its faults and failings, is still free, and great because it is free. On Thursday your vote decides whether that freedom shall survive or not. You dare not entrust it to any government but a Conservative government.

On Thursday, the Conservative Party was elected with a majority of 36 over all other parties in the House of Commons, and of 42 over the Labour Party. It seemed that the Heath revolution had been ushered in by the voters.

CHAPTER SEVEN

The Unquiet Revolution
(1970–1972)

The Conservative victory of June 1970 was all the more to be savoured because it was unexpected. The opinion polls, which had come to dominate the minds not only of journalists but of politicians, had seemed to promise Harold Wilson a favourable wind. By comparison with Wilson, Heath was lacklustre on public platforms. In those days, though not at the time of writing, Heath was an intensely private man. He drew around himself from the moment of his election to the leadership of his party a small group of confidants. Of necessity, these included the then Conservative Chief Whip, William Whitelaw, but the two politicians closest to him at that time were junior and without ministerial experience of any kind. They were his Parliamentary Private Secretaries, Peter Walker and Jim (now Lord) Prior: they were immediately rewarded with Cabinet rank on his assumption of office, Walker as Secretary of State at the newly-created Department of the Environment, and Prior as Minister for Agriculture. Within days the new government suffered a staggering blow. The only orator among its members, Iain Macleod, who had suffered indifferent health for years, died suddenly at his home. Macleod thus had no opportunity to present a Budget, and made only one speech as Chancellor of the Exchequer. Heath, moreover, had decided that he wanted Quintin Hogg to return to the House of Lords as Lord Chancellor, Hogg having given up his peerage to contest the leadership election in 1963.[1]

Macleod had prepared himself with great thoroughness for the post of Chancellor of the Exchequer. His powers of oratory, and his ability to attract those who worked with him, were expected, in my view quite rightly, to be enormous assets to a new government so many of whose members were untried.[2] Moreover, those functionaries closest to Heath, and those whom he most trusted, were not, at that time, proven to have any marked feel for politics.

They were his Political Secretary, Douglas Hurd, who came from the Foreign Office and who has since acquired a considerable and justified reputation as a politician; Brian Reading, an economist; and Michael Wolff, Heath's chief speech writer.[3]

The death of Macleod presented Heath with a particularly difficult problem because it was so soon after the election victory. He recalled Anthony Barber from his duties as chief negotiator with the Common Market, to take Macleod's place, and appointed Sir Geoffrey (now Lord) Rippon in his stead. Barber had been Minister of Health in the Home government and so had brief Cabinet experience. Heath also decided that he and the Cabinet should spend the whole summer contemplating the legislative programme which the government would present to the House of Commons when Parliament returned in October after the long recess.

Barber needed time to come to grips with his new job, and the Prime Minister concentrated his efforts above all on the issue of securing membership of the EEC. Thus it was that the underlying trend of inflation, and the steady expansion in the money supply went virtually unnoticed: these two factors bedevilled the Heath administration until its fall in February 1974. It was not that Heath lost immediate sight of the aims enshrined in the Conservative manifesto. The clearest pronouncement of those aims after he became Prime Minister was made at the Conservative Party Conference in Brighton in October 1970. 'We were returned to office', said Heath, 'to change the course of history of this nation – nothing less.' He went on to say, 'At every turn we face limitations of heavy international indebtedness, of enormous and increasing public expenditure, of a high and damaging level of taxation . . . of outmoded industrial relations . . . of wildly excessive wage demands . . . of a stagnant economy and roaring inflation.' He went on, in his peroration, to use a phrase (written by Michael Wolff) which was to give the speech the title which has survived to haunt him. He promised 'a revolution so quiet and yet so total that it will go far beyond the programme for a Parliament to which we are committed and on which we have already embarked; far beyond this decade and way into the future'.[4]

Referring to party conferences, Jock Bruce-Gardyne states that 'on these occasions the Leader of the Party is always assured of a loyal response from the assembled Party workers: this time Mr Heath would have been cheered to the echo when he addressed the final rally on the morning of October 10th if he had announced his intention to nationalise the means of production, distribution and exchange.'[5]

The Prime Minister, too, was lacking in sustained experience of high

Cabinet office. He was made Minister of Labour (as the Department of Employment was then called) in 1959, and in 1960 he was transferred to the Foreign Office with the title of Lord Privy Seal. At the Foreign Office he had been number two to Lord Home, but his sole responsibility – which was very dear to his heart – was negotiation with the EEC in the effort to secure British membership of the Community. When Home became Prime Minister in 1963 he revamped the old Board of Trade, renaming it the Department of Trade and Industry, and Heath was appointed Secretary of State to this new Department. He also had responsibility for regional development, but it was already clear that a General Election was less than a year away, and he could scarcely be blamed for being unable to concentrate on the broad sweep of government activity, in spite of the fact that there was no doubt that he was a possible future Prime Minister. Indeed, in a trenchant leading article, Sir William Haley, the then editor of *The Times*, advocated that, Macmillan having gone, the Conservative Party should skip a generation and choose Heath as its Leader. Heath immediately wrote to Lord Home to say that he was not a contender. But, since he did not write to the Chief Whip confirming this (as Ian Macleod did in 1965), which would have been in accord with traditional party procedure, it was clear that he was both convinced that Home would succeed Macmillan and that the Conservatives would lose the next General Election, in which case any support or sympathy that Home would give him in the next leadership contest would be valuable.

One must remember that Heath's legacy in June 1970 was a horrendous one. Between 1964 and that year the Wilson government had increased rates of taxation by over £300 million a year. They had introduced new taxes such as Selective Employment Tax, Corporation Tax and Capital Gains Tax. The trade deficit by 1968 was, in real terms, the worst since 1951, and although Roy Jenkins as Chancellor had begun to effect repairs in the economic structure, these repairs were barely complete by the time of the general election. The rate of economic growth at the time of the general election was 2 per cent, which was also its average over the Labour years: Conservatives eagerly pointed to the fact that between the General Election of 1959 and 1964 the growth rate averaged 3.8 per cent. Since the Wilson campaign of 1964 had been based fundamentally on a promise to achieve higher growth than had been possible under the Conservatives, this was the most dramatic failure of the two governments which Wilson had headed.

Worse still, from the point of view of a Labour Prime Minister, unemployment, which had reached the then unimaginable figure of

600,000 by 1967, was still rising at the time of the 1970 General Election. This, of course, did no good at all for the Wilson government's relations with the trade unions, and alienated many of Labour's traditional voters. Thus it was that large numbers of natural Labour voters abstained in the General Election: they could not bring themselves to vote Conservative – indeed, they feared Heath's apparent radicalism – but, their hopes having been so cruelly disappointed during the Wilson years, they could not vote Labour either.

Just as the electorate had welcomed Harold Wilson as a reformer in 1964, so they welcomed Edward Heath as a reformer in 1970. The promises in the Conservative 1970 manifesto were indeed wide-ranging. Taxation was to be reduced; public expenditure was to be curbed; saving was to be encouraged; private industry was to be supported, though with as little subsidy as possible; industrial relations were to be reformed, and trade union power curbed; and regional development would be encouraged. There were further promises not emphasised in the manifesto. One of these was to offer finance to immigrants to return to their countries of origin. Another was to encourage the sale of residential council property by local authorities to their tenants. These last two proposals, though not of great significance in the overall performance of the economy, were highly emotive issues – concern with immigration was running high, and the appeal of owning one's own home was a broad one. Nonetheless, no more than minimal government effort was put into prosecuting them. Early on, therefore, it is demonstrable that both Prime Minister and the Cabinet lacked a sure touch for popular feeling which was to cost them dear in the troubles of 1973 and 1974.

Barber's first budget, in March 1971, cut various taxes by some £680 million a year. His most fundamental innovation, which was to become fully effective in 1973 however, was the replacement of Purchase Tax and Selective Employment Tax by a Value Added Tax: the introduction of VAT was, of course, a necessary part of the Prime Minister's campaign to join the EEC. The Chancellor did, however, immediately halve the rate of SET and the following July introduced a mini-budget which slightly reduced Purchase Tax. He gave a further indication of the direction in which policy was moving by undertaking not to allow the prices charged by any nationalised industry to rise by more than 5 per cent. This was a popular move. It was not, however, generally realised either by politicians or the public that it was a dangerous indication of the government's willingness to continue to control broad swathes of industry from the centre. There were no substantial proposals for de-nationalisation or, as it came to be called in later years, privatisation. The

Prime Minister's promise of a revolution, whether quiet or not, began to have a hollow ring.

I will return to the evolution of domestic policy under the 1970 government, but the most fundamental commitment of the Prime Minister, a commitment to which he held with a passion he betrayed on no other issue, was to British entry into the European Economic Community. His burning ambition to achieve entry was greatly facilitated by the resignation of General de Gaulle, following his narrow defeat in a referendum on the reform of the French Constitution in April 1969. His successor, Georges Pompidou, besides being a personal friend of Heath's, was highly sympathetic to the British application – though he was determined to drive a hard bargain. Heath's main worry as he proceeded, for the second time, to negotiate with the continental powers, was the perceived difficulty of getting through the House of Commons the necessary legislation to enact any treaty which he signed.

Heath was able to move quickly because, after the veto of 1969, Wilson did not withdraw the British application, but left it on the table. Thus negotiations opened in Luxembourg on 30 June 1970. For the most part these were conducted by officials, though under political supervision and, all the while, there was intense diplomatic activity between European Community capitals and the capitals of the other applicants, Britain, Denmark, the Republic of Ireland and Norway.[6] For the next year there was preliminary skirmishing. A strong anti-membership lobby came into being in the United Kingdom with as one of its major objectives the protection of the trading interests of the Commonwealth, and particularly the white Commonwealth. Under this pressure the Prime Minister was compelled to do rather more than the Community powers wanted in this respect. At the same time the Commonwealth countries themselves, and Australia and New Zealand in particular, fought hard in London to protect their interests, and especially their privileged access to United Kingdom markets. In the event, they accepted with great reluctance the few concessions that Heath and Rippon had won, and in succeeding years increasingly turned to Asia and the United States in search of markets. Thus a great historical tradition was, save for the link between the Antipodeans and the sovereign, ended.[7] In June 1971 the outline agreement between the applicants and the member states of the EEC was signed. Officials were left to dot the i's and cross the t's, and the government set to to prepare the legislation. Heath had achieved his lifelong ambition, first formulated when he was a schoolboy, of forging greater unity in Western Europe.

Within a month of agreement being reached the government published a White Paper, *The United Kingdom and the European Communities*. Heath's nervousness about the strength of the opposition to his policies – all opinion polls showed a substantial majority of the electorate against membership – was assuaged by an eight to one vote in favour at the Conservative Party Conference on 13 October 1971. He was even more encouraged when the House of Commons supported the White Paper by a majority of 112 on 28 October 1971. This gave a somewhat false assurance, however, since 68 Labour MPs, led by Roy Jenkins, supported the government. It was intimated by Jenkins, who was in constant touch with the Conservative Chief Whip, Francis (now Lord) Pym, that it would be impossible to sustain this position through the line-by-line scrutiny that a Bill, when presented, would require. However, Heath felt that his position was strong enough for him to sign, on 22 January 1972 at the Egmont Palace in Brussels, the Treaty of Accession. Actual membership was to take effect shortly after the House of Commons passed the legislation.

The Prime Minister had two remaining worries. The first was the probability that the legislation would be lengthy and complex. The fact that the draft Treaty required it to be passed without even the slightest amendment flew in the face of all House of Commons tradition. The second worry concerned Enoch Powell, for long a redoubtable opponent of entry. The Prime Minister had not forgotten 1968, when the Labour Government had introduced a scheme to reform the House of Lords which, following talks between the Leader of the House, Richard Crossman, and the Conservative Leader in the Lords, Lord Carrington, the Conservative front bench decided to support. In spite of that formidable alliance, a much smaller one between Powell and Michael Foot, on the left of the Labour Party, eventually forced the Bill's withdrawal, largely because, an endless stream of amendments having been tabled by the two of them, the government was forced to the conclusion that the rest of its business would be disrupted if it continued the debate.[8] The power of Powell rested ultimately on his still immense popularity in the country, and Heath feared that wavering Conservative backbenchers would, under pressure from their constituents, vote on his side. Just as the Conservative government contemplated with concern its anti-Market backbenchers, the Labour opposition contemplated with worry its pro-Market backbenchers.[9] Powell's efforts, and the efforts of his followers, could not have defeated the Bill had the Opposition front bench not determined to oppose it.

However, the Attorney-General, Sir Geoffrey Howe, came up with an idea sharply to curtail debate, which, even though amendments were ruled out, could have continued almost indefinitely on the substance of the Bill if it were of the expected monumental proportions. The idea was to present a Bill of modest length. It ran only to a few pages. 'We can do it in twelve clauses,' he said, and they did. It was divided into three parts. The first dealt with the constitution and finance; the second with aspects of Community law; and the third with Britain's monetary obligations. Its essential theme was to provide that, where there was conflict between British and Community law, Community law would prevail.

The first dangerous hurdle that the government faced was on 17 February 1972, when the European Communities Bill was laid before the House of Commons for second reading. By then most of those Labour MPs who had supported Roy Jenkins and the government in the debate on the White Paper had, under intense pressure from their Whips, decided to change sides: Jenkins was no longer the powerful ally of the Cabinet that he had been earlier in the year because, although he still supported the government himself, he could no longer deliver the numbers from the opposition benches. There were, however, a handful of Jenkins supporters who were prepared to defy their whip in the event of the government being in danger. Jenkins, having made his support for the government public, felt obliged to resign the Deputy Leadership of the Labour Party on 10 April. Enoch Powell who, with the late Neil Marten and John Biffen were the leading Tories opposed to the Bill, also saw an erosion of their backbench support, which had numbered 41 in the debate on the White Paper. There were, however, a number of waverers, and the Tory Whips were fearful that in this most crucial of votes the government could lose. The Whips cajoled and threatened. The threat was that in the event of the government being defeated, Heath would seek a dissolution and, in the political circumstances of the time, it seemed clear that he would lose a General Election. He had intended not to speak but merely to vote at the end of the debate, but in the event he came down to the House of Commons towards the end of the debate and made it absolutely clear that the Whips' threat was not an idle one and that if defeated he would seek an audience of the Queen the following morning and ask that Parliament be dissolved and a General Election called. Nobody could doubt his resolution and many Tories feared for their seats but, even in these fraught circumstances, the government's majority that evening was only eight.

The Committee of the Whole House debated the Bill intermittently until July. Powell and his closest allies fought it inch by inch, in the country as well as in the House. But after the government victory on second reading it was clear that the Tory rebels were fighting a rearguard action. Once Jenkins had resigned the Labour Deputy Leadership in April the government could be completely confident that he and his friends would be available if they were needed, and the number of Conservative rebels steadily diminished. There were a few close calls as the opposition and the Tory rebels sought, in spite of the government's determination to avoid any changes, to amend the Bill. On 13 July the Committee stage was concluded and the Bill was given its third reading in the House of Commons. On 17 October the Bill received the Royal Assent. For good or ill, the United Kingdom (and Denmark and Ireland) agreed to the terms by which they would join the EEC. Membership would take effect on 1 January 1973. A vital turning point had been reached in British history, and from now on the primary thrust of British political strategy under governments of both parties would be in the direction of the continent.[10]

During the debate the opponents of entry expressed deep anger at two items in government propaganda in favour of entry. The first was the statement in the Conservative manifesto regarding what would be a Tory government's stance towards Europe. The particular words were, 'Our sole commitment is to negotiation; no more, no less. As the negotiations proceed we will report regularly through Parliament to the country.' As the negotiations proceeded it became clear that no government headed by Edward Heath would approach the continental powers with any such openmindedness as the manifesto, *A Better Tomorrow*, implied. Even earlier, not long before the General Election, Heath, alarmed by the rising tide of national opposition to membership, in an address to the British Chamber of Commerce in Paris, prevaricated about his intentions. He wanted to imply that there were certain circumstances in which he would break off negotiations if British interests were not met:

> Whatever the government in power in Britain I do not myself believe that Parliament will approve of a settlement which in the opinion of its members is unequal and unfair. In making this judgement they will have in mind, as is natural and legitimate, primarily the effect of entry upon the standard of living of the individual citizens that they represent. *Nor would it be in the interest of the Community that its enlargement should take place except with the full-hearted consent of the Parliaments and peoples of the new member countries.* [My italics].

Throughout the debate on the European Communities Bill, opponents of the government quoted this promise again and again. Some of them even believed that, if the Bill was passed, Heath would call a General

135

Election to test its acceptability to the electorate. There was, of course, no chance whatsoever of this happening, for the Prime Minister, in my view correctly, judged that he would lose such an election.

I will now turn to domestic matters. The essential character of the 1970 government was its concentration on administrative reform, not all of which required legislation. The Prime Minister believed that the economic renaissance which he sought would be procured, first, by entering the European Economic Community and, second, by comprehensive reform of national institutions. What he liked to call 'the machinery of government' was a particular obsession of the Prime Minister. The first expression of this obsession was the creation of the new Department of the Environment, which, over the years, has grown larger and larger and gathered to itself more and more powers, including powers over local government, the structure of which Heath was determined dramatically to change.[11] An innovation at the heart of government by which he set great store was the creation of the Central Policy Review Staff (popularly known as the 'Think Tank'). This was chaired by Lord Rothschild, and consisted predominantly of young people from outside the civil service whom the brilliant, but frequently eccentric, Rothschild considered would provide him with material essential to the radical restructuring of central government.[12]

On every major issue which came up between 1970 and 1974 except that of membership of the European Economic Community, the Heath preference was for a solution which exalted administration above policy. On the EEC, Heath was – and remains to this day – an idealist. There was no time between his election as Leader of the Conservative Party in 1965 and the signing of the Treaty of Brussels in 1972 when Heath wavered in his determination to bring the United Kingdom into the Common Market. Certainly, there were minor (as he would see them) tactical and rhetorical adjustments, but the Prime Minister's resolution on membership of the Community remained constant throughout. His steadfastness in this regard is worthy of memory, and even admirable, although the government he headed collapsed in chaos in February 1974.

The main challenges that the Heath government faced from victory in 1970 to defeat in 1974 concerned Northern Ireland, local government, and the economy, the last being indissolubly linked to the great matter of the reform of trade union law.

To understand the situation which the Heath government faced in Ulster it is necessary to look at the recent history of that unhappy province. The Northern Irish problem had festered – but festered quietly – from 1922, when Partition took place between the six Ulster counties and the twenty-six counties which were, eventually, to form the Republic of Ireland, until 1968. During this time Northern Ireland had a parliament of its own, based at Stormont Castle, which was responsible for all of the domestic affairs of the province, defence and foreign affairs remaining under the control of London. Initially hostile to the idea of being anything other than a fully integrated part of the United Kingdom, the Protestant majority in Ulster came eventually to cherish its degree of independence. That independence was used both to organise Stormont constituencies so as to increase the already preponderant Protestant majority in parliament and to discriminate against the Catholic minority in economic affairs. Over the years, Catholic politicians came close to despair at any possibility of gaining influence, let alone power, at Stormont. From time to time the Irish Republican Army, then a discredited and almost insignificant force, managed to mount terrorist attacks against the government at Stormont. However, successive Unionist governments provided themselves with an instrument to crush such dissent. This instrument was the B-Special force of armed police, theoretically under the authority of the Royal Ulster Constabulary but, in effect, operating independently.

The essential nature of working-class Catholic animosity to the Union was surly, and not hopeful. By the 1960s, however, a new, and more aggressive, generation was emerging. Its focus was Queen's College, Belfast, a university in its own right and open to Catholics as well as Protestants. Gathered together in its lecture rooms, were young Protestants as outraged by perceived injustice as were their young Catholic confrères. In April 1968 a young undergraduate in the Sociology Department, Bernardette Devlin, had made an impassioned speech against religious discrimination, which led to the foundation of a civil rights organisation called People's Democracy. The fundamental belief of this movement of young people was that change in Northern Ireland could be achieved solely by peaceful demonstration. However, on 28 April 1968 a march by People's Democracy crossing Burntollet Bridge on its way to Belfast was not merely disciplined but attacked by the RUC.[13] The emerging civil rights movement in Ulster had attracted a certain amount of attention from British, Irish (meaning the Republic of Ireland) and, more important, American television. The scenes of youngsters being beaten by truncheons were shown around the world and Ulster was brought to the attention of government in Westminster. The poisoned chalice which had been set on the table of British government in 1922 then had to be sipped.[14]

By one of those curious ironies of history, the events of the spring of

1968 had coincided with the first in a series of meetings to discuss cooperation between the government of the Republic of Ireland headed by Sean Lemass and that of Northern Ireland, headed by Captain Terence O'Neill. It was judged in Dublin remarkable that Lemass agreed to travel to Belfast to meet O'Neill and thus, by implication, to set aside the Republic's claim to sovereignty over Northern Ireland.[15]

In so far as, at that stage, the affairs of Northern Ireland concerned the government at Westminster, they were regarded as peripheral compared to the major problems which any London government, of whatever party, had to address. The national economy was in a parlous state; the nation's defence policy was uncertain, and subject to constant budgetary revision; and the trade union movement was aggressive. The government headed by Harold Wilson and the opposition headed by Edward Heath had agreed on a policy of benign neglect towards Ulster, and the fact that relations between Dublin and Belfast seemed to be improving overcame worries about, first, the consequences of the RUC's brutal crushing of the nascent civil rights movement and, second, the emergence of the Irish Republican Army, and various Protestant para-military groups as forces in the politics of Northern Ireland.

Following the events at Burntollet Bridge, the IRA made a claim to be the defender of the Catholic minority in Ulster. Then there emerged the Ulster Defence Force and the Ulster Volunteer Force as defenders of the Protestants.

Dr Ian Paisley came forward with, for the first time, a formidable electoral platform. The Ulster Unionist Party was divided against itself. The Northern Irish situation came to resemble a cracking iceflow, and the RUC lost not only respect, but credibility. Riots increased in number and terrorism began to show its ugly face. In February 1969 the Home Secretary, James Callaghan, had decided that the only way to suppress disorder in Northern Ireland was to send in troops from the mainland and to take away from the RUC the responsibility for keeping the peace.[16]

Initially, the Army had been received not merely with approbation but with enthusiasm by all sections of the community. In Catholic and Protestant areas alike patrolling troops were offered tea and biscuits by housewives along their route. This period of euphoria was not, however, to last. Civil disorder and terrorism increased, in spite of the best efforts of the security forces.[17]

All this was a part of Edward Heath's unhappy inheritance in 1970. At the beginning he chose to leave Northern Ireland to the charge of the Home Office, as it had been since 1922. His chosen Home Secretary,

Reginald Maudling, was a man of ineffable charm, sharpness of mind, and inability to understand the kind of dark passion that lurked beneath the surface of Ulster politics. The general Westminster belief, then as now, was that a spirit of compromise could be made to prevail in Ulster. Maudling seemed the perfect man to bring this about. Nothing he did, however, seemed to work. So Heath, beset by many other problems, decided, in 1972, radically to alter relations between London and Belfast. In keeping with his fundamental belief that efficient administration was the solution to almost all political problems he took responsibility for Northern Irish affairs away from the Home Office, and with the *Northern Ireland (Temporary Provisions) Act* gave it to a wholly new Department of State, the Northern Ireland Office.[18] The Act provided for the suspension of the Stormont Parliament and of all prescriptive powers of local authorities in the province. (This latter provision was important because of Catholic complaints of discrimination against them in matters of council housing.) Henceforward every decision about developments in Ulster was to be taken at Westminster. The idea that there could be conciliation between the rival religions still prevailed. Heath appointed as the first Secretary of State for Northern Ireland the senior Conservative politician most renowned for his ability to bring warring factions together, William Whitelaw.

1972 was the year which marked the turning point of the Heath government. It would be idle to pretend that the fundamental restructuring of the government of Northern Ireland had any basic influence on the electoral politics of the mainland, but the fact of the matter is that 1972 saw major reversals of policy by the government elected in June 1970. Of these Northern Ireland may serve as a symbol.

CHAPTER EIGHT

The Collapse of the 'Quiet Revolution'
(1972–1974)

All oppositions tend to division. This is a matter of human nature. Politicians want power and, once they are elected, need power. Power can be actual, as when a Member of Parliament holds governmental office, or reflected, as when he or she holds a seat while his or her party is in office. Quite apart from matters of ideology, the sheer frustration of being unable, except on rare occasions, to influence events bedevils an opposition party which reasonably feels that it could have formed a government.

The division endemic to opposition is, in this country, more dangerous for the Labour Party than for the Conservatives. The reason for this is that Labour has always contained within itself powerful and potentially contradictory elements, both ideological and practical. After an election defeat there are always many within the Labour Party who believe that defeat was occasioned by a failure to cling to the tenets of socialism: that is the ideological side.[1] On the practical side, the Labour Party was – and remains at the time of writing – financially dependent upon the trade union movement. There is, moreover, an instinctive sympathy between most Labour politicians and the leaders of the trade union movement. No such problems exist for the Conservative Party, the great majority of whose members and supporters care little for principle or policy as long as the party is in power. Whereas committed Labour politicians not infrequently feel that their ideals or the desirability of supporting the trades unions are more important than the acquisition or retention of office, most Conservatives feel that that acquisition, or that retention, is an end in itself.[2]

The difficulties of opposition can be reduced by the presence as Leader of the Party of someone who enjoys either great prestige or a consummate grasp of political tactics. Between 1945 and 1951 the Conservative

Party sheltered under the prestige of Churchill. Between 1970 and 1974 the Labour Party enjoyed the advantage of having at its head, in the person of Harold Wilson, the most skilled political tactician of the age.

However, Wilson held his party together in the first two difficult years after Heath's triumph only by abandoning or blurring practically everything the Labour government, and his party, had stood for in the 1970 election. At the beginning of his memoirs Wilson sounded a plangent note. Writing of his defeat in June 1970, and of the ambitions and hopes he had entertained in 1964, he said:

> If in all these things we had not gone as far as we would have wished, we achieved far more than most would have expected. As we went forward for a mandate to continue what we had begun, we were determined to use our newly developed economic strength as a basis for faster economic expansion, based on full employment, and for a more rapid rate of improvement in the welfare service.
>
> In the event, we were denied that mandate; once again, a Labour Government was prevented from building on the foundations which it had laid.[3]

Just as the Conservative victory was all the more sweet for being unexpected, so Labour's defeat was all the more devastating for the same reason. On election day, 18 June 1970, the Prime Minister travelled north to his constituency of Huyton, accompanied by a number of journalists. He was affable and concerned, behaving more or less as *pater familias* to the nation. He smoked a cigar, and observed to his travelling companions that he could now abandon the pipe, which had become his trade mark over the years. He fell to reflecting on the fate of Edward Heath and canvassed opinion on what job he could provide for his beaten rival: his own view was that the post of British Ambassador to the United Nations would be suitable for the defeated Leader of the Conservative Party.

Wilson's confidence in the result of the election was rampant, though he has since claimed that he had doubts.[4] Upon his arrival at Huyton, Wilson went to the Huyton Hotel. Two floors had been taken by the Labour Party, one to accommodate the Prime Minister and his entourage, the other for the press. Joe Haines, the Prime Minister's Press Secretary, had promised journalists interviews with Wilson as soon as the result became clear. By midnight, however, it was evident that the Labour Party had lost the General Election. Haines cancelled the Prime Minister's meetings with the press. Wilson took an overnight train to

London to tender his resignation to the Queen. By lunch on 19 June Edward Heath was installed at 10 Downing Street.[5]

It cannot too often be stressed how great was the shock to the Labour Party of its defeat. It is only mildly exaggerating to say that the party fell into a catatonic trance. For months the opposition was almost completely ineffective and, Parliament being in recess, the new Prime Minister had time to prepare his proposals for enacting the new measures which, he believed, would bring about a fundamental change in the condition of the country and, in what his predecessor was later to call the governance of Britain.[6]

Between 1970 and his return to office in February 1974 Harold Wilson made three crucial decisions. The first was, while not abandoning his ambition for the United Kingdom to join the European Economic Community, to state as a matter of policy that the terms negotiated by the new Conservative government were unacceptable and that revised terms would be submitted to the electorate in a referendum when Labour returned to power. This renegotiation was more fiction than fact, for the alteration in the terms of agreement with the continental powers made by the 1974 Labour Government was not material: it was left to Margaret Thatcher substantially to change Britain's contribution to the EEC budget. From the point of view of the Labour Party, however, Wilson's commitment to alter the terms which Edward Heath had negotiated with the existing members of the EEC had the advantage of placating the left wing of the Labour Party.[7]

The second important adjustment that Wilson made to the Labour Party's tactics was to turn a blind eye to what came to be called 'entryism'. For many years the Labour Party National Executive Committee had maintained a list of organisations whose members would be forbidden entry into the party. Wilson abolished this prohibition and thus consolidated yet more support from the left: senior Labour Party figures such as Tony Benn and the late Eric Heffer were very much in favour of the 'broad church' theory which sought to engage as allies any organisation or pressure group hostile to the Conservative Party.[8] At the time Wilson's tolerant attitude towards left-wing organisations was scarcely noticed by public opinion or the media, for it was assumed that Marxist and Trotskyite groupings were marginal in the overall scheme of British politics. It was not until the 1980s that a suddenly alarmed Labour leadership under Neil Kinnock realised that doctrinaire left-wing organisations were a serious threat not only to the health of the Labour Party itself, but to its electoral chances.

The third major decision as to opposition tactics was, in practical terms, made for Wilson. Heath, his parliamentary colleagues and the many outside advisers whom he had consulted between 1966 and 1970, had all reached an agreed conclusion, to the effect that the severe limitation, if not the abolition, of trade union privileges, was essential to national economic recovery. To this end, after protracted consultation, Steven Abbott, of the Conservative Research Department, working closely with Robert Carr, drafted an elaborate Trade Union Law Reform Bill, to be introduced immediately after Parliament reassembled following a Conservative electoral victory. The Bill was ready by the end of 1968. It was tabled at the beginning of the 1970–71 Parliament, and was deeply and even virulently opposed by all trade unions, but particularly by the two most powerful figures in the trades union movement, Jack Jones, the General Secretary of the Transport and General Workers Union, and Hugh Scanlon, the General Secretary of the Amalgamated Union of Engineering Workers. Apart from any personal sympathy Wilson may have felt for Jones and Scanlon, the brutal fact he had to face was that their two unions were the major contributors to Labour Party funds. Indeed, at that time the headquarters of the Labour Party were in Transport House, a building owned by and also housing the headquarters of the TGWU. It therefore did not cause Wilson any great heartache to promise to repeal any legislation which the Heath administration put in the statute book.

British membership of the EEC was, as has already been observed, the policy closest to Edward Heath's heart. But so far as strictly domestic politics were concerned the most important Conservative proposal was the reform of trade union law, to be introduced by the Secretary of State for Employment, Robert Carr, with the Solicitor-General, Sir Geoffrey Howe, handling the details. The government's belief being that the majority of rank and file trade union members disliked strikes and, however passively, were opposed to their leaders, it was also assumed that the right legislation would reduce the incidence of industrial disputes, and thereby provide an electoral dividend. It has always been a matter of considerable puzzlement to the Labour Party and the trade unions alike that all available evidence demonstrates that a majority of trade unionists vote Tory. Disraeli, in the nineteenth century, when embarked upon the process of extending the parliamentary franchise to the working classes, called those classes 'angels in marble'.[9]

Acting on their historically accepted knowledge of a propensity by trade unionists to vote Conservative, those politicians and their advisers who prepared the Industrial Relations Act which came into effect in 1971 had as their principal ambition the removal of power from the national executives of trades unions to the individual worker.[10] The 1971 Act repealed legislation on the rights of trades unions going back as far as 1871. The Trade Union Acts of 1871 and 1876 were taken off the statute book. The Trades Disputes Acts of 1906 and 1965 were, likewise, abolished. The 1871 Act was the first to establish the right of trade unions to exist. Subsequent Acts of Parliament before 1971 extended trade union rights to include the right to strike and the right to strike sympathetically.

It is hard imaginatively to remember in the 1990s how breathtaking the industrial relations proposals of the 1970 government were. That a new Conservative government should make some changes in the law on trade unions was not unexpected; that the government should decide to repeal *all* existing legislation, and institute a completely new legal framework, not only enraged the Labour Party but astonished the most devout of Conservative supporters.

The substantive provisions of the 1971 Act ordained not only that the individual worker was under no obligation to join a trade union, but also that he had rights to appeal against unfair dismissal by his employer. The government's intention was that it should be seen to be even-handed as between employee and employer. A register of trade unions was, further, to be established, so that breakaway or, in the words of the Secretary of State for Employment, 'rogue' trade unions could not defy the law. Clause 15 of the Act contained a provision that sowed dragon's teeth for the government in years to come. It introduced the vague concept of 'unfair industrial practices'. This clause in particular – but the Act in general – was to be monitored by the National Industrial Relations Court (NIRC), a newly-created judicial authority. Its first head was Lord Justice Donaldson (now the Master of the Rolls). It has to be remembered that, at the time, the assumption was that most major industries would remain in the state sector and that therefore the new Court would, in effect, be mediating not merely between unions and employers but between unions and the government of the day. Recognising this, the government laid it down that a relevant Secretary of State should have the right to ask the Court to enforce a 90-day 'cooling off' period before any industrial action took place with a right to ask for a further 60 days cooling-off period in the event of a dispute not having been resolved in the first period. The government did not grasp the fact that, while it had given itself the power to impose fines on unions which declined to add their names to its register, it had left Lord Justice Donaldson only recourse to imprisonment for unions which declined to obey his cooling-off period.

In September 1971, the Trade Union Council instructed its members not to register under the Act. In April 1972 Lord Justice Donaldson fined the Transport and General Workers Union £55,000 for its refusal to register as a trade union. The Amalgamated Union of Engineering Workers likewise refused to register and were fined the same amount. Furthermore, the two main trade union leaders, Jack Jones and Hugh Scanlon, were utterly determined in their opposition to the legislation. Scanlon was even more determined than was Jones. In October 1973 his union, the AUEW, was fined a further £75,000 for its continuing refusal to register. In May of the following year, the union still not having paid its second fine, an anonymous donor, who remains anonymous to this day, paid £47,000, the rest being contributed in smaller amounts by other, likewise anonymous, donors. Hugh Scanlon still refused to register his union under the Act and relied upon further donations to pay the fines his union was bound to incur.

The National Industrial Relations Court had the power to vary the length of the cooling-off period. On 21 July 1972 the Court, given the fact that the Transport and General Workers Union was refusing to pay further fines imposed upon it, sent five shop stewards to prison for blacking container depots in the Port of London, thereby in effect going on strike without observing the cooling-off period as stated in the law. The court action arose because John Gouriet,[11] decided to mount a private action against the dock workers, in an attempt to enforce the 1971 Act. This was immensely embarrassing to a government which was already beginning to understand that the law it had passed with such enthusiasm might well not be enforceable. Whether with or without government consent and encouragement, the Official Solicitor intervened to procure the release of the dock workers.[12] This defeat of the NIRC's attempt to administer justice – as justice was determined by the 1971 Act – meant, in effect, the end of the Heath administration's reform of industrial relations legislation. In 1972 the National Union of Mineworkers decided to strike. The government and the National Coal Board gave way to the union's demands. In my judgement the successful intervention of the Official Solicitor signalled the inevitable downfall of the Heath government.

In 1973 the NUM again announced its intention to strike, not only for money but for improved working conditions. Its General Secretary, Joe Gormley, and the man certain to succeed him, Arthur Scargill, made it clear that they were determined to ignore all the provisions of the 1971 Act. Scargill went further than Gormley by declaring that it was his intention to bring down the Heath government. He succeeded.

There was at the time, and we can see this ever more clearly in retrospect, a tragic character to the decline and fall of the government elected in 1970. Aristotle it was who first defined tragedy as the consequence of personal failings in a ruler. Edward Heath entered office in 1970 with the highest of hopes. These were not merely hopes for himself, but hopes for his country. He did, it is true, fall victim to the lures and trapping of office but, essentially, he was concerned with a greater good than could be summarised in the world of ministerial limousines and an ever-attendant and efficient secretarial staff.

The dilemma in which the Heath administration found itself quite shortly after it was elected can be expressed simply. Heath's main electoral promise was to liberalise the economy and restore freedom over their own lives to individuals – not merely to trade unionists, but to taxpayers. The Prime Minister's difficulty was that to introduce his quiet revolution he required – and was inclined, by his nature, to adopt – a number of measures which seemed to him to need central control. His most brave dash for freedom was the decision on 23 August 1971 to float the pound.[13]

As already mentioned, in January 1972 the National Union of Mineworkers, led by Joe Gormley, decided in the face of rising inflation, rising unemployment, and the virtual impossibility of exporting coal, to strike. The dispute was to go on for six weeks. Under the influence of Reginald Maudling, the Home Secretary, Heath agreed to ask Lord Wilberforce to examine the validity of the NUM's claims. On 18 February 1972 Wilberforce reported, with a recommendation that the miners' full claim for a 22 per cent wage increase should be met. The government met it. The rate of inflation at the time hovered around 10 per cent. Heath thus abandoned his earlier policy that wage increases should not exceed the going rate of inflation. The settlement was a tremendous triumph for the NUM and, naturally, was followed by similar demands from the other major unions. The various wage demands led to the unofficial but very significant creation of the annual wage round. By the autumn of 1972 the wages demands of the most powerful unions had created not merely a run on the pound but a serious increase in inflation, approaching 20 per cent. Moreover, the United Kingdom was on the verge of its full entry into the EEC, via the Treaty of Brussels. This, it was known, would impose upon the country a very heavy financial burden, while the benefits – if there were any – would not take effect for some years to come.

Therefore, on 26 September 1972 the Prime Minister announced an anti-inflation programme. From being in favour of a free market in labour and currency, Heath decided to change course. Thus, he called a press conference at Lancaster House on 26 September 1972 to announce a freeze on pay and prices, to take effect from midnight on that day and to be monitored by two new Quasi Autonomous Government Organisations,[14] the Prices Commission, and the Pay Board. It was predictable that these measures would excite the hostility of the Labour Party, which regarded them as proof positive of the failure of the government's economic policy. In addition, however, there was deeply-felt, cross-party hostility to the Prime Minister's decision to make his announcement at a press conference rather than to Parliament. The fact that Heath was later to say that these measures were so urgent that he could not wait either to recall Parliament, or until Parliament reassembled in October was taken as further evidence that he had allowed the economy to get out of control. Thus it was that he undermined the most powerful claim of his party to electoral credibility – the idea of economic competence.

Heath, naturally, denied that any fault in his conduct of economic policy had produced the situation in which he felt obliged to freeze increases in prices and incomes. Nonetheless, and whoever was at fault, the economic situation continued to deteriorate and inflation was, month by month, adding to the financial burden on British households. Heath pressed ahead with what he considered to be structural reforms in the national economy. In the April 1972 budget Value Added Tax supplanted all other indirect taxation, including Selective Employment Tax: SET was a tax levied on employers; VAT was a tax levied on consumption. The imposition of VAT was, of course, a requirement of British membership of the EEC. But it was also from the point of view of government an easy tax to administer. However, the Heath government faced severe embarrassment: none of the proposals which it had laid before the people in 1970 seemed to produce an upturn in the national economy, and the electorate is always inclined to blame the government of the day for any failure in the management of the nation's financial affairs.

For a brief period it seemed that the government was to be held accountable for everything that was going wrong in the economic field. But, then, on 6 October 1973 – Yom Kippur or, in English, the Day of Atonement, the most sacred day in the Jewish calendar – President Anwar Sadat of Egypt launched an attack on Israel. For two weeks the fate of the Jewish state hung in the balance. In order to reduce the support for Israel of Western nations, the Arab oil-producing countries sharply lifted the price of oil. The price of Middle Eastern-produced oil went, overnight, from $15.00 to $56.00 a barrel: it was later to rise to a price on the Rotterdam spot market to somewhere between $90 and $100 a barrel. The desperation of Western, but specifically of European countries was such that Rotterdam prices rose steadily in hours as well as days. By the formal ending of the war, with yet another outstanding Israeli victory, the price of oil extracted from wells in the Middle East remained at a level which had hitherto been considered unimaginable. The oil-producing Arab nations had already formed the Organisation of Petroleum Exporting Countries, but OPEC only realised that it had muscles to flex during and immediately after the war.[15]

No Western nation wanted, or would court, a new Middle Eastern war. The Israelis were convinced, moreover, that, having been so convincingly beaten in 1948 and 1967, their neighbours would not again challenge them. The Egyptian attack on 6 October 1973 found the Jewish state unprepared for conflict. However, for all that the battle it was to wage for the next eleven days was cataclysmic in terms of international relations, it brought a measure of relief to the British government. Whatever his failings of policy or administration, Edward Heath could now blame the war for increased inflation and unemployment.

The promise of the quiet revolution which the Prime Minister had made at the Conservative Party Conference in 1970 was certainly well meant. But what happened between 1970 and 1974 was in the issue anything but quiet. Heath's idea was to produce a total transformation of the structure of British government. To this end, and apart from the dramas of industrial relations and wars between foreigners, he was determined radically to change the nature of local government, and at the same time the management of the National Health Service. It is important to remember here that the NHS, in its fundamental character, was regarded as sacrosanct by the incoming government in 1970. The Conservative Party, having been persuaded to accept the fundamental principles of the 1945 government's provision for health care, was profoundly opposed to altering the principle of a service free at the point of use. Certainly, they were prepared to tinker with the level of prescription and dental charges; but they were not prepared to change the basic structure. During the period of opposition beween 1966 and 1970, Sir Keith Joseph, initially Shadow trade and industry spokesman, had devoted a great deal of time, and the energy of many people, to drawing up proposals for managerial reform of the NHS. It was thought after Iain Macleod's death that Joseph might be made Chancellor of the Exchequer. It was certainly expected, after the June 1970 victory, that he would be Secretary of State for Trade and Industry. To widespread surprise, however, he was given the job of Secretary of State for Social Services, and told by the Prime Minister that as a priority he should embark upon making the NHS efficient[16]. Unexpectedly, he proposed only one simple reform. This was the introduction of a management tier in the NHS, which would be staffed by hospital administrators who would not necessarily be doctors or nurses and which would work closely and effectively with Local Health Authorities.

This reform was designed to be part of a general restructuring of local government. Ideas for local government reform had been in the political air for some years, stimulated particularly by growing demands in Scotland and Wales for some form of devolution.[17] However, the 1970 government was also determined, quite apart from the issues of devolution and the NHS, to change the structure of local government root and branch, for the first time since 1889. On 11 June 1969, Lord Redcliffe-Maud had produced a Royal Commission report envisaging eight provincial Councils for England.[18]

While the Redcliffe-Maud Commission was hard at work the Conservative Party was devising its own proposals for change in local government. These proposals, drafted by Chris Patten, then a desk officer in the Research Department, under the supervision of Lord Jellicoe, Vice Chairman of the Party responsible for local government, issued eventually, in the first basic reorganisation for nearly a century, in the Local Government Act of 1972. The existing system, outside Greater London where no changes were made, was abolished. In its place came a top tier of metropolitan authorities in the six conurbations and the 47 non-metropolitan counties. Under the administration of the top tier authorities came 36 metropolitan districts within the areas of the metropolitan counties and 333 districts in the rest of the country.

Heath's policies on entry into Europe and on local government and NHS reforms were, generally speaking, unpopular. But they can be considered merely as minor irritations when compared to the consequences already described of the industrial action by the National Union of Mineworkers in June 1973. The Prime Minister's major problem was his inability to enforce restraint on prices and incomes, even though these restraints had statutory force. On 8 October 1973 he announced an extension to the period of controls. The NUM made it clear that it would not observe the government's rules. Therefore, on 13 December 1973, the Prime Minister announced to the House of Commons that he was invoking the authority available to him under the Emergency Powers Act of 1920. This was in effect the implementation of the state of emergency he had announced in November and meant that, subject to a majority vote in the House of Commons, he could take whatever measures he considered necessary to ensure the economic survival of the nation. He decreed, by Order in Council, the commencement of a three-day working week from 1 January 1974, the object of which was to conserve energy resources, which were, for the most part, controlled by the NUM. He also announced the creation of a new Department of State, the Department of Energy, to be headed by Lord Carrington.

Thus began Heath's rush to electoral defeat. Heath was inclined to feel that he should seek a renewal of his mandate from the electorate. In this view he was encouraged above all by Carrington. The principal opponent of the calling of an early General Election was William (now Lord) Whitelaw, recalled in January 1974 from the Northern Ireland Office to run the Department of Employment, and thus to take charge of negotiations with the NUM. His fabled powers of conciliation were to be stretched beyond their limits. He found that the NUM's policy was to say to the government, in the mythical words of the highwayman, 'stand and deliver'. Every offer – always moving in the direction of the NUM's financial demands – was rejected. 'By this stage, however, the NUM was not prepared to accept anything but a cash on the table deal.'[19] Whitelaw believed that negotiations should continue and felt 'unhappy and reluctant' at the prospect of a snap General Election. Heath, however, chose to heed the advice of Carrington and, on 7 February 1974, went to the Palace and received the Royal Assent to an immediate dissolution of Parliament. His view was that, with what he confidently believed would be a solid endorsement of his economic and industrial relations policies, he would be able to outface the trade union movement in general, and the National Union of Mineworkers in particular. In the event, the opportunity to test this theory was not to be granted to him.

Joe Gormley, one of the most shrewd, as well as honourable of trade union leaders, was, having taken soundings, confident of the loyalty of his members. He therefore felt it safe to call a ballot of the National Union of Mineworkers, asking for the authority to call an all-out strike if he wished. From November 1973 the NUM had eschewed overtime, which, in effect, meant that there was no work done at weekends and, thus, the safety of pits could not be ensured. The ballot endorsed the General Secretary's authority with a plurality of 81 per cent of the total membership of the union. Gormley stated that he would therefore take the steps necessary for all-out industrial action. Due, however, to the intervention of Harold Wilson, the NUM agreed to suspend all action and resume negotiations with whatever government was elected on 28 February. The Heath government was thus wrong-footed: they had assumed that Gormley could not gain so preponderant a majority among his members. David Butler and Dennis Kavanagh quote an unnamed

Minister at the Department of Employment as saying 'it could all have been solved if our intelligence had not been so bad'.[20]

The, at least temporary, ending of industrial action was a severe blow to Heath and a massive fillip to Harold Wilson. The brutal fact which faced the Prime Minister was that the Leader of the Opposition appeared to have more authority in industrial relations than he had himself. The traditional idea that only a Labour government could deal with the trade union movement was given substantial reinforcement. Heath, promptly and in response to Wilson, began to prevaricate on the government's attitude to trade unions in general, and the NUM in particular. Having sought the support of the people in order to enable him to defeat the trade union movement, he then began to offer compromises to that movement. These compromises – which particularly involved increased perks to miners, notably increased income for 'unsocial working hours' – were clearly in breach of Phase Three of the Incomes Policy.

Worse was to come. Again, it should have been foreseen. On 15 January Enoch Powell had denounced the proposals being made for an early General Election on the grounds that the government had a sufficient parliamentary majority to carry through any measures which they deemed necessary to deal with the problems of the nation. On the day on which Heath called the General Election Powell announced, to the Chairman of his Constituency Association, his determination not to stand as a Conservative candidate. 'I consider', he wrote, 'it an act of gross irresponsibility that this general election has been called in the face of the current and impending industrial situation.' He went on:

> The election will in any case be essentially fraudulent; for the object of those who have called it is to secure the electorate's approval for a position which the government itself knows to be untenable, in order to make it easier to abandon that position subsequently.

The campaign having once begun, the government was in retreat throughout. First came the ending of the 10.30 p.m. curfew on television broadcasting (imposed as part of the restrictions under emergency powers). Then the Prime Minister announced that the miners' pay claim would be examined, yet again, under a new procedures – the so-called 'relativities procedure' – by the Pay Board. It was made clear, both at press conferences and in individual briefings to journalists, that any recommendation made by the Pay Board in favour of the miners would be considered with sympathy. On 8 February, Harold Wilson said, more or less exactly, what Enoch Powell had said, 'For the first time in history, we have a general leading his troops into battle with the deliberate aim of giving in if they win.' On 10 February, Jeremy Thorpe threw his tuppence into the battle. 'Why', Thorpe asked, 'did an election take higher priority in his [the Prime Minister's] mind than the honourable settlement which he would have obtained for the nation? The nation is entitled to know.' The tide of opinion turned irresistibly in support of the Powell proposition that the General Election was unnecessary.

Wilson, as ever, showed his sure grasp of political tactics. He suggested that he, the Prime Minister, and the Leader of the Liberal Party should sit down with the TUC, the CBI and the NUM to discuss a solution to the industrial relations crisis. To this end he asked that the election should be postponed. To an electorate already confused by the different signals coming from government, the Wilson appeal seemed eminently sensible. The Prime Minister turned down the Wilson proposal. Meanwhile, both the AUEW and ASLEF (the Associated Society of Locomotive Engineers and Firemen, the main railway workers' union) called off threatened strike action until after a General Election: this was done in deference to Harold Wilson's wishes. The run on Heath's credibility as a dominant Leader was now serious, for it seemed increasingly clear that Wilson could manage affairs with the unions, and that Heath could not. It was essential, throughout the campaign, for Heath, whatever compromises he was offering, to insist that the authority of democratic government depended on beating the NUM. On 18 February, however, the Deputy Chairman of the Pay Board, Derek Robinson, said, through the Press Association, that coal miners were paid 8 per cent below the national industrial average and that, therefore, their current claims were more than justified. Later the Director-General of the CBI, Campbell Adamson, accepted this statistical analysis. Harold Wilson was given the news later in the evening, and altered his prepared speech to opine that 'something funny is going on'. What these rapidly unfolding events suggested to the electorate was that a government which prided itself on administrative efficiency did not in fact know what was going on.

As the tide of opinion seemed to turn against the government, the Conservative Party was at least relieved that Enoch Powell – still by all available measures of opinion the most popular political commentator in the country – had kept his silence. With devastating effect he broke it, first at Shipley on 25 February; then the following evening, when he told Thames Television that he had already registered his postal vote at Wolverhampton South West in favour of the Labour Party; and, finally, to enormous national attention, at the Bull Ring in Birmingham the following Saturday. For the following five days most national newspapers carried news about Powell's opinions on their front pages. In my judgement[21] the Powell intervention was decisive in tipping the balance against the Heath administration. Nonetheless, on election day, 28 February 1974, the opinion polls all suggested a Heath victory. The Harris poll gave the Conservatives a 5 per cent lead, which, if it were accurate, would more than double their majority.

Worry in the Conservative camp began to develop on election night, when the BBC, having for the first time interviewed voters leaving the polling stations, came to the conclusion by 11 p.m. that the government had lost. The Conservatives had won 297 seats and the Liberal Party 14. Smaller parties had won 23. However, the Labour Party had been triumphant in 301 constituencies. Heath spent the following weekend endeavouring to make an agreement with Jeremy Thorpe, whereby the Liberal Leader would become Home Secretary. While Thorpe was willing, his party was not. Thus, at midday on the Monday Heath presented his resignation to the Queen.

Heath's manoeuvres with Thorpe cannot be described by any other word than sordid. The Prime Minister had appealed to the country to endorse himself and his actions. Whatever else was unclear, or uncertain, about the result on 28 February, it was certain that the endorsement had been denied him. Even had he procured the support of the Liberal Party, he would not have enjoyed an overall majority in the House of Commons. A functioning majority had, thus, been thrown away to no purpose. The Prime Minister's prolongation of his residence in No. 10 Downing Street was not merely undignified, but to no purpose.[22]

CHAPTER NINE

The Beginning of the End

(1974–1979)

Throughout the General Election campaign of February 1974 Harold Wilson was in exceptionally lacklustre form. In truth he did not expect to win, in spite of the fact that the tide of affairs in general seemed to be flowing against the Heath government. In the event, although he was able to form a government, it was clear that he had no serious mandate from the electorate: the voters had clearly called down a plague upon both Labour and Tory houses. My own conviction is that Wilson clung on to the leadership of the Labour Party between 1970 and 1974 almost solely in the hope of gaining revenge on Heath. When in power between 1964 and 1970 he was ever full of initiatives – specious though most of these turned out to be – but he at least gave the impression that he was always moving forward to meet new challenges. However, in his third administration, from February 1974, he seemed able only to roll with the punches of political life and, by the end, to be punch-drunk. The contrast between the Wilson of the sixties and the Wilson of the mid-seventies is perhaps best illustrated by another sporting metaphor which he was fond of using in conversations and interviews. He likened himself, in his first incarnation as Prime Minister, to a goal-scoring centre-forward; when he returned to No. 10 Downing Street in 1974 he proclaimed his ambition to be a sweeper – that is a defender who mops up the attacks of the opposing team but does not himself take any initiatives. It was an accurate metaphor, for Wilson had no choice but to react to the difficulties which confronted him – difficulties which were in part the consequences of his inheritance from Heath, but in considerable part, also, the result of the compromises he had made in order to keep the Labour Party together after the defeat in 1970.

His problems were manifold. The threat of an all-out strike by the NUM remained. This problem the Prime Minister solved simply by

154

granting all the demands of the union. This was a tactical move; but it was full of potential for disaster. By appointing Michael Foot – who could never see that there was so much as a mote in the eye of any trade unionist – as Secretary of State for Employment Wilson signalled his intention to give the trade union movement almost anything it wanted, whatever the cost to the economy. Foot began immediately to draft a bill which would, first, repeal in total the legislation introduced by the Heath government and then extend to the unions privileges hitherto undreamt of. This was the most graphic demonstration of the supposed truth of the then current belief that no government could run the country without the consent of the union movement. The fact that the unions had to be accepted as at least equal, and often superior to, government and Parliament suggested the arrival of the corporate state. Since the bruised Conservatives, having failed to make effective the reforms of trade union law which they had espoused, also believed that union power could not be defied, their criticism of anything Foot did could not be more than feeble.

Then there was Europe. Wilson and the new Foreign Secretary, James Callaghan[1], were faced with a difficulty which might turn out to be dangerous. They had promised a renegotiation of the terms on which Heath had procured Britain's membership of the EEC: in order to placate the anti-Marketeers within their party, they had to appear to be tough. On the other hand, both men were more than anxious to stay within the ranks of the Community, so they did not wish seriously to offend their fellow-Member States, who were perennially suspicious of British motives. It was necessary to tread warily. Lord Callaghan records that Hans-Dietrich Genscher, the German Foreign Minister, was sympathetic to the British government's problems, but unable to alleviate the financial burden imposed on Britain by membership of the Community because he 'claimed that Germany could pay no more'.[2] Callaghan nonetheless found continental politicians far more sympathetic to his domestic problems than were the members of the Commission in Brussels. The Labour manifesto had promised that renegotiation of the Heath terms would be complete within a year of the return of a Labour government and immediately submitted to the electorate by way of referendum. As with all matters concerned with the EEC, everything took rather longer than was initially bargained for; but the referendum did take place 18 months after the General Election, a fact of which both Wilson and Callaghan were inordinately proud.

But, as always with post-war British Prime Ministers, the economy presented the new government with its most acute problems. Wilson inherited an inflation rate approaching 20 per cent per annum. Until the International Monetary Fund decided, in 1976, to stop Britain's access to international credit, a spending spree by the government continued, and every economic indicator showed that the economy was in free-fall. No small contribution was made to the rate of inflation – which, when the IMF stepped in had reached 26 per cent – by the virtually free hand given to trade unions in wage negotiations. Trade unions demanded then – as they demand to the present day – annual wage increases exceeding the rates of inflation current at the time of negotiation. They regarded the public purse as bottomless and, since the largest industries in the country were nationalised, the major claims always went eventually to the Treasury, which invariably surrendered. No senior trade union leader seemed to realise that the more he entered demands higher than the rate of inflation, the more he increased inflation.

Wilson did, nonetheless, enjoy one distinct advantage. This was the fact of Conservative disarray. They had a Leader who had lost two out of three General Elections. This is not a situation which, to put it mildly, Conservatives find tolerable, and a movement to replace Heath immediately began. Cool heads, most notable among them Willie Whitelaw, Edward du Cann and Airey Neave, pointed, however, to the electoral situation. 'Wilson wants to do a '66', said Neave. By this he meant that Wilson, finding himself in a position not dissimilar to that in which he had been in 1964, would call an early General Election in the hope of repeating his triumph of 1966. Many senior Tory figures, who would have been happy to see an end to the Heath reign, attended to Neave's prophecy that Wilson would seek a firm mandate in October. Since it was known, and much repeated by his own acolytes, that Heath would struggle with every fibre of his being to retain his leadership, it seemed folly to plunge the party into a leadership battle with a General Election looming on the horizon. 'Let Ted lose again,' said Neave, 'and then we'll have him.' Airey Neave was beginning to emerge as the most formidable political tactician on the Tory benches.

The struggles ahead for the Conservative Party were to be profound. In many respects the defeat of February 1974 hit the Party harder than their humiliation in 1945. This may seem a paradoxical observation, given that Clement Attlee came to office with a majority of 145, and Harold Wilson was forced to form a minority government. But the circumstances were different in an instructive way. When the Conservatives were comprehensively thrashed in 1945 they were, under the guidance of Butler, made to be receptive to many of the ideas promulgated by the Attlee government. There was no question, after the war, but that the Labour Party was making the intellectual running. The Conservatives, in their pragmatic way, were perfectly prepared to adjust to a wholly new social and political environment, so long as it gained them office again.

In 1974 the situation was wholly different, largely because of the brave effort made by Edward Heath after he became Leader in 1965. Whereas Churchill, Woolton and Butler set their policy sights according to Attlee's compass, Heath decided to set out in an entirely new direction. The 1945–51 opposition was seeking consensus; the 1965–70 opposition was seeking radically to change its own nature. Heath introduced, in opposition, proposals for economic, legal and structural reforms which were considered by many to be alien to Tory traditions. These comprised plans for liberalising the economy, for reducing the power of central government, and for making the individual more responsible for his (or her) affairs than at any time since the nineteenth century. However, the ability of nineteenth century governments sharply to limit public expenditure, and to reduce the state's role to a regulatory rather than a coercive one was possible only because the nation was unquestionably – indeed incredibly – prosperous, and because society was so stratified. Heath came to power in a quite different world – one in which social distinctions, if they had not disappeared, were certainly losing their power to affect the affairs of the nation.[3] His own elevation to the leadership of the Conservative Party demonstrated quite clearly how much things had changed.

Edward Heath decided, therefore, to review the whole nature of Toryism, and to bring it into rapport with a world in which internationally Britain had been reduced to the level of a medium-sized power, and economically could not compete with either the United States or her allies in Europe. This left the Conservative Party in 1970 possessed of a new, modern, and capitalist ideology, but bereft of many of its historical traditions.[4] Heath was to reverse most of the major policies on which he was elected in 1970. After its defeat in February 1974, therefore, the Conservative Party found itself rudderless. It was no longer attuned to the old paternalism which Heath had rejected, but it also found that the new plans and ideas introduced by Heath in the second half of the 1960s seemed to have failed of their effect. The fact of the matter was that between 1972 and 1974 the government and the party had lost all clear sense of direction. When the pall of opposition fell upon it with Wilson's return to office no idea and no policy could be relied upon. Nor was it open to Heath and the Shadow Cabinet to do in 1974 what Churchill had done after 1945. To criticise the attempts by Wilson and Callaghan to renegotiate the terms of the Treaty of Accession to the Common Market would seem unpatriotic; to support the renegotiation programme would be to admit that Heath had been remiss in his initial exchanges with the European powers which led to that Treaty. The Tories opposed the government's plans for again changing trade union law – but they could hardly effectively do so on the basis of a defence of the law they had passed, for that law had conspicuously and ignominiously failed. As to the general handling of the economy it was hard for the opposition effectively to oppose the government's plans to inject larger and larger sums of public money into manufacturing industry. After all, that was what the Heath government had been doing between 1972 and 1974. The disarray in opposition ranks was vividly demonstrated in April 1974 when a financial measure subsidiary to the Finance Bill came before the House. Heath first decided to oppose it, and then to abstain. In the event roughly a third of Tory members abstained. Rather more than a third voted against the government, and rather less than a third voted with the government. The Leader simply could not lead.

Such events as the April vote quickened the Tory conviction that a new start was required. In due course Wilson did what Airey Neave had prophesied he would do and called an October General Election. The result surprised the Conservatives, and deeply disappointed the Labour Party. Labour, it is true, was returned with a majority overall, but that majority was only three. However, given that the government could generally rely on support both of the Liberal Party and of the Scottish and Welsh Nationalist Parties, Wilson seemed reasonably secure for some time. In these circumstances the Tories, reconciling themselves to spending some time in opposition, could set about the business of finding a new Leader.

Heath was not so foolish as to imagine that he was not in danger; but he moved quickly to consolidate his position. In order to ensure his continued control over the party machine he created the new post of Director-General at Conservative Central Office and appointed to it his closest confidant and chief speech writer, Michael Wolff. Wolff's brief was to keep a close weather eye for signs of dissent or disloyalty in the ranks of the party's paid servants, and to act appropriately. Under the guidance of Kenneth Baker and Peter Walker, Heath began to try to repair the damage to relations with the backbenchers that his inattention had caused during his years as Prime Minister. He then awaited the inevitable challenge.

Initially, Heath believed that he had at least a year of grace and that he would not be challenged until after the Party Conference in 1975. He was quickly disabused of this notion. The putative coalition against Heath, which began to form in March 1974, was a shifting one. Therein lay its weakness. It consisted, first, of those who deplored the reversal of economic policy in 1972; second, of those who were opposed to, or at least sceptical about, Britain's membership of the EEC; and, third, of those who believed, simply, that Heath was not an election winner. These – on the whole amicable – divisions in the ranks of those opposed to Heath reflected the profound traumas which afflicted the Conservative Party. The uncertain pragmatists, many of whom had no particular views on policy, constituted what might be called the floating vote. Those who differed deeply from Heath on economic policy – soon to be called 'monetarists' – were not all against membership of the Common Market. Those who were against membership of the EEC were not all enamoured of tight control of the money supply and deregulation of industry which the monetarists favoured. However, the latter two groups faced one certainty: neither of them had any chance whatsoever of preferment as long as Edward Heath was Leader. This meant that any challenger could depend absolutely on their support.

Initially, the standard bearer of the economic Right was Sir Keith (now Lord) Joseph.[5] Joseph declined to accept a shadow post which would require him to devote his time and energy to the affairs of a particular Department of State: he would join the Shadow Cabinet only if he was allowed to speak his mind over the whole gamut of Opposition policy. This proposal Heath, being acutely aware of his own vulnerability, accepted; and Joseph used his roving commission consistently to undermine the intellectual position of his Leader in the months that followed.

His insistence on his independence was, of course, taken to mean that his hat would be in the ring in any leadership contest. Between February and November he made a series of deliberately challenging and provocative speeches. Heath's supporters embarked upon a whispering campaign against him, and even his own supporters doubted his resolution. Nicholas Ridley wrote:

> We greatly admired Keith Joseph. He had a fine intellect and was exceedingly brave in stating his opinions. I think that he was right not to offer himself for the Leadership. I think that even he would admit that he was less incisive in taking action than Margaret Thatcher turned out to be. He could never quite bring himself, as a minister, to embark on the brave courses upon which he had called on us to embark.[6]

Margaret Thatcher, now Deputy to the Shadow Chancellor, Robert Carr, remained steadfast in support of Joseph. Meanwhile, she was winning golden opinions for her performance on the front bench: she was helped in making her mark by the fact that Carr was utterly inept in economic matters. Joseph, however, decided that he could not stand the strain of constant exposure and, moreover, came to doubt whether he had the ability to be Prime Minister. On 21 November 1974 he called on Mrs Thatcher and told her that he was no longer a candidate for the Leadership of the Party. Impulsively, she decided to make what was initially to seem a forlorn bid on her own behalf. 'Somebody from our lot[7] has got to stand', she said, 'and I suppose it's got to be me.' She immediately informed Heath of her intention. His only observation was, 'You'll lose'.

Meanwhile, other events were afoot. On 14 October the nine-man Executive of the 1922 Committee met at the Lord North Street house of its Chairman, Edward (now Sir Edward) du Cann. It is my conviction that every member of the Executive believed that Heath should be replaced, though opinions varied on who should replace him.[8] Du Cann went immediately to see Heath to tell him of the unanimous view of the Executive that there should be a ballot for the Leadership in order to clear the air: under the Rules as they then obtained, only the Leader could set in train the moves needed to hold a contest. Heath rebuked du Cann, and insisted that he had no authority as Chairman of the Executive, since that authority had terminated with the calling of the October General Election and could not be re-asserted until a fresh Executive was chosen at the annual election.[9] This contention, he thought, would give him breathing space and time to organise a campaign for the election to the 1922 Executive of his own supporters. (This he did, although in the event it was totally ineffective in that all nine existing members were triumphantly re-elected.)

In the face of Heath's view the Executive, having taken advice from Philip Goodhart, the MP most versed in the history of the 1922 Committee, reconvened and decided to draft a letter to Heath arguing that he was wrong. Heath replied, curtly and formally, saying that he was prepared to discuss his leadership, but only with a freshly elected Executive.

Parliament reconvened on 1 November. The following day the full 1922 Committee met.[10] Members were, naturally, depressed by a second General Election defeat within a year. They were also, naturally, deeply distressed about the question of the leadership. But their feelings were inchoate: for the most part they did not know whether they wanted

Harold Macmillan arriving at the Conservative Party Conference
at Brighton in October 1961.

Harold Wilson leaving Downing Street for Chequers, May 1969.

Edward Heath when he was Prime Minister, July 1972.

Enoch Powell in October 1976.

James Callaghan on the first full day of his appointment
as Prime Minister, 6 April 1976.

Neil Kinnock at a Labour Party Press Conference, June 1987.

Margaret Thatcher.

John Major in February 1992.

Heath to continue, or whether they wanted a new Leader. They also faced the same problem that Edward du Cann and their Executive had already faced. That is, that only Heath could set in motion the process of election. However, their instincts were given focus in a short, but devastating, intervention by the then Member for Rutland, Kenneth (now Sir Kenneth) Lewis. He inquired whether the leadership, which had been held by one man for nearly a decade, was to be regarded as a freehold or a leasehold. The response was overwhelming and almost unanimous: the backbenchers decided that it should be a leasehold.

This display of opinion greatly increased the pressure on Heath. He and his advisers thought of a delaying tactic. Since it was clear that the leasehold versus freehold argument was uppermost in backbenchers' minds, Heath decided to invite Lord Home to advise on what changes should be made in the method of choosing a Tory Leader. It was assumed on the part of the Heath camp that Home would recommend that an annual ballot could be held if the Leader of the day faced a challenger. They further assumed that Heath would have no difficulty in being elected in the early part of 1975 and would then face no further challenge until the autumn of that year, thus giving him ample time to consolidate his support and benefit from the problems which the government was facing.

All these assumptions proved to be mistaken. Home decided to go well beyond the simple leasehold issue. He recommended that there could be at most three ballots for the Leadership. If a contestant (whether the incumbent Leader or someone else) failed to gain 50 per cent plus one *of all those entitled to vote* the matter would go to a second ballot, and, at this stage new candidates could put themselves forward. It was this provision in Home's report that spelt doom for Edward Heath, because it provided for a strong stalking horse in the first ballot who, if he (or, in the event, she) damaged Heath would open the way for a convincing replacement. Thus, William Whitelaw, whose principles of loyalty were such that he could not bring himself to stand against Heath on the first ballot, could seize his opportunity on the second on the assumption that Heath had not gained a convincing victory first time round.

Confusion and discontent remained, however, rampant within the party. 'It was', Whitelaw later wrote, 'certainly the worst time in my political life. I remained Chairman of the Party and so observed from one particular vantage point the bitterness, dissension and general bad feeling in the Parliamentary Party.'[11] He did enter on the second ballot, along with Sir Geoffrey Howe, Jim Prior and John Peyton. But Margaret Thatcher, though without gaining the required majority on the first ballot, so convincingly trounced Heath that the Parliamentary Party came to the view that she could not be denied the Leadership. She beat Heath by 130 votes to 119 and, later, Whitelaw by 146 to 79.

The bitterness and dissension which Whitelaw detected concealed the fact that the fight between Margaret Thatcher and Edward Heath was about much more than a clash of personalities. Certainly there was a clash of personalities: Heath detested Mrs Thatcher; and she returned that dislike in full measure. The Heath campaign team went to somewhat extraordinary ends, mainly by way of tittle-tattle. The Thatcher campaign was concerned above all with propounding an ideal of Conservative government.

The period between October 1974 and May 1979 was one of profound instability in British politics such as had not been seen since the 1920s and the early 1930s. Both major parties were divided on both policies and personalities.

The Labour government elected in February 1974 was committed both to accepting all the wage demands put forward by the National Union of Mineworkers, and to repealing the reforms in trade union legislation enacted by the Heath government. It was also committed to holding a referendum on whether or not the United Kingdom should continue to be a member state of the European Economic Community. On both of these matters the governing party was deeply divided. There were those who, like the Prime Minister himself, had been sedulous supporters of Mrs Barbara Castle's attempts to reform trade union law between 1968 and 1969,[12] and those who had been opponents. Among the most ardent proponents of restoring to the trade unions, not merely the powers and privileges that they enjoyed in 1970, but of greatly increasing those powers and privileges, were the Foreign Secretary, James Callaghan and the Secretary of State for Employment, Michael Foot. In order to hold his party together Wilson had, in opposition, offered Foot *carte blanche* to return the unions to their former eminence.[13]

The promise of a referendum on EEC membership more openly, and savagely, divided the Labour Party. The two sides were represented by, on the one hand Michael Foot and Tony Benn and on the other Roy Jenkins and Shirley Williams. All four were, at this time, powerful figures in Labour Party politics, and all four threatened resignation if the Cabinet failed to espouse their views. The Prime Minister arrived at a typically Wilsonian compromise. He decided, for the nonce, to dispense with the doctrine of collective Cabinet responsibility: each Cabinet Minister would be free to say precisely what he or she thought on the question of EEC membership.[14] Since any question of government policy could be drawn in to the ambit of British policy towards the EEC, this meant, in effect, that no Cabinet Minister could rely on the discretion of his colleagues; and could feel free to say what he liked on any subject to his journalistic contacts. The recipe was one for chaos.[15]

These two deep – and, as it sometimes seemed intractable – divisions, coupled with the freedom of Ministers to say what they liked to whom they liked, meant that the machinery of government ground almost to a halt.

However, the Conservative Party was not, immediately, equipped to strike anything remotely resembling a deadly blow at a weak government. It, too, was divided on policy. Those who had been closest to Mrs Thatcher in her campaign for the leadership were, to put it at its mildest, sceptical about Britain's membership of the EEC, and, at its strongest, utterly opposed to that membership. On trade union law, most of the senior figures from the days of the Heath administration were convinced that, the Heath reforms having failed of their effect, there could be no going back on the reversal of those reforms being introduced by the fourth Wilson government. Margaret Thatcher was underestimated – and often derided – partly because she was a woman and partly because of her lack of senior ministerial experience.[16] There was also the difficulty that she favoured the kind of capitalistic and free-enterprise policies on which Edward Heath had been elected in 1970 but which he had subsequently chosen to abandon. The men who had been closest to Heath in government believed that she could not succeed and that, although the rather romantic drama of the Conservative Party electing its first woman Leader – and becoming the first Western nation so to do – had an immediate effect in terms of public relations, she was not an election winner.[17]

Margaret Thatcher, therefore, embarked on her leadership with many question marks hanging over her authority. Almost immediately, however, she took four decisions designed both to shore up that authority and to unite a party which was divided on doctrine and subject to constant sniping from Edward Heath and his acolytes.

Although she dismissed Geoffrey Rippon and Peter Walker from the Shadow Cabinet,[18] she, amid general surprise, decided to recall Reginald Maudling as Shadow Foreign Secretary, and kept a majority of the adherents of Edward Heath in Shadow office.

Her second decision was to appoint William Whitelaw as her Deputy Leader. This was only the second time that a Deputy Leader had been appointed.[19] The right wing was distressed, for Whitelaw was, rightly, believed to be at the opposite pole of politics from the new Leader. Whitelaw was surprised but delighted. He wrote:

> From that moment on, she did everything in her power to make my position easier. And so started a relationship which I, at any rate, have enormously appreciated. She has always treated me with a kindness and understanding which have meant much to me and which have enabled me to feel that I have played some part in her remarkable achievements as Prime Minister and Leader of our Conservative Party.[20]

Whitelaw's appointment was a shrewd one. Not only was he a former and exceptionally successful Chief Whip but he was held in high personal regard by the great majority of Conservative MPs. Moreover, loyalty was one of the determining principles of his life. He decided that he 'would serve Margaret Thatcher in any capacity that she wanted, and that I would give my undivided loyalty to her as Leader. On that basis I made up my mind that I would do my utmost to work with her.'[21] For the next twelve years he was an invaluable lieutenant, resolute in support of her policies and diplomatic in soothing potential rebels. He also had a gift, priceless in a politician, of spotting trouble well before it arrived. It is not, I believe, an exaggeration to say that, when retirement was forced upon him on 14 December 1987 because of a stroke the government lost its rudder.

Her third decision related to the management of the party machine. Almost immediately she dismissed Michael Wolff, the recently-appointed Director-General of Conservative Central Office. Finally, her fourth decision was another which caused surprise. It was clear that she would not keep Lord Carrington as Chairman of the Party, not only because he was a bad administrator but because he had been singularly unwise in the advice he had given to Heath in the months before the February 1974 General Election. Carrington's replacement was Lord Thorneycroft. Thorneycroft had held several senior ministerial posts until his dismissal from Heath's Shadow Cabinet in 1968. From then on he had been on the outer fringes of politics, and never expected to return again to the limelight. However, the party's finances were in some disrepair and the new Leader believed that Thorneycroft, as a highly successful businessman, could rectify the situation. Moreover, he had made a deep impression on her many years before, when he was the first distinguished guest speaker to address the Oxford University Conservative Association during her presidency of that body in her student days.

Having entered the February 1974 campaign with no great expectation of victory the Labour Party was delighted to find itself back in office, albeit without a House of Commons majority. Nobody doubted, of course, that the new government faced tremendous difficulties, but apart from the joys of office there was also the joy of observing the turmoil in the Conservative Party.

An incoming Labour Prime Minister has a particular constraint imposed upon him by the constitution and conventions of his party. In opposition the members of the Shadow Cabinet are elected by the back-benchers. The annual elections, which take place at the beginning of each parliamentary session, are eagerly awaited by politicians and journalists alike, for they give a running indication of how the contestants are regarded by their parliamentary colleagues. Although, theoretically, a new Labour Prime Minister is wholly free to choose whomsoever he wishes as members of a Cabinet it is, in practice, impossible to ignore the claims to office of those last elected by the backbenchers. In February 1974, as we now know, Wilson wanted the United Kingdom to remain within the Common Market.[22] It would therefore have been highly convenient for him to leave Tony Benn and Peter Shore out of the government which he formed in February 1974: Michael Foot, like Benn and Shore opposed to Britain's continued membership, was indispensable because of the close links he had formed with the trade union movement. A Conservative Prime Minister would have suffered no such handicap: in opposition and government alike the Leader of the Conservative Party has a completely free hand in the choice of opposition spokesmen or government Ministers. Of course, as time goes by, a Labour Prime Minister can drop or appoint Ministers as he thinks fit. But his earliest opportunity to make changes is the first occasion after an election victory on which he reshuffles his Cabinet. Again theoretically, it would be possible for a new Labour Prime Minister to follow a powerful convention by appointing to Cabinet office all those elected in opposition, and to dismiss some of them a week later. In practice, however, this is impossible. Quite apart from the disruption this would cause to the machine of government, feeling in the Labour Party is always such as to demand that new Ministers should be given a chance to show their mettle. In the event Wilson did not reshuffle until after the European referendum in 1975.[23]

The handling of the economy was, of course, the most urgent problem facing the new government: that has been the case with every new British government since the war. The first decisions taken by the Wilson administration were, however, such as to exacerbate rather than to alleviate the difficulties. After a month of negotiations the National Union of Mineworkers, being the most intransigent of all trades unions, insisted on continuing their strike until, on 11 March, the new Secretary of State for Employment, Michael Foot, agreed to their terms: the settlement involved a wage increase of 26 per cent – 6 per cent above the current rate of inflation – as well as various ancillary benefits. By the end of the year the average wage settlement for industrial workers was 29 per cent. Retail prices, meanwhile, had risen by 19 per cent and industrial production had fallen by 3 per cent.

With such figures as these it was clear that the British economy was tottering towards destruction. No government can for long sustain a large general increase in public expenditure over state income, particularly if measures which promote inflation are accompanied by a fall in production. The pure Keynesian theory of economic management ordains that, in times of high unemployment, it is both desirable and practical for a government to increase public expenditure and thus public borrowing in the belief that such expenditure will produce growth. Between February 1974 and July 1975 the government was having the worst of both worlds. Costs were escalating at an alarming rate and productivity continued to fall: the Keynesian theory did not work. Now, when confronted with an economic problem, a Labour government is prone to resort to measures of control imposed from the centre. By the middle of 1975 wages were rising at the annual rate of 33.3 per cent. It was therefore decided to cap wage settlements. The White Paper, *The Attack on Inflation*, ordained that wages, whatever the industry, whether nationalised or private, should rise by no more than £6 a week.

The most dramatic action taken in the closing months of the Heath government had been the introduction of the three-day week. Heath, and the Cabinet, believed that some such measure was required to conserve energy for industry, most at risk from industrial action by the National Union of Mineworkers. It seemed to them, also, to be politically advantageous: the feeling of a nation under threat from powerful trade unions was highlighted by the reduction in the working week. The Heath government believed that the three-day week would convince the electorate that draconian measures had to be taken to preserve the nation from anarchy. Although the Labour Party, before and throughout the General Election campaign, had publicly attacked the three-day week, in private their senior figures believed that it was probably necessary. Wilson would have liked nothing better than to restore the full working week immediately on his election, but his own acceptance of the necessity for emergency measures required him to keep them in place. However, somewhat both to their bafflement and their pleasure, the new Prime Minister and the new Chancellor of the Exchequer, Denis Healey, were presented with Treasury papers demonstrating to their satisfaction that the three-day week had had a neutral effect on industrial production. They therefore felt free to abolish it on 8 March. Just as Heath had believed that this visible demonstration of the power of the trades unions would pay electoral dividends, so Wilson and Healey believed that the ending of the state of emergency would pay electoral dividends for them in another General Election that could not be long delayed.

In the tangled history of post-war British politics, but particularly in the 1970s, British governments have again and again been faced not only with manifold difficulties – not always of their own making – but also with their own conflicting promises. Harold Wilson inherited a disastrous rate of inflation; but he also determined to keep his promises to the trades unions which would inevitably have the effect of increasing that inflation. On 12 August 1975 it was announced that the monthly retail price index had risen by 26.9 per cent – the highest figure recorded since the war. On 20 November 1975 it was, therefore, announced that cash limits, not as yet defined, would be applied to all public expenditure. Thus the Labour government abandoned the programme announced in its manifesto of increased industrial subsidisation and increased social expenditure. The question was raised as to how long the government could survive. It was not until James Callaghan became Prime Minister the following year that the means of survival appeared.

The trouble with the two Labour governments which lasted from February 1974 to May 1979 was that they had no serious fundamental proposals for tackling the malaise of the British economy. In 1964 the central proposition of the Labour manifesto was that greater efficiency, organised by central government, and the use of the National Economic Development Council, together with the National Enterprise Board, to channel government subsidy to industry would produce a rejuvenation of the British manufacturing base. There can be no doubt, in spite of Harold Wilson's special pleadings in his memoirs,[24] that the 1964 government was an almost unmitigated failure. But on his return to 10 Downing Street in February 1974 Wilson and his colleagues had no fresh ideas to offer: it was simply the mixture as before. True, the government did not attempt again to create such exotic and otiose institutions as the Department of Economic Affairs; but the whole thrust of policy was in the same direction as had obtained a decade earlier.

Only one element of the 1960s package was lacking in the opening stages of the third and fourth Wilson administrations, and in the

Callaghan administration which succeeded them. This was a policy on incomes. As we have seen, the first step towards a full-blown incomes policy was taken in July 1975. But its efficacy depended on exhortation and agreement with the unions. It is a sad but fundamental truth about modern democratic government that an administration which spends more than the nation earns, and borrows to finance that spending, invariably ends up with first a voluntary, and then a compulsory, attempt to control incomes. This was true in all four governments headed by Harold Wilson and of the government headed by Edward Heath from 1970 to 1974 – in spite of the fact that Heath had given the most solemn undertakings both in the 1970 manifesto, and in the course of the campaign, that incomes policies were anathema to him.

Wilson was, after February 1974, fortunate in having in Denis Healey a Chancellor with an exceptionally tough character and a total lack of principle. Healey's self-esteem could be punctured neither by criticism nor by failure. He took reversals of policy in his stride. Thus, on 19 February 1976 he published a White Paper on Public Expenditure proposing cuts of a billion pounds in the current financial year and 2.4 billion in the year following. The Labour Party was outraged; and divisions began to emerge in the Cabinet, with Tony Benn, an increasingly formidable political figure, leading a group of Ministers – including Antony Crosland, Harold (now Lord) Lever and Peter Shore – in their stern opposition to the deflationary policies proposed by the Chancellor. However, the putative rebels had different solutions to the crisis, and in their differences lay their weakness. At one extreme, Benn wanted a far more Socialist form of government, with more and more central controls, and ever stricter governmental monitoring of the system of industrial subsidy. At the other extreme, Lever advocated still higher borrowing, on the Keynesian principle that very high public expenditure was justified in times of difficulty because it would produce confidence in industry and, eventually, a boom in manufacturing. His was a very high-risk policy.

Another problem for Healey's critics was the fact that there were two former Chancellors in the Cabinet – the Foreign Secretary, James Callaghan, and the Home Secretary, Roy Jenkins. Both of these men had been over this ground before, and they had been badly bruised by their experiences. Callaghan had been forced to resign in 1967. But Jenkins, by applying measures not dissimilar to those advocated by Healey, had procured a distinct improvement in the general economic situation by the time of the June 1970 General Election. Unfortunately for him, the good he had wrought had not produced benefits for the individual in time to save Labour at the General Election in which Edward Heath was victorious. But in the increasingly frenetic Cabinet debates of 1974 and 1975 – debates which were echoed on the backbenches and in the press and broadcast media – the shared experiences of Wilson, Callaghan and Jenkins gave them immense moral authority, though the matter was not finally settled until the International Monetary Fund intervened in Britain's economic affairs in October 1976. It is fair to say, however, that Healey appreciated the necessity for a programme of economic austerity before the IMF acted. But the fact of the matter was that, though he had most of the required measures in place, the economy had not had time to react to them. The IMF's decision to withdraw international credit from Britain – a decision so quickly made public – provided a salutary shock to the system, frightened most Labour supporters, and added influence to those, like the Chancellor, arguing for deflationary action.

Upon his return to power in February 1974, Harold Wilson had informed the Queen that he would retire in the following year. He was succeeded, on a vote of the Parliamentary Labour Party, by James Callaghan who, with Denis Healey, had to bear the brunt of the economic storm that was breaking over Britain.

None of Healey's measures worked. Further cuts in public expenditure were made, and in the April 1976 budget it was proposed that taxation be reduced by 1.6 billion. But this reduction was made to depend on the agreement of the TUC to a new pay norm. This agreement was given, and subsequently broken. In March 1976 sterling fell below $2.00 for the first time, and in October of the same year the pound was worth $1.5675: this was the lowest point ever for sterling.

The Callaghan government – like the Wilson government before it – was always bound to have to live on a knife's edge. For this reason, its members, for the most part, managed to conceal their private differences in public. The referendum on continued membership of the EEC being over, Ministers realised that survival was the order of the day. However, in 1977, Callaghan did make an important change in the composition of the government which he headed, by replacing Roy Jenkins with Merlyn Rees. Roy Jenkins had opposed him for the succession to Harold Wilson, and the two men were temperamentally quite exceptionally incompatible. In my opinion, the Prime Minister, easily though he had beaten Jenkins for the leadership, felt a sense of inferiority to his Home Secretary. The Jenkins life style – the taste for fine wines, the writing of elegant books and, perhaps above all, the condescending manner of speech – all irritated Callaghan profoundly. At this point in his career, further, Jenkins had to face the fact that he now had no chance of

169

fulfilling his ambition to become Prime Minister. Indeed, he was considerably less than enthusiastic about taking on the Home Office for, although that Department is one of the three senior offices of state, it is inferior in esteem to the Chancellorship of the Exchequer, which Jenkins had already held. There was no doubt, therefore, that Jenkins was an increasingly disillusioned man from 1974 onwards. Indeed, he says as much in considerable detail in his memoirs.[25]

However, a solution agreeable to both men was before long to come to hand. In 1976 Jenkins was invited by the European Council, with the encouragement of Callaghan, to become President of the European Commission, with effect from January 1977. Though he remained Home Secretary for a further ten weeks after this invitation, this was essentially his farewell to the Labour Party. Jenkins was an intensely enthusiastic pro-European. He was delighted with his new job – 'starry-eyed' is his own description of his feelings.[26] It was not, however, the end of his connection with British politics. In 1981, at the conclusion of his term at the Commission, Jenkins played a crucial part in the foundation of the Social Democratic Party.[27]

Callaghan still had to face the serious problem of his vestigial majority, which was gradually being eroded by by-elections. While the October 1974 election had given Labour a comfortable plurality – 319 to 277 seats – over the Conservatives, there were also 13 Liberal seats, 3 taken by Plaid Cymru, 11 by the Scottish Nationalists and 11 by the Ulster Unionists. There was also one representative of the Northern Ireland Social Democratic and Labour Party. On 17 March 1977, Mrs Thatcher tabled a motion of censure for debate on 23 March. It seemed not unlikely that the government would fall as a result of the vote on this motion and that the Prime Minister would be forced into a General Election which he thought he would lose. He therefore decided to open negotiations with the minority parties.

It should be stressed that he was not holding out the offer of a coalition, in this respect unlike Edward Heath's negotiations with Jeremy Thorpe in 1974. What he wanted to do was to ascertain on what terms the smaller parties would pledge their votes in the House of Commons to keep his government alive. Different negotiators were appointed to sound out each of the leaders of the smaller parties, and talks began immediately, lasting until 20 March. Merlyn Rees, a former Northern Ireland Secretary, and much esteemed by the Catholic community in Ulster, was appointed to deal with the single SDLP Member, Gerry (now Lord) Fitt. Another former Northern Ireland Secretary, with a reputation for tough dealing with the IRA, Roy Mason, was, along with the

Leader of the House, Michael Foot, given the task of negotiating with the Ulster Unionist parties.[28] Cledwyn (now Lord Cledwyn) Hughes was charged with speaking to the leader of the Liberal Party, David Steel, and with Gwynfor Evans of Plaid Cymru. The Prime Minister himself concentrated on the Scottish National Party.

The essence of the government's offer in these negotiations was to give the minorities almost anything they wanted, apart from government office. The Liberals – who, in any event, were sympathetic to Labour's social policies – were won over by a promise of consultation on all areas of government, and the eventual appointment of a Speaker's Committee to enquire into the possibility of proportional representation.[29] The Welsh and Scottish Nationalists were offered a Bill providing for devolution in both countries to be followed by two separate referenda on its terms. The central Ulster Unionist demand, formulated by Enoch Powell, who accompanied Molyneaux to all his talks, was for an increase in the number of parliamentary seats in the province to bring it into line with the mainland. There were two further demands. The first was to return to local authorities in the province the same powers as were enjoyed by their equivalents on the mainland. The second was that the system introduced at the time of the imposition of direct rule of legislating for Northern Ireland by Order in Council, rather than by the normal process of putting a bill through Parliament, should be abandoned.[30] Fitt wanted an undertaking to step up negotiations with the government of the Irish Republic on the question of Northern Ireland. Ministers undertook to legislate to increase parliamentary representation for Ulster and to consider all the other requests put before them. The Callaghan government was thus able to survive for a further two years until another censure motion by Mrs Thatcher on 28 March 1979 when, deserted by the minorities, the government fell by one vote.[31]

Of the minority parties, the only ones that can be said to have got anything substantial in the long run were the two Ulster Unionist parties. Special legislation was introduced which increased the number of Northern Ireland seats from 12 to 17.[32] The Liberals were never given their Speaker's Conference and, although they certainly enjoyed the heady business of having ready access to and regular consultations with government ministers, they had no serious influence on the evolution of policy. The continuing difficulties in which the government found itself led them to fear that they would be tarred with the brush of the government's failure. Thus, during the summer recess of 1978, the Liberal Party announced that it would withdraw from its agreement with the government the following November. This did not mean that the

171

Liberals would invariably appear in the opposition lobbies but merely that they were under no obligation always to support the government.

At first sight it seemed that the Scottish National Party and Plaid Cymru had the best opportunity of all the minority parties for achieving a major success. Of course, the SNP wanted – as they do at the time of writing – full independence for Scotland, but they were prepared to accept devolution as a half-way house. Devolution had been advocated for a number of years by senior members of both the major parties and with greater vigour by the Liberals. The Callaghan commitment to the nationalist parties was, essentially, to speed up the legislative process to provide for the devolving of certain substantial powers from Westminster to a Scottish Assembly in Edinburgh and a Welsh Assembly in Cardiff. The discussions – which were of great complexity – preceding the introduction of the Bill were concerned with how many powers were to be transferred. The basic paper on which all parties could work was the report of the Kilbrandon Commission, which had been published in November 1973, and the principle was embodied in the Labour Party manifesto for the General Election of February 1974. Throughout 1974 and 1975 the Leader of the House, Edward Short (now Lord Glenamara), sought to create a framework of legislation based on Kilbrandon. But the Nationalists concluded that his work was far too desultory. Therefore, though they did not doubt that the Labour government favoured devolution, they were anxious in the 1977 negotiations to ensure speedy action. Michael Foot succeeded Short in April 1976. Foot was an enthusiast for devolution and, even in advance of legislation, made some firm proposals for powers that would be devolved to the Assemblies, including the handing over of control of the Scottish and Welsh Development Agencies. The second reading of the relevant bill was on 13 December 1976. The government and the Scottish and Welsh National parties foresaw squalls ahead, for there was strong opposition within the Labour Party to the whole idea of devolution.

The voting figures on the second reading are interesting. Ten Labour Members voted against their government and 29 abstained. By this time, of course, Margaret Thatcher was Leader of the Conservative Party and showing a distinct inclination to withdraw from the principle of devolution made by her predecessor, Edward Heath. In the second reading vote 5 Conservatives supported the government and 28 abstained. It is unnecessary here to go into minute detail in discussing a bill which was destined to fail. But some of the more prominent details are important. Foot decided that he would allow 30 days of debate and then seek to guillotine the bill.[33] On 22 February 1977 the debate on the guillotine motion was held. Callaghan tells us[34] that his Chief Whip, Michael (now Lord) Cocks, predicted that the government would lose by 30 votes: the actual figure was 29.[35] It was therefore vitally important for Callaghan in his negotiations with the Nationalists the following month both to undertake to reintroduce the bill, and to take stern measures to ensure that it would be passed.

A young Scottish Labour MP, John Smith – later to rise to eminence in the Labour Party – was given the task of drafting the new bill in agreement with the Liberal Party and the two nationalist parties. Smith is a lawyer and was held in high regard for his skill in drafting legislative proposals. Michael Foot, quite apart from his manifold responsibilities as Leader of the House, was not noted for precision in argument; and it seemed sensible to the Prime Minister to hand over the intricacies of drawing up a new bill on devolution to a man with forensic skills. Callaghan still bore the scars of the failure of a previous Labour government's attempt to reform the House of Lords.[36]

Although the Liberal Party had voted against the previous attempt to guillotine a devolution bill, they remained in principle in favour of devolution. John Smith persuaded David Steel that if the new bill was divided into two sections, one concerning Scotland and one concerning Wales, and that the record of debate on the devolution bill which had failed was taken into account, a guillotine motion would be acceptable. That guillotine was announced on the first day of the new debate. Seventeen days were allotted for Scotland and eleven for Wales.

Just as Enoch Powell and Michael Foot had outmanoeuvred the government of the day in its attempt to reform the House of Lords,[37] so Callaghan and Smith were outmanoeuvred in a subtle way by two Labour MPs, George Cunningham, the then Member for Islington, and Tam Dalyell, Member for Linlithgow. Cunningham moved an amendment which argued for a requirement that in a referendum on devolution in Scotland there should be a majority of 40 per cent of all those entitled to vote.

No government likes to see amendments to its legislation, and the Callaghan government was no exception. Thus it was the wish of the government that the Cunningham amendment should be defeated. However, by this stage, the Conservative opposition had decided to vote against the bill, Mrs Thatcher having become increasingly averse to any form of devolution. Moreover, 34 Labour MPs voted against their government. As a result the amendment was carried by 15 votes. This was to have profound consequences for the fate of the devolution policy, and the ultimate fate of the Labour government. Callaghan writes:

I have since wondered whether those thirty-four Labour Members would have voted as they did if they had been able to foresee that their vote on that evening would precipitate a General Election in 1979, at the least favourable time for their Government.[38]

However, the legislation was carried, and received the Royal Assent on 31 July 1978. Referenda were held in Scotland and Wales on 1 March 1979. In Scotland 1,230,937 voted in favour of devolution and 1,153,502 voted against. The yes majority constituted only 32.9 per cent of those who had a right to vote and thus devolution for Scotland fell, for the moment at least, by the wayside. In Wales, however, devolution proved singularly unpopular. In the Principality, 243,048 voted for devolution and 956,330 voted against, the relative percentages being 20.2 per cent and 79.8 per cent of those voting.

It has to be said that, apart from the constraints imposed by his desire to remain in office, Callaghan did believe in the rectitude of the devolution policy. However, even more fundamental to his view of how to run a government was his conviction that business should be conducted in alliance with the trade unions. Callaghan, when Home Secretary, had destroyed Harold Wilson's plans for a reform of trade union law that would have restricted the unions' privileges.[39] He had a visceral feeling for trade unions and their leaders. He had an almost mystical belief that the major union leaders were their members and that, therefore, if they agreed with him on a particular policy, that policy would be respected by all union members. Essentially, what he required was trade union support for restraint on incomes; and this the two major trade union leaders, Jack Jones and Hugh Scanlon, promised him. Callaghan did not seem to grasp the significance of the facts both that Jones and Scanlon were approaching retirement, nor that smaller unions were beginning to resent the assumption that the great industrial unions would always be able to determine the conduct of the non-industrial sectors of the TUC. Callaghan had no marked theoretical view of politics: like Herbert Morrison, he believed that Socialism was what a Labour government did.

A Labour government finds it more difficult to confront conflicting economic indicators than does a Conservative government. It is true, of course, that many economically disadvantaged people vote Conservative; but they do not, in general, do so solely because they expect a Conservative government to improve their financial lot. The essential assumption of Labour politics, however, is that the party exists to serve the working classes as defined in Labour mythology. The nascent trade union movement created the Labour Party because it wanted a voice in Parliament.

174

Thereafter it was assumed, not unnaturally, that there would be two engines propelling the advancement of those at the lower end of the social scale – the Labour Party (ideally a Labour government) and the trade union movement. Serious problems arise when some economic indicators bode well, and others bode ill and a Labour government is in power. In those circumstances it is difficult for Labour supporters to appreciate that the government cannot immediately deliver on the promises not merely of its manifesto but inherent in its nature.

Over 1977 and 1978 the economic indicators were in conflict. Unemployment had risen to well over 1.5 million. On 7 September 1977 the TUC therefore agreed to support the policy of restraint on incomes advocated by the government. On the other hand, in January 1978, UK gold and dollar reserves rose to $20.6 billion, which was their highest point ever. The following month inflation fell below 10 per cent for the first time since 1973. However, the state of industrial relations continued to deteriorate as the non-industrial unions increasingly declined to obey the fiat of the TUC. Firemen struck in 1977, motor workers in October 1978, printworkers in December of the same year, lorry drivers and public employees in January 1979, and civil servants in February. This was what came to be known as 'the winter of discontent'.

It is a singular characteristic of the British political system that, subject to the judgement of the Sovereign, the Prime Minister chooses the date for a General Election – provided only that it cannot be more than five years from the date of the previous General Election. The opinion polls having been favourable through the summer and early autumn of 1978, it was almost universally assumed not only in Labour but in Conservative ranks that Callaghan would go to the country in October. The Prime Minister procrastinated: at the last Cabinet meeting before the summer recess he informed his colleagues that he would tell them of his decision on 6 September. He was engaged to speak at the TUC Conference in Brighton in September, and he therefore asked senior trade union leaders to his Sussex farm on 1 September. All of the union leaders were in favour of an immediate resort to the voters; but the Prime Minister was not clear in his own mind as to which date offered him the best chance of success. It must be remembered that, eager though he was to win his own mandate as Prime Minister, Callaghan enormously enjoyed his job, and was unwilling to put it at risk.

For various reasons concerned with ministerial diaries, the autumn Cabinet was postponed for a day. Meanwhile, media speculation about his intentions had mounted to fever pitch. On 7 September Callaghan told his Cabinet colleagues that he would make a statement later in the day. In his speech to the TUC that day he made it clear that there would be no early General Election. He then got in touch with the broadcasting authorities and sought time for a ministerial statement on radio and television, in which he declared to the electorate that he was postponing the day of decision. From that day to this it had been debated whether his decision was wise: as he points out himself,[40] the Labour Party enjoyed an average opinion poll lead of 5.5 per cent through October and November.

His decision once made, the Prime Minister told all of his Cabinet colleagues that it was his determination to soldier on until the new year.

Intensive discussions now took place between Ministers and trade union leaders, Callaghan being determined above all to reduce inflation to, at most, 5 per cent. While, in general, the major trade union leaders were sympathetic, it rapidly became clear that they could not speak for their members.

Callaghan's problem was that most of the strikes that were taking place during the winter of 1978/79 were in service industries. The spectacle of hospital patients turned away, riotous behaviour on the part of members of the National Union of Public Employees, and bodies unburied appeared on television night after night. The Prime Minister nonetheless decided to fulfil his engagement to attend a summit meeting of Western leaders at Guadeloupe on 5 and 6 January 1979. Whether he decided to go to Guadeloupe or to stay at home, the Prime Minister could not win the public relations battle. If he stayed he would be accused of panicking in the face of trade union dissent; if he went he would be accused of gallivanting on the world stage while there were serious troubles at home. The summit discussions were concerned with matters of no great consequence, but of incomprehensible technicality. Moreover, the British press and television, in general, took particular delight in reporting on Callaghan's enjoyment of West Indian sunshine while so much at home was miserable.

It is now quite clear that the Prime Minister simply did not appreciate the seriousness of the situation in which the government was placed. Upon his return from Guadeloupe he seemed impervious to danger. He was still convinced that the problems of industrial relations which confronted him were of a trifling nature. But he had now lost the allegiance not only of the Liberal Party but of the Nationalists, who bewailed his refusal to accept Michael Foot's recommendation to revoke the results of the Scottish and Welsh referenda on devolution by placing before the House of Commons the Order in Council required by legislation and voting it down.[41]

Still, though, the Tory hour had not struck. For most purposes of ordinary business the minority parties were willing to support the government; and most of Mrs Thatcher's colleagues doubted the wisdom of laying down a motion of no confidence. Whatever the public thought of the government, the Prime Minister, in his avuncular persona, was widely judged to be popular and it was not in many Conservative circles thought to be prudent to pit Mrs Thatcher against him. However, her closest adviser, Airey Neave, thought otherwise and, under his guidance, she decided, again, to put the matter to the touch. On 28 March 1979 the crucial vote took place. Every effort was made, particularly by Michael Foot, to persuade the minorities to keep the government in office. Mr Speaker announced the result of the vote at eighteen minutes past ten. 310 Members of Parliament were found to have confidence in Her Majesty's Government; 311 had not. The Prime Minister rose and said:

Mr Speaker. Now that the House of Commons has declared itself, we shall take our own case to the country.

Thus James Callaghan began his walk into political oblivion; and Margaret Thatcher began her march to No. 10 Downing Street.

CHAPTER TEN

The Breaking of the Mould
(1979–1985)

Any Prime Minister inheriting a difficult economic situation has one major disadvantage, and one major advantage. The disadvantage is that he or she has to find ways of tackling the problems, seemingly perennial, of the economy. But the advantage is that a new Prime Minister, coming from opposition to government, can disclaim responsibility for all that has gone before. The 1979 General Election at once gave Margaret Thatcher an invaluable starting point: the Conservative majority over all other parties was 43. Her victory, moreover, was unexpected. Most commentators, still amazed at the choice by the Conservative Party of a woman leader, believed that the electorate would choose the party led by the safe figure of James Callaghan. It was not, at that time, realised that the old house of Labour was gradually being destroyed by left-wing termites within it. Only with the election of Neil Kinnock as Leader of the Party in October 1983 did a temporary recovery of its fortunes begin. Thereafter it became a very different party from that defeated in 1979 – though it required a further General Election defeat to convince Kinnock of the necessity of changing not merely personalities but policies.

The new Prime Minister had fought a doughty campaign. Her determination was all the more admired because of the murder, in the second week of the campaign, of her closest adviser and campaign manager – also the head of her private office and Secretary of State designate for Northern Ireland – Airey Neave. But, in truth, it is my belief that her victory was decided before the campaign began. The country was in the mood for radical change. Mrs Thatcher had promised to break the grip of the trade union movement on the British economy. Many, even in the ranks of her own party, thought that this was an Herculean task impossible of achievement: she determined to go ahead. Her majority was such as to ensure that there could be no serious opposition in Parliament to the drastic economic measures that she and the Chancellor of the Exchequer, Sir Geoffrey Howe, proposed to take. She had the will required to enforce a seriously deflationary economic policy and the benefit of an increasingly deeply divided opposition.

However, there were risks of divisions within her own party on one specific area of international concern. One of Mrs Thatcher's first overseas engagements was the Commonwealth Prime Ministers Conference in Lusaka in July and August. At the top of the agenda was the problem of trying to find a solution to the civil war that had been raging in Rhodesia since even before the Unilateral Declaration of Independence by an all-white government headed by Ian Smith on 11 November 1965. Large sections of the Tory Party were desirous of washing their hands of the whole problem. During the second half of the 1960s and through the seventies the solution passionately advocated by the right wing of the Tory Party was to recognise the all-white government of Ian Smith. However, there was a general desire that blacks should have a share in government; and this desire appeared to be gratified by Smith in April 1979 when he stood down as Prime Minister in favour of the Methodist bishop, Abel Muzorewa. The general international opinion however – in my view a correct one – was that Muzorewa was merely a puppet to be manipulated by Smith and his party, the Rhodesia Front.

Mrs Thatcher had no experience whatsoever in foreign affairs. Her first instinct was to recognise the Muzorewa government and to abandon the sanctions which Britain had imposed upon Rhodesia since UDI. However, when Muzorewa came to London in June she formed an extremely low opinion of his capabilities. Towards the end of June she attended her first international economic summit in Tokyo and, on the way back, stopped in Canberra to discuss with the Australian Prime Minister, Malcolm Fraser, the Commonwealth Summit in Lusaka due to take place the following month. She and Fraser had known one another for some time: they had both been Education Ministers in the seventies. They had shared views of economic policy and before the 1979 election he had seconded one of his most senior advisers to Conservative Central Office. She was somewhat surprised to discover how vehemently Fraser opposed any move towards even the most vestigial accommodation with Muzorewa.

On 25 July she made her first speech on the subject in the House of Commons in the debate on the adjournment for the summer recess. At the time, because of industrial disputes, neither *The Times* nor *Hansard* was being printed. The other newspapers did not note that the Prime Minister's speech marked a major change in what was assumed to be her policy of recognition of Muzorewa. In effect she advocated a black majority government. Lord Boyd of Merton had, on behalf of the Conservative Party, carried out an investigation into the new Rhodesian dispensation and had concluded it to be firm and fair. She rejected his conclusions, but among her backbenchers only Julian Amery saw the change that had taken place in her policy. Mrs Thatcher's arrival in Lusaka was preceded by that of the Queen, who had been on a tour of Commonwealth African states. The Queen was immensely popular in Zambia; but Commonwealth leaders in general expected Margaret Thatcher to be more than usually unpopular.[1] She herself expected a hostile reception and, indeed, such a reception was prepared for her. However, discreet communication of the meaning of her speech in the House of Commons was conveyed to Dr Kenneth Kaunda, the then President of Zambia and Chairman of the Conference, and hostile demonstrations which Mrs Thatcher had feared were called off. In the event, she formed an exceptionally warm and effective relationship with Dr Kaunda, who was the leading black African head of government in the fight to secure majority rule in Rhodesia.[2] It was agreed that a constitutional conference should take place in London between all the conflicting parties in the Rhodesian imbroglio. It should be mentioned here that the government of Rhodesia was not represented at Lusaka. Nonetheless, the British Prime Minister's ability to procure, during many late-night discussions, the agreement of Commonwealth governments to the London conference was a remarkable demonstration of sure-footed diplomacy, particularly as it came from somebody who had no previous ministerial experience of foreign affairs.

In 1980 the conference took place at Lancaster House. It was presided over by the British Foreign Secretary, Lord Carrington, but Carrington had, more than once, to summon Mrs Thatcher to upbraid the delegates when agreement appeared to be unobtainable. Robert Mugabe, who was to emerge as the first President of Zimbabwe (as Rhodesia shortly came to be known), at one stage flew to Mozambique to appeal for continued support by the President of that country, Samora Machel, and Ian Smith departed for Salisbury (now Harare) to advocate a continued white defiance of the possibility of black majority rule. Nonetheless, the combination of the Prime Minister's conviction and Lord Carrington's technical skill ensured the peaceful passage of Rhodesia into a new age.[3] The successful outcome of the Lancaster House negotiations ensured the establishment of Mrs Thatcher as a serious and powerful figure on the stage of international politics. The Rhodesian problem, having defeated more experienced politicians, notably Harold Wilson and Edward Heath, was finally resolved by an inexperienced woman.

Nonetheless, the delicacy of Mrs Thatcher's position at home should not be underestimated. She felt it necessary, for example, to bring Peter Walker back into the Cabinet as Minister for Agriculture and, further, felt that the reform of trade union law should be approached with the utmost caution. The one thing, however, that she was determined upon was the institution of a budgetary policy which was severely anti-inflationary. This required a greater resolve than that shown by any post-war Prime Minister hitherto and, particularly, that shown by her immediate pre-decessor as Leader of the Party, Edward Heath. At the end of May 1979, for example, Sir Geoffrey Howe and the Chief Secretary to the Treasury, John Biffen, suggested that the monetarist cause would be served by cuts in public spending amounting to £500 million: she insisted on cuts of £3,500 million. The new Prime Minister's decision to ignore rising unemployment – which was, in some part at least, the consequence of her monetary policy – also required a will of steel. But she was fortunate in the unwavering support of the Chancellor of the Exchequer. Sir Geoffrey Howe's first budget, in June 1979, duly proposed drastic reductions in public expenditure well over and above the reductions demanded of Denis Healey by the International Monetary Fund.

But in democracies – and particularly in Britain – while a policy of austerity is often accepted as inevitable, it is also expected to produce reasonably quick results. By 1981 there seemed, however, not even the smallest glimmer of sunlight on the horizon. Unlike Edward Heath in 1972, Mrs Thatcher decided that there should be no turning back, and Sir Geoffrey Howe put before the Cabinet a further package of deflation-ary measures judged harsh even by friendly reporters. A number of members of the Cabinet, notably Ian Gilmour, Peter Walker and James Prior, were horrified at the prospect that lay ahead: unemployment was rising precipitously and was eventually to reach the previously unimagin-able post-war figure of three million. The Prime Minister would brook no opposition. The day before the budget speech was made she invited dissenting Ministers to resign. None did.[4]

That the Thatcher-Howe economic policy met with resistance in government ranks was hardly surprising, given the number of opponents to her economic views that she had included in her first Cabinet. Of all her initial appointments the most unexpected seemed to be that of James Prior as Secretary of State for Employment. Prior had been one of Edward Heath's most devoted adherents. He had started his rise to high office in 1965 as Heath's Parliamentary Private Secretary. Upon Heath's election victory in 1970 Prior became Minister of Agriculture. It is rare for a PPS to go straight into the Cabinet, but Prior's loyalty to the new Prime Minister was so ingrained, and his experience as a farmer so relevant, that the promotion could readily be justified. When Heath changed the economic policy of the government in 1972 there was no more stout supporter of his decision than Prior. Prior remained steadfast, but also came to the conclusion that Heath's initial attempt to reduce the powers and privileges of the trade unions had been mistaken. Here again he was listening to his master's voice.

No politician, therefore, was more amazed, in view of her plans for trade union reform, than Prior when, in May 1979, Margaret Thatcher offered him the job of Secretary of State for Employment. Later he wrote:

> Within twenty-four hours of my appointment at the Department of Employment I knew exactly what she thought of me from her remark that she was determined to have 'someone with backbone' as my junior Minister. Neither the Party, the press nor the unions needed a crystal ball to predict that I was going to have a rough passage. With Margaret as Prime Minister and my view being regarded as well to the left of the Party, there were bound to be question marks over my credibility – would I last long on the front bench? Was it really worthwhile for the unions to bother to get to know me?
>
> Throughout my entire time in the job I was having to fight on two fronts – I was striving to impose some form of legislation on the unions while repelling the right-wing demands for extreme measures which were extreme [sic].[5]

The only piece of legislation which Prior introduced was the Employment Act of 1980. It provided public funds to be available to meet the cost of ballots among trade unions members before a strike was called. This was not a measure favoured by trade union leaders, who believed that they should be able to take decisions on whether to call strikes or not, and expected their members loyally to follow them. But, since it was a measure a great deal less stern than the Prime Minister's rhetoric had promised, they became reasonably content to live with it. Neither they, nor the Secretary of State himself, knew what was to come.

On 12 September 1981 the Prime Minister decided to reshuffle the government. Prior, having, however unwillingly, served her purposes, was offered the choice of Secretary of State for Northern Ireland or leaving office. He asked for time to think about this choice; but Mrs

Thatcher was implacable. Prior was faced with an extremely difficult decision. If he refused the poisoned chalice of Northern Ireland he would seem to be unpatriotic. If, on the other hand, he agreed to leave the Department of Employment without taking another office he would inevitably put at risk the trust he believed he had built up with trade union leaders; he was immensely proud of the good personal relations he enjoyed, not only with Len (now Lord) Murray, the Secretary-General of the TUC, but even with such fundamentalist left-wing trade unionists as the Communist Ken Gill of the AUEW.[6] He therefore asked the Prime Minister to retain his position as a member of the Economic Committee of the Cabinet, thus preserving an influence on economic and industrial relations policy. But the position of Secretary of State for Northern Ireland is virtually all-consuming in terms of time and energy. Mrs Thatcher concluded, shrewdly, that she could readily agree to Prior remaining formally a member of the Committee, reckoning that he would have no time to devote to its affairs. On these terms, however, Prior agreed to accept the Northern Ireland Office. It was the end of his influence on mainland government policy. Realising the hapless nature of his situation, he decided, in 1984, to leave the Cabinet and announce that he would resign from the House of Commons at the next General Election.

Mrs Thatcher's central conviction on the matter of trade union law was that the legislation introduced by the Heath government was fundamentally correct, but that it had been too hastily introduced, was too much for the trade union movement to take in one dose, and would excite universal opposition. She was determined, therefore, to bring in a very similar set of reforms, but piece by piece. One man in the government which she headed had long hungered for the job of reforming trade union law. This was Norman Tebbit. Tebbit replaced Prior and brought to his new job certain very distinctive psychological advantages. He was fundamentally a man of hard personality. Affable enough in private, he could be vicious in public debate: he was once described in the House of Commons by Michael Foot as a 'semi house-trained polecat'. His origins were irrefragably working class, but he had none of the sense of deference often found in ambitious Conservative politicians of working class origins; moreover, he had about him none of the sense of guilt which often attaches itself to Tories of patrician origins. He embarked upon the business of breaking the power of the trade unions, not merely with enthusiasm but with relish; and it was hard for them to gainsay him. Behind the hard, though humorous, exterior there was a shrewd operator. He later wrote that he 'was determined not to enact unenforceable

183

legislation – the memory of the collapse of the 1972 Industrial Relations Act was very much in my mind'. He continued:

> I had a very clear plan for my programme of reform before I made the first move but it existed only in my mind and I had no intention of exposing more than one move at a time. I was determined first to form public opinion and then to be always just a little behind rather than ahead of it as I legislated.[7]

The Prime Minister and the new Secretary of State for Employment had two movements of fact and opinion in their favour. The first was rising unemployment. This weakened the power of trade union leadership, not least because a man or woman who becomes unemployed cannot continue to be a member of his or her trade union. The second was the sea-changes which had been taking place in the trade union movement as a whole. These changes were evinced most notably by the rise in power of the electricians' trade union, then led by Frank (now Lord) Chapple. There was a remarkable symbiosis between the intentions of the government and the ambitions, for his members, of Chapple – ambitions which were to be further pursued by his successor, Eric Hammond and, later, by the leaders of the AUEW, Bill Jordan and Gavin Laird.

Norman Tebbit introduced and guided the passage of one important piece of legislation on trade union law, and prepared another vitally important bill, which was seen through Parliament by Tom King, who succeeded him in October 1983. The Employment Act of 1982 provided that the Treasury would compensate employees judged to have been unfairly dismissed. The significance of this Act was that it represented the first move to protect workers victimised by the institution of the 'closed shop', whereby, in any major industry, it was virtually impossible to retain employment without belonging to a union. The Trade Union Act of 1984 was, it could be argued, the most consequential piece of legislation passed during Mrs Thatcher's time in office. It made the existing legal immunity of a trade union taking strike action dependent on a secret ballot of members. This meant that when Arthur Scargill, General Secretary of the National Union of Mineworkers, decided to call a strike in March 1984 without a full ballot of his members, he was open to court action.[8]

By the spring of 1982 it had become clear that the programme which Mrs Thatcher would pursue in government was the same as that outlined by her in opposition. The austere economic policy was in place. Nobody, not even the most optimistic or self-confident of trade unionists, believed that there would not be further legislation on industrial relations. Moreover, the government had begun to implement its plans for the sale of council houses to their tenants. The strictest of monetarists grumbled somewhat, since property was being offered for sale on very favourable terms. But this was a policy very close to the Prime Minister's heart. In 1955 Anthony Eden had proclaimed the Tory ideal of a 'property-owning democracy', but he had no plans for disposing of local authority housing. In the 1970 Conservative manifesto an undertaking was given to facilitate the sale of council houses, but only a very small number had been sold by the time the Conservatives lost office in 1974. From 1979 onwards, however, sales rocketed.[9] This policy should properly be seen, not merely as an implementation of Mrs Thatcher's social policy, but as the beginning of the massive wave of what has come to be called privatisation.

In 1982, however, there was to be a dramatic distraction from mundane domestic affairs, the evolution of which threw a great deal of light on the operations of the British system of government. On 2 April Argentinian forces landed at Port Stanley in the Falkland Islands. Successive United Kingdom governments had believed that, while British sovereignty obtained in the Falklands, a *modus vivendi* could be reached with whatever government held power in Buenos Aires, whether that government was democratic or dictatorial. For many years British and Argentinian diplomats – and from time to time Ministers as well – squabbled politely on the matter of sovereignty. But there was an air link between the mainland and Port Stanley, and a number of Falkland children went to school in Argentina, their education being paid for partly by the United Kingdom and partly by the Argentinian government.

The assumption of the British Foreign Office was always that the same kind of civilised minuet could be indefinitely conducted between London and Buenos Aires as was, and still is, being conducted between London and Madrid over the future of Gibraltar. Discussions about Gibraltar went along in a happily fractious way when Spain was a dictatorship and, later, when Spain became a democracy. There was no prospect either under General Franco or King Juan Carlos of a Spanish resort to violence. The Foreign Office believed that the same rules would apply to the dispute with Argentina over territory in the South Atlantic.[10]

The Thatcher government did not, however, grasp the depth of feeling that existed in Britain generally and in the House of Commons in particular against any compromise with Argentina on the future of the

Falklands. This was in spite of the fact that two years earlier the junior Foreign Office Minister with responsibility for South American relations, Nicholas Ridley, had come to the conclusion that the islands could be made into some variety of condominium between the United Kingdom and Argentina and this might well take the form of Argentinian sovereignty being accepted but with Britain leasing them back for at least 99 years from Argentina. After a visit to Buenos Aires and Port Stanley, Ridley reported back to the House of Commons on 2 December 1980. The only word that accurately describes his reception is savage.[11]

The Argentinian government had been convinced over many conversations with British Ministers that the United Kingdom was not at all unsympathetic to a takeover by Argentina – in whatever kind of face-saving deal could be designed – of the Falkland Islands. Ridley's reception in the House of Commons disabused them of that notion. But, in the course of 1981, they had other evidence to support their conclusion that the government of the United Kingdom had little care for its remote dependency. The Foreign Office, having been complacent about the course of negotiations, nonetheless became alarmed at the proposal of the Ministry of Defence to withdraw HMS *Endurance* from the South Atlantic. *Endurance* was essentially an Antarctic survey ship, but she was also armed and served as a testimony to the British commitment to the Islands. Carrington protested vigorously about the withdrawal of *Endurance* because of his fear that this would send the wrong signals to Buenos Aires. The MOD, however, in alliance with the Treasury, insisted on the saving of £2 million a year, which the return home of the ship would procure. This unhappy period was therefore characterised by an unseemly dispute between two major Departments of State, which was to have profound consequences. At no time, furthermore, did the Joint Intelligence Committee, whose duty it is to collate, and report to the Cabinet on, intelligence information from around the world affecting British interests, take seriously the advice of the British Embassy in Buenos Aires to the effect that the government headed by General Galtieri was contemplating invasion.[12] Moreover, had the JIC done its job properly, it could have availed itself of its right to report directly to the Prime Minister.

Meanwhile, across the Atlantic, General Galtieri's junta, while facing increasingly serious domestic problems, was enjoying a period of intense courtship by the United States, which was anxious above all to prevent any serious threat of Latin American countries embracing Communism. In spite of American help, however, inflation had reached 200 per cent, and was rising. Moreover, General Galtieri and his colleagues faced mounting agitation about the fate of the so-called '*desaparecidos*' – the men and women who had been abducted, tortured and often killed by the Argentinian military in support of their campaign against Communism, supposed or real. The junta therefore believed that they could regain popular esteem by capturing the Falkland Islands, while relying on the supine nature of British policy and the, at least covert, support of the United States. They reckoned without Mrs Thatcher and the close personal alliance she had formed with President Reagan.

Mrs Thatcher had one formidable ally at home. Upon hearing that the Argentinian fleet had set sail, the first Sea Lord, Sir Henry Leach, left his office and, in full uniform, went to the House of Commons to see a troubled Prime Minister. She was closeted with a handful of advisers, notably the Secretary of State for Defence, John Nott, all of whom advised her of the impossibility of launching a military operation at such distance. The assumption was that the British government would make many protests at the United Nations but agree eventually to an Argentinian takeover of the islands. Having had no military experience herself, the Prime Minister was uncertain how to proceed. Leach, having been asked to wait, insisted on immediate access to the meeting. By her own account she asked, 'First Sea Lord, if this invasion happens, precisely what can we do? . . . I shall never forget the quiet, calm, confident, answer:

> I can put together a Task Force of destroyers, frigates, landing craft, support vessels. It will be led by the aircraft carriers, HMS *Hermes* and HMS *Invincible*. It can be ready to leave in forty-eight hours.'[13]

On 2 April, fortified by Leach's utter conviction that the United Kingdom could reclaim the islands, she convened a Cabinet meeting, and opened proceedings by saying, 'Gentlemen, we shall have to fight.' It is fair to say that few, even of the Prime Minister's closest political allies, thought that a war should or could be fought successfully at a distance of so many thousand miles. Lord Whitelaw, the Home Secretary and Deputy Prime Minister, had, after all, fought in the Second World War and had been awarded the Military Cross after the Battle of Caumont in July 1944. But, again, her will prevailed.

The House of Commons was in recess. It was summoned to meet on Saturday, 3 April for the first time since the Suez Crisis in 1956. It was, as Lord Whitelaw puts it, 'an unhappy day for the government. The mood in the House of Commons on all sides was ugly. John Nott, as Defence Secretary, was severely mauled.'[14] It could hardly be said that the Prime Minister was at her oratorical best on that fraught Saturday morning; but since she had taken the decision to send the Task Force she proved herself to be sufficiently belligerent to command the support of Parliament and country. It was particularly important, furthermore, that the Leader of the Opposition, Michael Foot, decided to back her in the decision to recapture the islands. In my judgement, had the Prime Minister not authorised the despatch of the Task Force her government would have fallen. It is also my judgement that no conceivable alternative Prime Minister would have taken this drastic action.

The government had a happier passage in the House of Lords, and Lord Carrington was therefore astonished when Whitelaw reported to him that the lower house had dealt venomously with his record as Foreign Secretary.[15] Carrington told Whitelaw on Saturday afternoon that he was of a mind to resign. The press on Sunday and Monday was even more harsh than had been the House of Commons, and on Monday, in spite of Whitelaw's attempts to dissuade him, Carrington tendered his resignation, as did the junior Foreign Office Ministers, Humphrey (now Lord) Atkins and Richard (now Sir Richard) Luce. John (now Sir John) Nott, the Secretary of State for Defence, also wanted to resign, particularly as he was responsible for the crucial decision to recall *Endurance*. His resignation the Prime Minister refused to accept, on the grounds that he was the only senior politician with an intimate knowledge of the defence forces, and it was therefore his duty to see the conflict through. Once that conflict was over, however, Nott decided to retire altogether from politics.

Mrs Thatcher made an instant decision to appoint the Leader of the House of Commons, Francis Pym, as Foreign Secretary. While Pym's speeches in the House of Commons during the long voyage of the Task Force were stentorian, it quickly became apparent that he was far more favourable than was the Prime Minister to a negotiated settlement, either for the old lease-back idea or for a United Nations suzerainty over the islands. The United States government was more than a little unhappy about the prospect of armed conflict between its foremost European, and its foremost Latin American, ally. The US Ambassador to the United Nations, Mrs Jeanne Kirkpatrick, was not merely a Latin American specialist, but somebody who had played an important part in the formulation of the policies which had won the White House for Ronald Reagan. Her position was vastly more sympathetic to the views of Argentina than to those of Britain. Secretary of State General Alexander Haig was more even-handed, but he desperately wanted, if it was at all possible, to avoid a war. To this end he flew, as it seemed almost ceaselessly, between Washington, London and Buenos Aires. He came eventually to the conclusion that the Argentinians would not withdraw, and therefore implemented fully the agreement reached on the telephone between the Prime Minister and President Reagan to place at Britain's disposal all available American intelligence about Argentinian capacity, as well as the naval base at Ascension, which was to prove an important staging post for Admiral Woodward's fleet.

On 12 April the British government declared a maritime exclusion zone around the Falklands: this meant that any Argentinian ship found within the zone could, legitimately, be sunk. On 21 April the Task Force attacked South Georgia, recapturing it four days later. On 30 April a total exclusion zone was declared, and on 1 May initial landings on the main Falkland Islands were made by the Special Air Service and the Special Boat Squadron, followed within days by other main elements of the Task Force. On 2 May, in an action which arouses controversy in British politics to this day, the Royal Navy sank the Argentinian battleship, *General Belgrano*. Admiral Woodward wanted to take this action but he did not feel that he could do so without the direct sanction of the War Cabinet. This sanction he speedily received. It had the particularly enthusiastic endorsement of the Prime Minister, even though she knew that the *Belgrano* was sailing away from the islands rather than towards them. It is this decision on her part which has provoked the controversy. For, at the time, the Peruvian government was seeking to add its weight to efforts at mediation between Buenos Aires and London.[16] Battle continued, often fiercely, and with considerable losses on both sides, until the surrender of all Argentinian forces on 14 June.

The successful prosecution of the war did wonders for Mrs Thatcher's popularity, and there were those who wanted her to call an immediate General Election, particularly since Labour ranks were deeply divided, with Denis Healey and Neil Kinnock, in particular, voicing strident criticism of the conduct of the war. The Prime Minister demurred, partly because she did not want to appear to be taking an unscrupulous advantage of the success of the Task Force, and partly because she realised how much more power victory had given her.

The constitution and operation of the War Cabinet was indicative of Mrs Thatcher's preferred style of government. The Foreign and Defence Secretaries, because of their particular responsibilities, had, perforce, to be included. But she also brought in the ever-loyal William Whitelaw and – to general surprise – the Chairman of the Conservative Party, Cecil Parkinson. The surprise at Parkinson's inclusion was occasioned by the fact that, since the Prime Minister was supported by a virtually totally united party, both at Westminster and in the country, there seemed no need for the Party Chairman to function as a barometer of party opinion. But, then, Parkinson was an out-and-out Thatcher loyalist, and she always liked to have on any important committee just such a man.

It would not be wrong to say that Mrs Thatcher intensely disliked the notion of Cabinet government. A Prime Minister is always, whatever the conventions say, the only voice in Cabinet which matters. But all post-war Prime Ministers except she have preferred to rule through a consensus of their senior colleagues. It is a remarkable fact that for the first two years of her premiership the full Cabinet was never given an opportunity to discuss economic policy. This, of course, was her intention: she knew that the majority of her Cabinet colleagues were either opposed to her economic policy or, at the very least, doubtful that it would work. She therefore implemented it with the aid of two men upon whom she could rely – Sir Geoffrey Howe and William Whitelaw. The rest of the Cabinet signified nothing. But the making of economic policy is a precarious business, since results can never be quickly seen. The Falklands War, for all that its prosecution required immense resolution, was, by comparison, a simple affair, in that, once the Task Force went into action, there was little the Prime Minister could do to affect the outcome. But there is no doubt that she found the experience of running a War Cabinet immensely agreeable. While she never doubted that her economic policies were right, her experience of war totally convinced her that the correct way to run government was through small groups of politicians amenable to her ideas.

A war on the domestic front was threatening. The discontent of the trade union movement had not ended with her election victory in 1979. In the middle of 1981 the Secretary of State for Energy, David Howell, proposed to close twenty of the National Coal Board's pits. The General Secretary of the National Union of Mineworkers immediately threatened strike action. Howell believed that Arthur Scargill and his cohorts could be outfaced, but the Prime Minister instructed him to cancel the plans for closure. Howell was amazed, for he believed that the rigorous economic policy on which Mrs Thatcher had been elected would include the closure of pits and that she therefore would be prepared to outface the NUM. She believed, however, that the time had not yet come to take on the NUM. 'I don't at all mind having enemies', she said, 'but not too many at the same time, please.' She was, after all, facing a major strike in the civil service and growing dissent in the Cabinet over economic policy. 'Next time,' she said, 'I'll be ready for them.' On 14 September 1981 Howell was replaced by Nigel Lawson. His instructions were to build up enormous coal stocks. On 11 June 1983 Lawson was himself replaced by Peter Walker. The Prime Minister's conviction was that Walker, a good manager and astute in the business of public relations, would be the ideal man to handle not only the detail but the presentation of what she saw as the coming confrontation with the miners.[17]

Walker was appointed after the General Election held on 9 June 1983. As already mentioned, the Prime Minister had been reluctant to call a General Election in June for fear that it was still too soon after the Falklands War for her to avoid being accused of capitalising on the victory. Some commentators still believe that the election victory she gained in June was in large part due to the war.[18] I am not, myself, among them. My view is that the size of the Conservative majority was affected by the Falklands War but that she would have had a comfortable majority anyway. In the event, the Conservatives' majority was 144 over all other parties and 188 over the Labour Party. She was now ready to tackle Arthur Scargill.

Peter Walker was convinced that any job he was offered would be of minor importance, for he had long given up hope of senior ministerial office. He decided to tell her that, rather than taking on the Department of Transport or the Department of Energy – the two offices he thought she might suggest – he would prefer to retire to the backbenches. What followed is best told in Walker's own words:

> She said she would like me to go to Energy, but before I could make my carefully prepared declaration, she added that she wanted me there because she believed the government was about to be challenged in a major battle with Arthur Scargill . . .

Walker goes on:

> She was properly nervous of the harm a miners' dispute could do to the economy. She had been with me in Ted Heath's Cabinet in 1974 and seen the damage done then. But the 1981 humiliation when she was Prime Minister was clearly scorched on her mind. She said she felt there was no one in the Cabinet who could conduct the battle with Arthur Scargill as well as I could. She thought I would have the political knowhow and the communications skill to explain the government case to the public. This was essential in a major conflict of this kind. Industrial unrest in the coal industry was probably the greatest threat to her government and I was the best person to see it did not happen.[19]

Walker took the job, and the battlelines were drawn.

The Prime Minister foresaw a major dispute with the NUM; and Arthur Scargill wanted a major dispute with the government. The significance of the confrontation that was to come went far beyond the usual trade union demands for more money, better working conditions and the restoration of legal privileges. Arthur Scargill saw, rightly, that it was the miners who had brought down the Heath government in 1974. He believed that he could bring down the Thatcher government in 1983. What has to be understood about Scargill is that he was no ordinary trade union leader, but a Socialist revolutionary. His model country was Fidel Castro's Cuba. A charming man in private – and a wonderful mimic – in matters of trade union business, and in his oratory, he was, and is, fanatical. Over the decade from 1974 to 1984 Scargill had made no less than three attempts to bring his union out on strike. But it was clear on all three occasions that he did not have the willing assent of his members. It is interesting to observe that the NUM had never in its history until 1984 taken industrial action without a ballot of its members. Scargill, who was in virtually total command of the NUM Executive, decided nonetheless to use the authority of that Executive to bring out the miners. Thus began an industrial dispute that lasted one long and bitter year, and resulted in the destruction not only of the NUM as a serious force in trade union and national politics but of Arthur Scargill's influence in the affairs of the nation. By the end Scargill cut, in the classical sense, a truly tragic figure. He was a man whose cause was lost by contradictions in his own temperament. He genuinely wanted to improve the lot of his members; but he also genuinely wanted to use those members as instruments of political revolution.

Arthur Scargill did not realise, as he embarked on industrial action, that the Prime Minister had set two traps, into both of which he walked. The first was the creation, as I have already mentioned, of huge stockpiles of coal. This meant that industry could continue functioning even with the miners on strike: Walker calculated that the government could sustain a strike of two years' duration. The second trap consisted of the legislation which outlawed strikes undertaken without a full ballot of members. This meant, above all, that if the union broke the law in this respect an employer could ask the courts to sequester the assets of a striking union, force that union to pay the costs of the action and impose damages. The NUM Executive, aware of these provisions, deposited a great part of its funds abroad, but this meant that it had no means of providing strike pay.

Other important factors worked against Scargill. The first was that political and public opinion alike took the view that Peter Walker's proposals for the settlement of the dispute were fair, and even generous. There were to be no compulsory redundancies. Early retirement was to be offered to miners over 50 on terms which were better than in any other industry. If a pit was to be closed its miners, if they wished to continue to work for the National Coal Board (now British Coal), would be offered employment at another pit and would be helped with resettlement costs. Younger miners who wished to leave the industry would receive what Walker rightly describes as 'handsome' redundancy payments. Finally, pay awards would be greater in pits which increased their productivity.

The next factor which worked against Scargill was the intimidation and violence which characterised the strike, and which was, in some cases, extreme. British public opinion had, until 1984, traditionally been sympathetic to miners, who were widely admired for undertaking a job that was at once dirty, dangerous and vital to the national economy. The conduct of the NUM throughout the strike lost it much of this sympathy.[20] It was a further shock to Scargill that the trade union movement in general and the Labour opposition, though shedding many crocodile tears, did not come with any effect to his aid. In my judgement, Scargill believed that his strike would lead to a general strike: he was wrong. Moreover, the refusal of the Nottingham miners to take industrial action was a severe blow to the unity of the union.

Peter Walker avers that 'it was total nonsense to suggest, as some on the left and in the Labour Party did, that the Conservative government wanted confrontation, but if it was forced upon us we intended to win.' There is little doubt that this was Walker's attitude, and he was certainly stronger in the confrontation than even Ian (now Sir Ian) MacGregor, the tough-talking Chairman of the National Coal Board. It was necessary, of course, that Walker, while demonstrating firmness, also showed a willingness to meet reasonable demands from the miners. But the Prime Minister took a more robust rhetorical line. Hugo Young[21] quotes a speech she made to the 1922 Committee on 19 July, describing the strike as 'a scar across the face of the country'. She went on:

We had to fight an enemy without in the Falklands. We always have to be aware of the enemy within, which is more difficult to fight and more dangerous to liberty. . . . There is no week, nor day, nor hour when tyranny may not enter upon this country, if the people lose their supreme confidence in themselves. . . . Tyranny may always enter – there is no charm or bar against it.'

As the miners' strike came towards its close it was clear that the government – and particularly the Prime Minister – would not, and did not have to, yield. All of Arthur Scargill's promises of success proved impossible of realisation. Families, certainly disadvantaged and, in some areas, even hungry, began to appreciate that, however much they had admired the man called 'King Arthur', and whatever lingering affection they had for him, he had failed them. Disillusioned and embittered, slowly at first, but in waves of increasing power, miners drifted back to work. It became apparent that Scargill had been comprehensively trounced. He did not, himself, openly accept the verdict of his own members; the fact of the matter was that the miners had voted with their feet, and the conclusion was that he had failed utterly.

While the economic policies pursued by Mrs Thatcher's first and second administrations were vital in redesigning the fundamentals of the British economy, the miners' strike produced dramatic evidence of her sense of purpose. It is not too much to say that the defeat of Arthur Scargill demonstrated that not merely the face but the very nature of British politics had been changed. Other trade unions came to the conclusion that the government's will could not be gainsaid. They therefore began to seek methods of pursuing the financial interests of their members other than industrial action. An intriguing aspect of the death of Socialist Britain was that, while the unions began to move away from even the most tenuous devotion to socialism, the Parliamentary Labour Party and Constituency Labour Parties were moving in the opposite direction, although they were later to learn the same bitter lesson.

CHAPTER ELEVEN

The Bitter Lesson
(1985–1987)

In addition to her resolution and political skill Mrs Thatcher enjoyed that most priceless of political gifts – luck. In 1979 she faced in James Callaghan, a Prime Minister whose great vice was complacency. In 1983 she faced a Leader of the Opposition, Michael Foot, who was a hopeless romantic. In 1987 she faced another Leader of the Opposition, Neil Kinnock, who started out as a romantic, but turned out to be a ruthless pragmatist. These three men, in their different ways, summarise the recent history of the Labour Party, and each led it to defeat.

When James Callaghan succeeded Harold Wilson as Prime Minister in April 1976 he was preoccupied, above all, with staying in office. He therefore failed to appreciate serious developments in the character of his own party. Both in the Parliamentary Labour Party and in the constituencies the ideological Left was on the march, its standard bearer being Tony Benn. On the other side of the political divide senior Labour politicians, notably David Owen, the Foreign Secretary, Shirley Williams, Secretary of State for Education, and William Rodgers, Secretary of State for Transport, were increasingly worried about the Left-wing volcano they feared would erupt. Both factions, however, remained quiescent as long as Callaghan was in office. Although the Labour Party is less interested in the raw pursuit of power than its Conservative opponents, its members do not, nonetheless, like carelessly to relinquish it. Incipient divisions in the party were therefore contained until its defeat in the General Election of 1979.

Once, however, Mrs Thatcher emerged victorious in the General Election of that year Callaghan concluded that, in his own words, 'Given the size of Margaret Thatcher's majority it seemed likely that Parliament would run its full course. I would then be in my early seventies, and the Party would be demanding a younger leader.'[1] In the event, the 'younger' leader was Michael Foot, who had been born just over a year later than Callaghan himself. Callaghan evidently had no heart for remaining as Leader of the Opposition. In his memoirs, he goes on to say:

> It was not a happy period. I was ready to accept criticism and to defend the Government's record when it was unfairly attacked. But I deeply resented the charges of 'betrayal' made by the left and used as an excuse to fetter the Parliamentary Party and to organise factions to replace Members of Parliament with whom they did not agree. The tactic nearly always failed but it fermented an atmosphere of mistrust and cynicism in which the motives and actions of Party Leaders were continually questioned.

So, in October 1980, Callaghan resigned.

Initially it seemed that the contest to succeed him would be between Peter Shore on the Left and Denis Healey on the Right. In matters of domestic policy there was little to choose between the two men. But Shore had the priceless advantages for the Left of being totally averse to British membership of the European Economic Community and enjoying the patronage of the most-loved of Labour backbenchers, Michael Foot. Healey, on the other hand, was identified with the Callaghan government's acceptance of the strait-jacket imposed by the IMF. While Shore was a man almost universally popular among his colleagues, Healey's tendency to bully anybody who crossed his path had earned him a great many enemies. Suddenly, however, Foot decided to withdraw his patronage from Shore and – at the behest of his wife[2] – to contest the leadership himself. Foot enjoyed a comfortable victory, with Neil Kinnock as his campaign manager. This was the last election in which the Labour Leader was chosen solely by members of the Parliamentary Party.

What was not fully realised at the time was that this was a battle for the soul of the Labour Party. Roy Jenkins in Brussels and David Owen, Shirley Williams and William Rodgers at home, were essentially politicians whose minds were formed by the influence of Hugh Gaitskell. They were what would be recognised more readily on the Continent than in Britain as Social Democrats. They believed, for example, in a strong defence policy, and they believed in a relatively free market. However, in so far as economic policy was concerned they believed in aiming for social and financial equality, which was to be procured by state intervention. Whereas the Conservative Party invariably stresses in its rhetoric, above all, freedom and opportunity, the inheritors of the Gaitskell tradition have emblazoned on their banners the doctrine of equality achieved through redistribution of incomes using the taxation system. But this is qualified by a willingness to allow a certain amount of freedom to private enterprise. The genuine parliamentary Socialist, the most articulate of which was, and is, Tony Benn,[3] believes that the interests of all, and particularly of the poor, are best served by the control of all but the smallest economic activities by central government, as well as swingeing increases in taxation for the above-average earner. It is only fair to add that Benn had, and has, a rather touching, if unrealistic, belief that a completely Socialist system would command the enthusiastic support of virtually the entire population. After each successive Labour defeat from 1979 arguments within the party have been between those who believed that it was, during successive campaigns, unelectable because it was too left-wing and those who believed that it was not left-wing enough.

A crucial figure in what was to happen was Roy Jenkins. On 13 March 1979, as Jenkins's term of office as President of the European Commission was coming to an end, Callaghan offered him a peerage and the governorship of Hong Kong. Jenkins declined both. He writes that he said to the Prime Minister, 'I want to come back and look around and keep options open'. Callaghan advised him that he 'might find it quite difficult to get back into the House of Commons. And you might not like it when you get there. It has changed. It has deteriorated a lot.'[4]

Jenkins was then invited to deliver, in January the following year, the Dimbleby Lecture, founded in memory of Richard Dimbleby seven years before. As he puts it, 'What was on offer was an hour of prime BBC-1 time with a specific undertaking that I could talk about anything I liked.' Jenkins believes that the BBC expected him to talk about European affairs. He decided to talk about British party politics. Throughout the second half of May 1979 he began to prepare his lecture which, essentially, would constitute an appeal to create a new central force in British politics. Initially he thought that such a force could best be created by his joining the Liberal Party. On 14 June, over dinner in Brussels, David Steel persuaded him that it would be wiser to support the formation of a new party. Steel's thinking was that a new party could attract a great deal of public support from hitherto apolitical voters. Moreover, he was convinced – rightly as it turned out – that Labour dissidents, with Owen, Williams and Rodgers at their head, would find it easier to make the break with Labour if they were to join a wholly new party than if their only alternative was to join the Liberal Party. Steel

197

believed that a new party, under whatever name, could work harmoniously with his own party. But he was quite clear in his mind that the effective leader of that party should be Jenkins. He was perfectly happy with this arrangement since his aim in politics was to destroy what appeared to be a Conservative monopoly of power, and a Labour Party that was increasingly doctrinaire.

Like the good historian he is, Roy Jenkins understood that every democratic party is a combination of factions. So long as they differ only on the detail of policy, and not on the fundamentals, they can work very well. This is what he calls a 'covert coalition'. His ideal is what he calls the 'Roosevelt coalition', for Franklin Delano Roosevelt is Jenkins's main political hero. Jenkins's test was whether a coalition either between parties or among conflicting interests within a party was honest:

> The Labour Party of the late 1970s, with the vast gulf between, say, Benn and Callaghan, failed this test. That was why the constitutional disputes which were currently raging in the party, about who should elect the leader, who should write the manifesto and how easily a small caucus could get rid of an MP, were not minor organisational points but part of a continuing left/right ideological battle which had crossed the divide from constructive tension and made internecine warfare the principal purpose of the party's life.[5]

Jenkins is not a man who readily displays passion. But, in the Dimbleby Lecture in January 1980 he gave the gravest possible warning of the danger of an imminent takeover of the Labour Party by its left wing. He feared that there was an insufficient awareness on the part of people of his own attitude of mind of the threat which they faced. He therefore chose to adorn the lecture with a quotation from some famous lines of William Butler Yeats:

> The best lack all conviction, while the worst
> Are full of passionate intensity.

Tony Benn, most certainly, did not lack passionate intensity. He was, as early as the autumn of 1979, the most intellectually formidable figure on the left of the Labour Party.

Michael Foot was elected Leader on 10 November 1980. But, earlier in the year the Labour Party held the first of two one-day conferences at Wembley, the second being in the following year. These concerned themselves essentially, not only with policy, but with the method of choosing a Leader. The rules adopted for changing the Leader totally altered the balance of power in the Party. Forty per cent of the votes in the electoral college were donated to the trade unions, 30 per cent to Labour Members of Parliament, and 30 per cent to the Constituency Labour Parties.[6] Disillusion had been growing for some time in the ranks of moderate Labour MPs, and the howling-down of David Owen at the 1980 conference convinced many that there was no further place for them in what was becoming a new Labour Party.

Throughout 1980, amid rumours that there would be a major break-away from the Labour Party, intensive discussion had been going on between dissident Labour MPs. The most important discussions, how-ever, were between David Owen, Shirley Williams, William Rodgers and Roy Jenkins. Of these four, William Rodgers was the only one who was a member of the Shadow Cabinet. He had been Shadow Secretary of State for Defence under Callaghan. He was more than anxious to hold the same post under Foot, for he believed that he could be effective in preventing the movement towards unilateral nuclear disarmament which, almost daily, was gaining ground in the party. Foot declined to satisfy his ambition, and offered him either Health and Social Services or Northern Ireland. Being denied the opportunity to continue to hold the defence portfolio was, probably, the breaking point for Rodgers.[7]

On the morning of 25 January 1981 the four gathered at David Owen's house in Limehouse. In the course of the day they were joined by various other potentially dissident Labour MPs. On the basis of an original draft by Jenkins they hammered out the terms of what was to become famous as the Limehouse Declaration. This was released to the press in the afternoon. While the declaration signalled a readiness to leave the Labour Party, it did not constitute the final breach. The final paragraph read:

> We recognise that for those people who have given much of their lives
> to the Labour Party, the choice that lies ahead will be deeply painful.
> But we believe that the need for a realignment of British politics must
> now be faced.

'Looking back on the Declaration we signed that day,' writes Owen, 'it is hard not to be struck by how orientated it was to the Labour Party.'[8] It certainly was so orientated, but it was also, as everybody present that day realised, a declaration of war on Michael Foot and his colleagues. The clear message was that either the Shadow Cabinet changed its policies or the four, and such allies as they could muster, would leave the Labour

Party.[9] This they did on 5 March, when they and twenty-nine MPs – including a single Conservative, Christopher Brocklebank-Fowler – formed the Social Democratic Party. Distressed though Michael Foot was by the threat of these defections, he would not alter, or even adjust, party policy, and it is fair to say that many on the Left rejoiced: they now had the party virtually to themselves.

It was clear that the new party would work in close harmony with the Liberals in what came to be known, for the purposes of the 1983 General Election, as the Alliance. The Labour Party, wrapped in its mantle of righteousness, did not realise how much damage the Alliance would do it electorally. But, on the other hand, the Liberals and the Social Democrats did not realise that the immediate popularity they enjoyed would prove to be evanescent. While it was relatively easy to agree on policy, the philosophy of the SDP was Gaitskellite, adjusted in detail to modern conditions. The principal advantages the new party enjoyed in winning over the public were its tone of civilised moderation and its novelty value. For some time the public was supportive of a party which was at neither extreme. Michael Foot and his closest colleagues were seen to be at one and the same time intellectually vapid and aggressively left-wing. Margaret Thatcher and her colleagues, on the other hand, were seen to be right-wing and strident. Moreover, the battles between the two main parties, particularly twice a week at Prime Minister's Question Time, were becoming increasingly raucous. Into this maelstrom strolled the smiling figures of sweet reason – David Steel, David Owen, William Rodgers, Shirley Williams and Roy Jenkins.

While SDP policy was easily formulated, the principal priority of the new party presented a more practical problem. It was necessary to find parliamentary seats for Shirley Williams and Roy Jenkins. Jenkins was first in the field: he fought Warrington in a by-election in July, and narrowly failed to overcome a substantial Labour majority. In November, Mrs Williams overturned a massive Conservative majority in Crosby, and in March 1982 Roy Jenkins took the Labour seat at a by-election in Glasgow Hillhead. Jenkins had never expected to win Warrington, but he was surprised and delighted by his thoroughly creditable performance in that constituency. He writes:

It had underpinned the nascent SDP, created an experience and a climate which were highly favourable to the fostering of the Alliance, and increased both my own sense of confidence with the electorate (after nearly five years of separation) and my authority within the party. The fact that I was still not in the House of Commons counted for little compared with this. I wanted to get back only to change the shape of British politics and not for the sake of being an MP again, and towards that end I had contributed much more by the Warrington summer campaign than by winning a quiet by-election.[10]

Jenkins knew, even after his defeat at Warrington, that he was the elder statesman of what was becoming the Alliance. To further illustrate this in his memoirs, he later makes an engaging reference to a dinner he gave in March 1982 for David Steel and Shirley Williams, in which he was 'in the mood of a nervous duenna who hoped that the young people would get on well together'. The following month David Steel, Mrs Williams and William Rodgers attended the Anglo-German weekend conference at Königswinter, where they had fruitful discussions with continental Social Democrats. These discussions essentially concerned the sort of policies a new-born British Social Democratic Party should espouse. The three then began to draft a declaration of principles, which was to become part of the Alliance manifesto. It was the manifesto, as Jenkins puts it, of

... an anti-party party, which would bring together a swathe of opinion, liberal and internationalist, concerned with conscience and reform, without attempting to bring together the cells of party fanaticism which showed themselves in Labour selection conferences or Conservative standing ovations for the Leader's annual conference speech which had done so much to repel many of goodwill and public spirit from the party game.

Jenkins and Owen took little part in the drafting of the declaration of principles. On Jenkins's part this was because he knew that anything along social democratic lines produced by the triumvirate would be acceptable to him; on Owen's part it was because he knew he could not dictate its terms. Already it was clear that the perceived unity of purpose of the SDP and the Liberal Party concealed divisions not only of policy but of personality, which were to reap a harvest of dragon's teeth in the General Elections of 1983 and 1987.

However, through 1981 and 1982 the wind seemed set fair for the SDP. The opinion polls, which at that time were taken seriously by all political parties, but particularly by the new SDP, suggested a steady growth in esteem for the SDP. That politicians of such high profile as Roy Jenkins and Shirley Williams could overturn, at by-elections, both Labour and Tory majorities was, therefore, not surprising, though it has to be said that Mrs Williams's victory in Crosby, where the Conservative majority in 1979 had been 19,000, was spectacular. It has to be remembered that Liberal and SDP candidates did not stand against one another so when, on 22 October 1981, Bill Pitt, the Liberal candidate in the Croydon North West by-election – not, as Jenkins puts it 'a conventionally good candidate' – came home victorious it did seem that the Alliance was truly on its way, particularly since the focus of the press and the broadcast media on the SDP and the Liberals intensified with each by-election, and publicity is the elixir of politicians. The Alliance began to believe its own propaganda.

Meanwhile, the Left was tightening its grip on the throat of the Labour Party. It was a fundamental belief of those whom the SDP had left behind that a truly socialist policy, clearly understood and expressed honestly and directly, would gain the support of the electorate. Thus Michael Foot presided happily over Labour's steady move to the left, without understanding that many of the Conservative government's policies commended themselves to traditional Labour voters. Above all, the leadership of the party and of the trade unions failed to grasp that the Conservative government's determination to enable tenants in local authority property to buy their homes was proving to be immensely popular.

So far as the leaders of Britain's trade unions were concerned, Michael Foot was a virtually ideal Leader of the Parliamentary Labour Party. For all that he was an intellectual idealist, he viewed every trade unionist through rose-tinted spectacles. When he had been the Secretary of State for Employment in 1974 he had not merely restored to them all the privileges of which Edward Heath had tried to deprive them, but had given them even more say in the conduct of the nation's affairs than they had enjoyed in the 1960s. They trusted Foot for what he had done for them; and were convinced that, in power, he would do more. Just as the parliamentary Left was convinced that clearly enunciated doctrinaire socialism would prove popular with the electorate, so the trade union leaders were convinced that a Foot government would allow them a say not only in matters concerning their members' livelihoods but also in the fields of education, defence and foreign policy.[11] The union leaders of the 1980s were as blind to the realities of the new Britain being created by Mrs Thatcher as were their parliamentary allies.

They also knew that, if perchance Michael Foot failed to win a General Election, they would have the preponderant say in choosing his successor. (Foot had made it clear that if he failed to win a General Election he would immediately vacate the leadership.) But they did not expect Labour to lose, and paid little attention not only to the appeal of Mrs

Thatcher and her policies but also to what many people considered to be the inexorably rising tide of social democracy.

Under Foot the Labour Party's rules were adhered to more rigorously than under any previous Labour Leader. In the formulation of policy, the annual Labour Party Conference is supposed, democratically, to determine what should be in the next election manifesto. Of course, this is no truly democratic procedure since trade union leaders present at Conference not only vote on behalf of their actual membership without consultation, but the number of votes allocated to each union often exceeds the number of members of a given trade union.[12] Should the Leader, his Shadow Cabinet, and the National Executive dislike a motion on policy which they judge to be popular with Conference as a whole they have two immediate recourses. The first is to put to Conference a composite motion which fudges the relevant issue. The second is to ask Conference to 'refer back' the disagreeable motion for further consideration by the National Executive Committee. However, if a motion is voted for by a two-thirds majority at Conference it is supposed immediately to become party policy, and thus part of the next manifesto. The National Executive Committee, consisting of members of the Parliamentary Labour Party, the constituency Labour parties, and the trade unions, is supposed to draft the manifesto. In practice, all Labour Leaders before Michael Foot drafted their own manifestos, taking an insouciant view of both the NEC and Party Conference. Whatever grumblings there might be, the imminence of a General Election invariably, until 1983, concentrated Labour minds wonderfully.

In preparing for the next General Election Michael Foot had no difficulty, in 1982, in following the dictates of Conference and a predominantly left-wing NEC, for the policies they advocated were ones which, in his heart, he agreed with. Thus Labour went in to the 1983 election committed to policies of increased taxation, greatly increased public expenditure, and vastly increased intervention by the state in the affairs of the nation and unilateral disarmament. The manifesto constituted, as Denis Healey said after the election, 'the longest suicide note in history', for the electorate concluded that none of these policies were workable, and most were undesirable.

From the moment the Prime Minister called the General Election in 1983, Michael Foot's campaign was disastrous. Foot was the last romantic hero of the old Labour Party ideal. He proclaimed himself to be a Socialist, but if he was such he had never – unlike, say, Tony Benn – thought the matter through. Rather, he pulled together in his mind a mixture of impressions of the worthiness of Marxist ideas and trade union honour. The unworldly nature of his political character became all too apparent during the campaign. Unfortunately for Foot, he was protected by his advisers from too much contact with the outside world. He did the minimum of television and radio interviews, and when he addressed a public meeting it was only to a hand-picked audience of the faithful. On every occasion he received a rapturous reception and this gulled him into believing that he could gain a famous victory. When, however, he and his policies were comprehensively rejected by the electorate, he resigned the leadership. With his departure began the final death-throes of British socialism. But death-throes can be prolonged.

The Alliance campaign was initially based on the conviction that the two parties could gain a substantial, and perhaps crucial, representation in the House of Commons. In the middle of the second week, however, alarm bells began to ring. Steel, Owen and Jenkins met at Steel's home at Ettrick Bridge in his constituency. The two younger men believed that the paterfamilias of social democracy in Britain had proved ineffective as a national, as opposed to a constituency, campaigner: in effect, Owen and Steel took over the election campaign, Owen providing the intellectual muscle and Steel the campaigning skill. But it was all too late, for Mrs Thatcher was sweeping to a decisive victory.

From 1983 to 1987 most Labour politicians believed that their 1983 defeat could be blamed on either Michael Foot's inability to present himself to the people as a convincing Prime Minister, or on the glory which accrued to Mrs Thatcher as a result of the Falklands War. Labour and trade union leaders alike ignored the significance of the haemorrhage of support they had suffered when the SDP was created. The fact that the Alliance did not do as well as they expected provided a certain consolation.

With Michael Foot's resignation it became necessary to have a new Leader of the Opposition, to be chosen by the new system.[13] David Owen, in particular, had been prepared to accept that Labour Party policy could be filtered through Party Conference, the National Executive Committee and the Leader's Private Office. When he was still a member of the Labour Party he could not accept the new system of choosing a Leader, for he could not believe that a Prime Minister should be chosen by anybody outside the parliamentary party. As he put it at the first Wembley Conference:

But I say to the Party this, the day this system is used to elect a Prime Minister the whole of the country will be watching the procedures, and then those procedures will be shown to be highly undemocratic. They will therefore be shown to be a totally illegitimate way of electing the Prime Minister of the country.

Any Leader of the second party in the country could become Prime Minister; but Owen's point was that such a Leader should be chosen by Labour Members of Parliament, although he would have accepted a system of election by the entire membership of the Labour Party throughout the country. He could not and would not accept that the leaders of individual trade unions could have a powerful, and indeed determining, influence on the choice of Leader.

Up to the 1983 election defeat what can only be called the intellectual Left and the trade unions had a common purpose in the adoption by the Labour Party of a left-wing platform. After Foot's resignation these two wings of the electoral college diverged, although both agreed to support Neil Kinnock for the leadership. The voice of moderate Labour – what might be called the Gaitskellite voice – was uttered by Roy Hattersley, who had the support of those in unions, constituencies and the Parliamentary Labour Party who believed that it was necessary at least to modify the left-wing policies on which Foot had stood. It had been thought that Hattersley might have defected along with Owen, Rodgers and Mrs Williams. He chose to stay within the cocoon of the Labour Party, but he was a formidable politician and took the view that he would be best advised to fight the moderate corner from within the Labour Party. He became Kinnock's Deputy and, surprisingly for a man who differed so much not only on policy but in temperament, they worked more or less happily together until both departed the scene in 1992.

Neil Kinnock was the preferred choice of the unions as Michael Foot's successor for several reasons. He was a totally committed supporter of trade union power: he was sponsored in his constituency by the Transport and General Workers Union. He had an attractive personality, and was a fine orator. He had never held ministerial office and thus became Leader without, as the unions saw it, a stain on his character. He had honed his techniques of political manipulation as Michael Foot's campaign manager. In a phrase, he was Michael Foot in a more youthful, and attractive, guise.

But at this stage Kinnock did not wish to change the policies on which his party had been defeated. It is always necessary to remember how important a part social camaraderie plays in relations between Labour politicians and trade union leaders. Kinnock appointed his Deputy, Roy Hattersley, as Shadow Chancellor. At first sight this seemed a brilliant appointment. While Kinnock could enunciate with his own individual, and remarkable, fervour the tenets of old-style class warfare and the more modern doctrines of left-wing ideological socialism, Hattersley could, it was thought, present a side of the party's policy that was at once caring and competent.

Alas for the Labour Party, this combination was to prove unconvincing. For the first time, the dread word 'unelectable' began to be used about the party.

Throughout the 1980s the Labour Party was locked in a time-warp from which it has not, at the time of writing, emerged. The party leadership was, of course, tarred with the brush of some Labour local authorities, not just because of the extreme doctrinaire socialism of those authorities, but because of their pandering to selected minority groups. This happened most notably in Liverpool and the London area. Although Kinnock proved, in the end, willing to tackle not only the extremist local authorities but also extremists within the Parliamentary Party, he had not, by 1987, convinced the electorate that he had been sufficiently effective. The Labour Party and the trade unions believed, furthermore, that the pursuit of the socialist and collectivist ideas which lay at the heart of their programme would, sooner or later, bring them to power: they did not realise that the time of those ideas had passed. At one stage they proposed the reclaiming of council houses already sold, but beat a hasty retreat when the unpopularity of such a policy became evident. They then proposed to reverse the measures the government had taken to privatise industry, failing to take account of the fact that many of the voters whose loyalty they counted on had become shareholders in those privatised industries. They remained committed to their old policy of unilateral nuclear disarmament. Moreover, they increasingly promised massive additions to public expenditure on popular institutions, such as the National Health Service, education and pensions, well above the levels ordained by the government, without giving any clear idea of how these would be paid for without inflation.

Mrs Thatcher's campaign against the trade unions proved to be one of her greatest successes. But a triumph which was far more difficult of achievement was her ability to demonstrate to the electorate that excessive national spending over national income led to inflation. She convinced the public that inflation was not only her bugbear but theirs. This battle cry, later to be taken up by her successor, was taken to heart by the voters.

At no stage between the 1983 and 1987 General Elections did Neil Kinnock grasp the fact that the policies which he espoused, while being acceptable to his own party, were, taken as a whole, deeply unpopular with the electorate at large. What the Labour leadership failed to understand was that, while some policies, most notably their spending policies, seemed popular with the electorate, they were not popular enough to encourage people to vote Labour. In the same way, the SDP and the Liberals failed to understand that their general philosophy of moderation was not enough to gain them such a breakthrough in numbers of parliamentary seats as would ensure them at least a major say in the formation of a new government, of whichever party.

Moreover, Kinnock confused presentation with electoral acceptability. The way in which Labour policy was put forward was totally modernised under Kinnock. Peter Mandelson (now a Member of Parliament) was hired as Labour's Director of Communications and Hugh Hudson, the director of one of the most famous British films ever made, *Chariots of Fire*, volunteered to produce Labour's party political broadcasts. The sheer technical professionalism of Kinnock's campaigning in the 1987 General Election campaign led him in to a tunnel of self-delusion not at all dissimilar to that in which Michael Foot had found himself in 1983. Foot's far more old-fashioned campaign ensured that, until the last moment, he felt that he would be victorious. During the 1987 campaign, Kinnock believed that old policies, wrapped anew in a glittering package and festooned with ribbons, would ensure electoral success. He was wrong; when the results of the General Election were declared the Conservatives were found to have a majority of 100 over all other parties, and 146 over Labour. Neil Kinnock's New Model Army had failed in its first serious engagement.

CHAPTER TWELVE

The Demise of Labour
(1987–1992)

During the 1970 General Election campaign Iain Macleod made an off-the-cuff speech on future economic developments. He had before him only a sheet of predictions from the Organisation for Economic Cooperation and Development. This showed Britain as ranking twenty-fifth of twenty-six listed countries in terms of economic development. The OECD predicted – and the then Labour government did not disagree – that, in the following year Britain would be at the bottom of the list. The Wilson government had made a great fetish of its proposals for more centralised economic planning. 'Imagine', Macleod said, in those stentorian tones of which he was the greatest political master in recent times, 'planning to make your country come last'. Labour did not know, between 1983 and 1992, that all its elaborate plans, first left-wing and later moderate, would result in it coming last in the only electoral battles that mattered, those between itself and the Conservative Party.

The years of Mrs Thatcher's power can be broken down into three parts, conveniently marked by General Elections. Between her first victory in 1979 and her second in 1983 the principal tasks facing the government were sharply to reduce inflation, mainly by cutting public expenditure, and to put in place the legislation designed to break trade union power. Of course, in this period, the grand design for the restructuring of the economy was being prepared. The period from 1983 to 1987 was the period of her greatest power, for it was during these years that her major reforms took effect. After her third victory in the latter year, most of the economic reforms she wanted had been institutionalised, and the opposition had no choice but to react to them. From 1987 until her fall from power she was bent on widening and deepening these reforms. She was also, alas for her, determined to keep a promise she had made between the two General Elections of 1974, when as Shadow

Secretary of State for the Environment she had undertaken to abolish the domestic rate and replace it with a more equitable system of local taxation. Thus, in fulfilment of an undertaking made many years before, she introduced the Community Charge – or, as it became almost universally to be called, the 'Poll Tax'. This led, ineluctably, to her replacement by John Major.

The stark fact that Neil Kinnock faced on the morrow of the General Election of 1987 was that the left-wing policies which he had espoused all his life made it virtually impossible for a Labour government to be elected. There were two elements in Kinnock's nature. The first was belief in socialism. The second was ambition. After the crushing defeat of 1987, ambition, in Neil Kinnock's mind, gained the ascendancy. One after the other the policies which he had espoused were jettisoned. Suddenly the Labour Party was in the business of promising, not to overturn reforms that had been put in place by successive governments headed by Mrs Thatcher but to refine them. Renationalisation gradually disappeared from the Labour agenda. Mrs Thatcher abolished the Greater London Council. Labour proposed not to reinstate it but to create some kind of looser authority overseeing the affairs of the capital. Kinnock, further, came to the conclusion that nuclear disarmament should be proceeded with on a multilateral, rather than a unilateral basis. The most dramatic change, however, in Labour policy was its increasingly fervent embrace of the European Community.

The Labour Party's record on British membership of the EEC is bewildering. In 1962 the party was for membership.[1] In 1964 it was against it. In 1966 it was for membership and made Britain's second application to join. In 1971 it was, again, against membership, but in 1975 was supportive of membership. By 1983, however, Labour had once again changed its mind, and by 1991 the party had reversed its position once more.

But, if the party in general was on the issue of Europe adopting the U-turn as a habit, Neil Kinnock was particularly prone to changing his views. In an article in *Tribune* on 2 May 1975 he described the Community as 'the robber of the real sovereignty of the people'. In an interview with the *News of the World* on 15 May 1983 he said, simply and bluntly, 'We want out of the Common Market'. After his 1987 defeat Kinnock came to the conclusion that Britain should stay within the Common Market and, finally, he still had the gall to tell the editorial staff of the *Independent*, 'I have never seen hostility towards the European Community in the Labour Party'. The lunchtime conversation was tape-recorded and published in the *Independent* on 4 February 1988.

As Kinnock proceeded to reverse policy after 1987, alarm bells began to ring on the left wing of his party. Thus, the following year, Tony Benn decided to challenge him for the leadership. Benn is one of the most intriguing characters in the history of modern Labour politics. He inherited a peerage on the death of his father, Lord Stansgate, in 1960. He had already been a steadfast campaigner for the abolition of the upper house and for the right to renounce a hereditary peerage. Having held the seat of Bristol South East in 1959, he was refused permission to continue as a Member of the House of Commons after the death of his father. After a protracted dispute a by-election was held in May 1961. Benn won, but the Election Court declared his victory to be invalid on the grounds that he was a peer of the realm, and the seat therefore passed automatically to the Conservative candidate.[2] His cause attracted a great deal of publicity, mostly favourable to him. That publicity was advantageous to Harold Macmillan, who wanted to enable hereditary peers to disclaim their titles, and legislation to this effect came into force in 1963. The sitting Tory Member in Bristol South East immediately stood down and Benn triumphed at the by-election which followed.

With his victory Benn established his credentials as a successful rebel, but when he became a Minister in 1964 his first love appeared to be technocracy. He believed, and demonstrated in successive Ministries in which he served from 1964, in the ability of the Civil Service, controlled by a politician such as himself, to run the economy efficiently. He was not a great success in any of the ministerial posts which he held, and he concluded, therefore, that his mistake had been a failure to appreciate the importance in British history of the trade unions, and through the leadership of those unions, the leashed power of their members. He believed that a socialist government could combine the managerial skills of the Civil Service with the enthusiasm of the working classes.

Since Benn believed that Neil Kinnock was determined on betraying the left-wing principles enunciated in the 1987 Labour manifesto, he decided to make his 1988 challenge. Benn thought that, while his position in the Parliamentary Labour Party was uncertain, he could rely on the Constituency Labour Parties: after all, it was as an elected representative of the Constituency Parties that he sat on the NEC. He also thought that he could rely on the preponderant support of the trade union movement, for he had delivered a practically endless series of speeches to trade union gatherings, which were exceptionally well received.

In the event, Benn discovered that he had no majority in any of the three sections of the electoral college. There were a number of reasons for the Labour Party's decision to persist with Kinnock. One was the conviction that, in the 1987 General Election campaign, he was saddled with the policies espoused by Michael Foot in 1983. It was therefore concluded that he should be allowed another attempt to win the supreme prize. Another factor was a widespread feeling throughout the party that the new and, as they saw them, moderate policies which Kinnock was beginning to espouse were right for the country. Finally, the majority in the party believed that Kinnock's policies would have greater electoral appeal than the platforms of either Tony Benn or Margaret Thatcher.

The divisions on policy between Benn and Kinnock attracted a great deal of public attention, and this was, inevitably, damaging to the party in the judgement of the electorate. In my view the Labour Party died in the course of 1988. Thereafter, it would never again be a potential party of government.

The idea adumbrated in Roy Jenkins's Dimbleby Lecture, that the Alliance could be a third force in British politics, possibly victorious but certainly able to influence in a crucial way the formation of government, started to fade away with Mrs Thatcher's victory in 1983. Jenkins then departed the leadership of the Alliance and ceased to be, what David Steel had called him, 'The Prime Minister in Waiting'. By the time of the General Election campaign in 1987 Steel and Owen had formed a dual leadership of the Alliance. It was not clear if the Alliance were to win the General Election which of them would be Prime Minister and, in any event, there were differences of temperament as well as policy between them. Yet again the combined forces of the Liberal and Social Democratic Parties failed to make an electoral breakthrough. David Steel thereupon retreated to his eyrie at Ettrick Bridge and from there, without consulting Owen, he issued a statement calling for a merger between his own party and Owen's. This was to lead to an acrimonious dispute between the two wings of the Alliance, which ended, after conference votes by members of both the Liberal Party and the SDP, with Steel forming a new party which was eventually to settle on the name of the Liberal and Democratic Party. David Owen strove for some years to keep the SDP alive, until he decided, in 1992, to retire from Parliament and endorse the party of Mrs Thatcher's successor, John Major, in constituencies where there was no likelihood of a Liberal Democratic victory. The split between Owen and Steel after the 1987 General Election ended the much-vaunted chances of a serious third force in British politics. The quotation from W. B. Yeats which Jenkins had used in the Dimbleby Lecture turned out to be all too true, for it ended: 'Things fall apart, the centre cannot hold.' After 1987 the centre could not hold, just as the left could not hold.

Steel still believed, however, that an effective alliance of the centre could be formed. Weary, however, of the stresses of being the Leader of a minority party and convinced that he was not the best person to bring into the ranks of that new party those who had passionately supported David Owen, Steel decided to stand down as Leader. He was replaced, after a leadership election, by Paddy Ashdown.

For some time, important sections of the trade union movement had been drifting away from the Labour Party. In 1984 Eric Hammond, the leader of the Electricians' Union, declined to support the National Union of Mineworkers. By the time of the TUC Congress in September 1985 Arthur Scargill was seeking to minimise the effects of the defeat he had suffered during the miners' strike, by tabling a motion calling for a future Labour government to release all miners jailed during the strike, to reimburse the NUM for all money confiscated by fines, receivership and sequestration, as well as to end all pit closures. As Eric Hammond puts it, 'What Scargill was after, really, was that he should be made immune from the effects of the law and the effects of the strike.'[3] Scargill won the vote at the Trade Union Congress by 64,000, the voting figures being 4,585,000 votes and 4,649,000. Of course, over 9 million people were not present in the conference hall, but this made no difference to the result because their votes were cast by their leaders on their behalf. In theory a motion supported at the Trade Union Congress binds all member unions to support a similar motion at the next Labour Party Conference. The following month, therefore, Scargill submitted his motion again to the Labour Party Conference. Neil Kinnock appealed to him to remit the motion for further consideration by the NEC. Scargill refused, and the motion was carried by 3,540,000 to 2,912,000. This was not a sufficient plurality to make the Scargill proposals Labour Party policy, but it was enough to call into question the authority of the parliamentary Leadership. The Conference was, however, distinguished by a speech made by Eric Hammond, the General Secretary of the Electricians' Union, in which he repeated a remark he had made earlier, that coalminers were 'lions led by donkeys'. This remark was regarded as a singular act of disloyalty. Ron Todd, the General Secretary of the Transport and General Workers' Union, then, as it still is, the largest trade union in the country, supported Scargill. In his speech he said, 'I have heard references this morning to lions being led by donkeys. Well, I am an animal lover. I tell you something. I prefer donkeys to jackals.' These remarks demonstrated the bitterness that was beginning to emerge in the different factions of the trade union movement.

But, as Ken Gill, General Secretary of the white-collar Manufacturing, Science, Finance Union, said recently, 'The trade union movement is the mother and father of the Labour Party.'[4] Fissures within that movement therefore have serious consequences for the general, and, particularly, the financial health of the party. It is true that, historically, the trade union movement was the mother and father of the Labour Party but, by 1985 the parents were getting ready to abandon their child. Against the tide of events Neil Kinnock strove valiantly to re-create his party in a moderate mould. He was able, by patient negotiation, to persuade the trade union leaders to support him on the National Executive Committee. Towards the end of his leadership he could count on the whole Committee, with the exceptions of Tony Benn and Dennis Skinner, to support any policy he chose to put before them. This enabled him to continue and develop his campaign of reform. He could make ringing public denunciations of evidently unpopular Labour Councils, most notably that in Liverpool, and withdraw official sanction from Labour parliamentary candidates, and even from a sitting MP, such as Dave Nellist in Coventry South East.

Thus, Kinnock thought he had secured his base. But he did not appear to grasp that it was not a base but a façade. The devastating defeat of the National Union of Mineworkers in 1985 and the acceleration of pit closures destroyed the power of his foremost trade union critic, Arthur Scargill, and thus gave him a good deal of peace of mind. It also, however, deprived him – given rapidly declining NUM membership – of the most stalwart cohort of his trade union army. From the defeat of the Scargill strike, increasing numbers of coalminers showed willingness to take redundancy on generous financial and retraining terms and either to move into other forms of employment or to set up their own businesses.

At the same time, under the influence of the Conservative government's trade union legislation and its creation of a market economy, major trade union leaders increasingly felt that the financial interests of their members could be perfectly well served by dealing directly with employers: this meant that they no longer felt dependent on the prospect, or reality, of a Labour government. The most dramatic sign of things to come was a meeting on 31 January 1985 between Eric Hammond and Rupert Murdoch. Murdoch, like his predecessor, Lord Thomson, had been plagued by disputes with the print unions at *The Times* and other newspapers which he owned. The print unions were resistant to his plans to introduce new technological methods of producing newspapers. Murdoch went ahead and built a new plant at Wapping, which was supposed to be the site for a new newspaper. Following the meeting of 31 January, Murdoch took Hammond and various of his confidants to see the way in which his American newspapers, using the new technology, were produced. Eventually Hammond agreed that his members not only could, but would, move to Wapping and produce all of Murdoch's national titles from there. This ended the stranglehold which the print unions SOGAT and the NGA had had on the British newspaper industry for a generation. All the other major newspapers followed Murdoch's lead. Hammond writes, 'Murdoch was to squeeze the print unions dry, and our union was to suffer the most vicious verbal and physical abuse ever endured by a union in more than a hundred years of TUC history.' Nonetheless, Murdoch and Hammond emerged triumphant. In spite of violent picketing outside the Wapping plant, not a day's production of any of the Murdoch titles was lost over the next year, at the end of which the pickets faded away into oblivion.[5]

Albeit in a self-satisfied way, Eric Hammond summarised the situation of the trade unions well when he wrote:

> Unions are not that much concerned with the future. They are, in the main, day-by-day organisations, reacting to events as they happen, or the initiatives of employers and governments. This is where my union has been different from the pack. We have tried to recognise what was happening in society and to adjust the EETPU to any changes. In all our arguments with the TUC there were a number of underlying trends which we recognised and others ignored. There was a crying need for greater recognition of individual rights. If unions were to survive they needed to be not only attractive to potential members, but also to have a relevance to employers. Bosses can, in innumerable ways, frustrate union organisation and prevent it existing within a plant or industry. At the very least, if they are hostile to the union involved, it can mean recurring confrontation and trouble.[6]

Hammond's realism was not shared by the majority of his trade union colleagues, and EETPU was dismissed from the TUC towards the end of 1985. The decision neither broke Hammond's heart nor his union's power to negotiate effectively on behalf of his members.

After the 1987 General Election the Conservative government could look with satisfaction on all that had occurred in the ranks of their rivals and, with a comfortable parliamentary majority, see themselves enjoying virtually untrammelled power. The Prime Minister did not anticipate how dangerous would be the storms ahead. Just as a cumulus cloud often signals rain, the affair of the Westland helicopter manufacturing company signalled the beginning of the end of Mrs Thatcher, though not of her heritage. The affair itself was simple. The Westland company was in dire financial straits. It was also an important provider of helicopters to the armed services, and therefore the government was necessarily anxious about its future. It had a choice between being bought by the American Sikorski company or by a consortium of European companies. The Secretary of State for Defence, Michael Heseltine, favoured the latter choice and the Prime Minister the former. Once the Cabinet decided to support the Prime Minister's policy, Heseltine, in the most dramatic manner possible, resigned: he walked out of a Cabinet meeting and announced his resignation to the press. This was taken to be a clear bid, not merely for the creation of a European helicopter industry, but for the leadership of the Conservative Party.[7] Heseltine clothed his defiance of the Prime Minister's will with various professions of his belief that there should be a EEC defence industry which would encompass Westland.[8] There can be no doubt of his belief in ever-growing unity between the member states of the European Community. But there can also be no doubt that by his resignation Heseltine staked his claim to the succession to Mrs Thatcher.

The Westland affair undoubtedly damaged the Prime Minister, not least because it was believed that her Private Office, in the person of her devoted Press Secretary, Bernard (now Sir Bernard) Ingham, had leaked an exchange of correspondence between the Department of Trade and Industry and the Ministry of Defence, revealing serious differences of opinion between government departments and No. 10 Downing Street. The then Attorney-General, the late Lord Havers, demanded a full public accounting of what had gone on,[9] but before this could take place the Secretary of State for Trade and Industry, Leon (now Sir Leon) Brittan resigned, thereby taking the blame for all errors that had occurred.

What was more important than the Westland affair, however, was looming economic recession. By 1988 Mrs Thatcher's economic dream of growth without inflation came under threat. At the same time she was preparing to introduce the Community Charge, which was to prove almost universally unpopular. The Charge was designed to replace a system of raising funds for local authorities based on property values by one levied per head throughout the nation. It was introduced first in Scotland and later in England and Wales. Although there was a generous system of rebates for those who could not pay, the fact of the matter remained that the method of calculation and the imposition of charges was not well understood. Many Conservative backbenchers sitting for marginal seats feared that the combination of economic recession, and the imposition of the Community Charge, could cost them their jobs. These fears were eventually to cost Mrs Thatcher her leadership of the party.

From 1975 there were elements in the Conservative Party who disagreed profoundly with Mrs Thatcher and also disliked her intensely. One of her most bitter critics, Sir Anthony Meyer, challenged her for the leadership at the beginning of the parliamentary session in 1989. Meyer was never a serious contender: he was merely seeing how much opposition there was to Mrs Thatcher's continuance in power. The following year, however, in the face of deepening recession, Michael Heseltine decided to risk all, and mount his own challenge. In the meantime, the Chancellor of the Exchequer, Nigel Lawson, resigned on the, in my view, somewhat spurious grounds that she was too much under the influence of her personal economic adviser, Sir Alan Walters. The dispute here was over whether Lawson's policy of shadowing the Deutschmark – that is to say, using the resources of the Bank of England to keep up the level of the pound against the strongest currency in Europe – was the right way of proceeding, or whether the Walters policy of a completely free-floating pound was right. Shortly thereafter, Sir Geoffrey Howe, once Chancellor of the Exchequer and later Foreign Secretary, but at this time Leader of the House of Commons, also resigned. The Thatcher administration appeared to be falling apart. Heseltine therefore felt it possible that he could overthrow Mrs Thatcher; and he was fortified by the fact that the new Chancellor of the Exchequer, John Major, had, with the agreement of the Foreign Secretary, Douglas Hurd, persuaded or cajoled Mrs Thatcher into joining the European Exchange Rate Mechanism, a more formal development of Lawson's Deutschmark policy. Since she had resisted, step by unforgiving step, all moves towards European monetary integration, the pro-European MPs on the Conservative backbenches were encouraged to join forces against her. The proximate occasion of Howe's resignation was the Prime Minister's lack of enthusiasm for greater European integration; but, in fact, I believe his disgruntlement stemmed from his dismissal as Foreign Secretary the year before.

The storm clouds were now well and truly gathered over Mrs Thatcher's hitherto impeccable political head. Heseltine made his move. In the first ballot for the leadership she beat him, but not by a sufficient majority to prevent a second ballot. She fell short by four votes of the majority required to sustain her in the leadership.[10] However, after anguished consultation with her supporters and Cabinet colleagues, she decided that the sentiment of the parliamentary party was insufficiently strong to sustain her in office, and therefore decided to resign. Thus, the most remarkable political career of modern times came to its close.

The rules for electing a Conservative Leader allow for the entry of new candidates on a second ballot. Two promptly declared themselves. They were the Foreign Secretary, Douglas Hurd and the Chancellor of the Exchequer, John Major who was, at the time, convalescing from an operation to remove an impacted wisdom tooth.[11] Both men had stated that they would in no circumstances stand against Mrs Thatcher. Once she was out of the race they were free. Hurd and Major appealed to different constituencies. Hurd could hope to draw away from Michael Heseltine some of the pro-European MPs in the Heseltine camp who nevertheless had reservations about his personality and his potential. Major, on the other hand, could hope to attract the support of all those who had backed Margaret Thatcher, not least because of his stringent policies on public spending, first as Chief Secretary to the Treasury, and later as Chancellor of the Exchequer. In the event, Major having come out two votes ahead of the combined opposition, the other two candidates most gracefully conceded.

Just as the Conservative Party had gazed with delight on all the disruptions in the Labour Party from 1979 onwards, so the Labour Party chortled at Tory divisions. They hated Mrs Thatcher, but they also feared her. This was reasonable, in that any opposition would fear a Prime Minister who had won three successive General Elections. Moreover, the pale rider who came by on the rails was not regarded by the Labour Party as a very formidable opponent. First, he was determined to continue with the privatisation programme, and the reform both of the state education system and the National Health Service. But, most important of all, Major had been both Chief Secretary to the Treasury and Chancellor of the Exchequer. He had therefore, both in a junior capacity and in a senior one, presided over the recession. Moreover, while Labour put most of its emphasis on increased spending in areas where it was perceived to be more popular than the government, the new Prime Minister, while proceeding with reforms in various areas, put his principal emphasis on the conquest of inflation. 'If it isn't hurting, it isn't working,' he said in one of his earliest statements after entering No. 10 Downing Street. Senior Labour politicians were delighted to make a contrast between this prophet of austerity and their own generous-hearted Leader.

In effect, the General Election campaign began with John Major's succession. It was open to him to go to the country in October 1991, after he had played himself in, but he could have waited until July 1992, the latest date available to him. Labour were not displeased with his decision not to take one of the early options for they believed that the longer he delayed the more time they had to expose his record as Chief Secretary and Chancellor.

Undoubtedly Major was anxious to escape from the shadow of Mrs Thatcher and acquire his own mandate. On the other hand, he was anxious to prove himself as a capable head of government. He had two important opportunities to show his mettle. The first was the war in early 1991 that followed Iraq's invasion of Kuwait. He demonstrated assurance and skill greater than could reasonably be expected from a tyro Prime Minister. The second was the Maastricht Summit of EC heads of government in December 1991. Major proved to be a tenacious negotiator and, in particular, persuaded the other European countries to allow Britain at least to postpone – and possibly never to implement – full European Monetary Union. He also made it quite clear that no government which he headed would accept the provisions of the Social Charter put forward by the President of the European Commission, Jacques Delors. Since this Charter proposed a great many measures apparently beneficial to workers, including the imposition on employers of a minimum wage, Labour embraced it eagerly, and believed it would prove to be a vote-winner. In their eyes Major had yet again proved himself to be so tight-fisted that he could not win a General Election. Furthermore, the budget presented by the Chancellor of the Exchequer in March 1992 seemed to offer little in the way of easement of the people's lot: it contained only a marginal measure of relief for the lower paid, and a cut in tax on the purchase of motor cars.

When Major called a General Election for 9 April 1992, Labour went into the campaign in good heart. The opinion polls either gave them the lead or, at best for the Conservatives, showed the two main parties at level pegging. It seemed possible that there would be a Parliament in which neither Labour nor the Conservatives had an overall majority. This prospect excited the Liberal Democrats for, Paddy Ashdown believed, they could then force the larger of the two main parties to adopt an electoral system of proportional representation which would be bound to benefit his own party.

Labour presented a manifesto studious in its moderation: for the first time, the dread word 'socialist' did not appear in its pages. The Labour campaign was designed both to show a party of compassion and competence, but also one with glamour: particular use was made of the many show business personalities supportive of Neil Kinnock's cause. The

Conservative campaign seemed, particularly in the first week, hesitant and unsure.

In the second half of the campaign, however, the Prime Minister emerged as an exceptionally forceful character. While Neil Kinnock's walkabouts were confined to audiences of carefully monitored party supporters, the Prime Minister – no doubt to the consternation of his security advisers – walked about among the general public. In touching reminiscence of his youth as a Councillor in Lambeth he addressed public meetings standing on a soapbox. He managed to project an image compounded of decency and authority. By all accounts, it was not until the last forty-eight hours of the campaign that the clammy hand of failure seemed to touch the Labour leadership. When all the results were in it was shown that Major had a majority of 21 over all other parties. Paddy Ashdown's dreams of a new electoral system were dashed, and Neil Kinnock's hopes of glory were destroyed. The following Monday, Kinnock announced formally what had been confidently expected since Friday – that he was resigning the leadership of his Party. In an interview with Bruce Anderson in the *Sunday Express* on 19 April the Prime Minister said:

Socialism of course is dead and gone: Finished, passed, out of the window. Nobody believes in it any more. Nobody. Not in this country, not abroad. It is now a museum piece, nothing more. Time has passed it by.

Notes

INTRODUCTION

1 A select bibliography can be found on Page 253 and works by most of the writers mentioned in this introduction are listed there. Some more discrete references will, however, be found in succeeding notes.

2 There are many essays on Seeley but the only substantial and – one must add the word – brilliant study is by Deborah Wormell, *Sir John Seeley and the Uses of History* (Cambridge, 1980). Dr Wormell, one of the finest scholars of her generation, died in 1979 at the tragically early age of thirty-three.

3 When, today, one reads Wallas's *The Rise of Japan*, published in 1906, one cannot but stand in mute admiration not merely of the general accuracy, but of the exact detail of his predictions.

4 An impressive attempt is now being made by the Institute of Contemporary British History to bridge the gap between what might be called historical narrative and political science. The work of the Institute involves the recording on tape of the views and experiences of immediately contemporary public figures, while the events of which they have been part are still fresh in their minds, and before hindsight or self-regard have clouded their perceptions. The Institute also holds seminars and publishes a journal, *Contemporary Record*. As it grows the archive of the Institute will enable students to fulfil the paramount demand of the traditional historian, that the writer should always have available at least two independent sources to support any particular judgement. The most substantial – and, indeed, impressive – work to have come out of the process which the Institute has inaugurated is by one of its founder members and the editor of *Contemporary Record*. It is Dr Anthony Seldon's *Churchill's Indian Summer: The Conservative Government 1951–55* (London, 1981).

5 London, 1969. A revised edition was published in 1971.

6 Ten of these pages consist of a list of those organisations and associations consulted by the National Curriculum Council.

7 The late Professor McKenzie's masterwork, *British Political Parties* was first published in 1955. In 1963, however, he brought out a second edition with an

additional chapter on events in the intervening years. This incorporated a reply to the critics of his first edition, notable among them R. H. S. Crossman, subsequently a Cabinet Minister in governments headed by Harold Wilson, editor of the *New Statesman* and author of vastly entertaining and largely unreliable diaries. It is fair to say that no student of politics, whatever his political opinions, finds McKenzie other than invaluable.

8 *The Growth of British Government* (London, 1975). Professor Finer is also the author of a host of illuminating articles and essays on British political matters. I do not often agree with his conclusions, but his work is, nonetheless, wonderfully stimulating.

9 *Modern British Politics* (London, 1965). Professor Beer published a revised edition of his book in 1971. My remarks about Professor Finer in the previous footnote apply equally to Professor Beer.

10 I have chosen 1972 because it was the year in which the Heath experiment was abandoned when the Prime Minister reversed the policies on which he was elected in 1970.

11 The British economy had been in relative decline since at least the turn of the century. The decline was occasioned first of all by the fact that competitor nations had caught up with the Industrial Revolution which was spawned by Britain, and, secondly, by the cost of sustaining the Empire, the contribution of which to the home economy decreased over the years. Even in the prosperous fifties shrewd commentators saw what was going on and, in the sixties, some of them made efforts to review the matter over a longer period than was then common. See a special edition of the magazine *Encounter* in July 1963 edited by Arthur Koestler: each of the sixteen essayists whom Koestler assembled were advocates of what I have called the revolution – that is, they wanted more and more centralised control of the economy and society. A counter-blast was produced by the advocates of what was to become the counter-revolution in Arthur Seldon (ed.) *Rebirth of Britain* (London, 1964). See also Samuel Brittan, *Steering the Economy: the Role of the Treasury* (London, edn. 1970). This is a substantially revised and expanded version of Mr Brittan's *The Treasury under the Tories 1951–1964* which was published in 1964.

12 The Conservative Research Department had the task of drawing up policy advice for Shadow Ministers and of briefing them and backbenchers for parliamentary debates. CRD did (and still does) undertake some publications of its own, but the principal engine for the education of the party in the country was (and still is) the Conservative Political Centre (CPC). CPC was deliberately conceived of as a rival to Labour's Fabian Society. It was used by Butler to inaugurate his 'two-way programme'. The method here was to send out briefs to a large number of CPC groups in the constituencies, invite their comments, and reconsider policy in their light. This was the first time in its history that the Conservative Party had sought to use its voluntary members for an intellectual, rather than merely a canvassing, effort.

13 Revisionist writing, tending to scale down the value of the contribution made by Butler and his youngsters to the revival of the Conservative Party and, by contrast, to upgrade the value of the work on organisation done by Lord Woolton

in his capacity as Chairman of the Party is on the increase. See Patrick Cosgrave, *R. A. Butler: An English life* (London, 1981), pp. 85 ff. A much more detailed account, given from the point of view of Butler himself, can be found in Anthony Howard's magisterial biography *RAB: The life of R. A. Butler* (London, 1987), pp. 140 ff.

14 In his last year of office as Prime Minister, 1954–1955, Churchill urged his colleagues to legislate to restrict immigration. But by then he no longer had the strength nor the authority to enforce his views. The first measure to curb immigration was guided through Parliament by the Home Secretary, R. A. Butler, in 1962. It proved ultimately ineffective and other measures were subsequently passed by both Conservative and Labour governments.

15 See F. S. Northedge, 'British foreign policy', in F. S. Northedge (ed.), *The Foreign Policies of the Powers* (London, 1968), pp. 150–86.

16 See Anthony Hartley, 'The new superpower?', in *The Sunday Telegraph*, 17 September 1989.

I   A PEACEFUL REVOLUTION

1 Churchill always hankered after coalition. He had, after all, been first a Conservative, then a Liberal, and then a Conservative again, so party allegiance sat lightly on his shoulders. When he rejoined the Conservative Party he observed 'any fool can rat, but it takes a certain amount of genius to rat twice'.

2 The British war hero, Group Captain Leonard (later Lord) Cheshire, VC, flew in the leading plane of the American squadron. Cheshire maintained ever since that the use of the bomb was wholly justified, something which surprises many of those who knew of him only in his post-war incarnation as an indefatigable worker for the disabled and founder of the Cheshire Homes. On the fortieth anniversary of the Hiroshima bombings the Japanese government made it clear that Cheshire would not be welcome in their country.

3 John Colville *Downing Street Diaries 1939–1955* (London, 1985), pp. 611 ff. In the General Election of 1906 a Conservative majority of 268 was replaced by a Liberal majority of 270. The Conservative Prime Minister, Arthur Balfour, lost his seat.

4 Colville, *loc. cit.*

5 Winston S. Churchill, *The Second World War*, Volume VI (London, 1954), p. 583.

6 The British electoral system allows a party with a relatively narrow overall plurality among those voting to gain a substantial majority in the House of Commons. Indeed, when Churchill returned to power in 1951 with a majority of 19, the Conservatives actually polled fewer votes throughout the country than the Labour Party. In 1945, however, Labour polled 11,995,152 votes as against 9,988,306 for the Conservatives. This was the first time that the Labour Party, although they had formed two previous governments, had had more voters on their side than had the Conservatives.

7 It was no consolation to Churchill that the man put in charge of this most ambitious piece of social engineering was his *bête noire*, Aneurin Bevan. In later years, when he heard that Bevan was ill, Churchill remarked, 'Nothing trivial, I trust?'

8 This ambition is enshrined in Clause Four of the constitution. At the Party Conference of October 1961, the then Leader, Hugh Gaitskell, sprung upon his party a proposal to expunge Clause Four, thus precipitating a vicious and ultimately sterile intra-party conflict. Gaitskell had been trounced in a General Election and sought to discard the trappings of the past in order the better to convince the electorate that a Labour government would be responsible and non-ideological. He failed.

9 In these days of high-powered and expensive public relations organisations being employed by all parties, it is salutary to recall the genesis of the 1950 and 1951 manifestos. Drafts were prepared for Churchill by the Conservative Research Department and officials at Conservative Central Office. He found those drafts unsatisfactory. He therefore, on each occasion, took the text into his own hands and rewrote it. See Martin Gilbert, *Never Despair: Winston S. Churchill 1945–1965* (London, 1988), pp. 653–72. It is hard to think of any successor to Churchill who could have written such dashing manifestos, virtually unaided. But then, of course, Churchill was a writer, and had earned his living, for many years, by writing, and broadcasting. Churchill's personal finances were often precarious, particularly in the years between the wars. But, as he wrote himself, much of his writing was dictated and, thus, 'I lived from mouth to hand, and with my happy family around me, dwelt at peace within my habitation'. See Winston S. Churchill, *The Second World War. Volume I. The Gathering Storm* (London, 1948), pp. 156–7.

10 One of the most energetic and influential of Labour thinkers was the publisher Victor Gollancz. Commercially very successful, Gollancz was able to use the spare resources of his company in order to fund an enormous quantity of Labour propaganda. See Ruth Dudley Edwards, *Victor Gollancz* (London, 1987), pp. 401–3. Dr Dudley Edwards provides an effective summary of all Labour Party propaganda efforts during and following the Second World War.

11 See David Butler, *The British General Election of 1951* (London, 1952), *passim*.

12 See Anthony Seldon, *Churchill's Indian Summer* (London 1981), pp. 154–86. Dr Seldon does, however, make the point that the Churchill government was unwilling to quarrel with the trades unions, and thus laid up many problems for its successors of both parties.

13 Dr Morgan's *The House of Lords and the Labour Government, 1964–1970* (Oxford, 1975), ranges far more widely than her title would strictly dictate. Her work is required reading for any student of post-war British politics. Salisbury's attitude had a considerable influence on his junior whip, Lord Carrington, and caused Carrington, much later, to collaborate with enthusiasm in the schemes of a Labour government for the reform of the Upper House and the elimination of its Conservative majority. See Patrick Cosgrave, *Carrington: A Life and a Policy* (London, 1985), pp. 52 ff.

14 Robert Blake and John Patten (eds.), *The Conservative Opportunity* (London, 1976), pp. 2 ff.

15 See Kenneth Harris, *Attlee* (London, 1982), *passim*. The case for the argument that Marxist doctrine is at the foundation of British socialism is effectively put in Stanley Pierson *Marxism and the Origins of British Socialism: The Struggle for a*

New Consciousness (Ithaca and London), *passim*. Lord Wilson of Riveaulx was very fond of his own coinage 'The Labour Party owes more to Methodism than to Marxism'. See his *The Labour Government 1964–70* (London, edn. 1974), pp. 52–67. A more sceptical – and scholarly – assessment is to be found in Robert Rhodes James, *Ambitions and Realities: British Politics 1964–70* (London, 1972), pp. 1 ff. It is worth observing, however, that Mrs Margaret Thatcher was brought up as a Methodist and her upbringing never inclined her to socialism.

16 There is a vast literature on the subject of Labour's attempts to capitalise on this instinct for goodness in the British people. Perhaps the most entertaining argument along these lines is to be found in Bernard Shaw *The Intelligent Woman's Guide to Socialism and Capitalism* (London, 1928), pp. 1 ff.

17 See Anthony Howard *RAB: The Life of R. A. Butler* (London, 1987), p. 149. Mr Howard uses two sources for these judgements. The first is the Butler archive, the second his own television programme on Butler, first shown on BBC2 on 13 July 1983, in his series 'Reputations'.

18 It is interesting to observe that until 1946 the graduates of the great universities enjoyed two votes at General Elections, one in their capacity as graduates and the other as voters in their home constituencies. The last University Member was the humorist and barrister, A. P. Herbert. Herbert was a reformer: to him is due, for good or ill, the radical beginnings of the reform of divorce law.

19 Peter Jenkins, *Mrs Thatcher's Revolution: The Ending of the Socialist Era* (London, 1987), p. 6. Dalton is nowadays remembered for having fostered the early career of C. A. R. ('Tony') Crosland. Crosland's *The Future of Socialism* (London, 1962) was encouraged by Dalton and became a vital influence on the thinking of centrist Labour politicians in the 1960s and 1970s.

20 See Ben Pimlott *Hugh Dalton* (London, 1985), pp. 524 ff. The indiscretion was in a conversation with John Carvel, a lobby correspondent for the *Star*. Carvel was accompanied by his son, Robert, later Political Editor of the *Standard*. Dalton told Carvel the details of the budget speech that he was about to make; Carvel phoned it through to his newspaper; and with the publication of the *Star* it became clear that the Chancellor had committed the unforgivable sin of leaking details of a budget before giving it to the House.

21 Trinity is unique among Oxford and Cambridge colleges in that its mastership is in the gift of the sovereign, and appointments are made on the advice of the Prime Minister. Harold Wilson liked in later years to say that his nomination of Butler had been Machiavellian in that, at one stroke, he removed from active politics the most important Conservative thinker of the time. It seems more likely, however, that Wilson, an essentially kindly man, saw an opportunity to gratify the last ambition of a man already tired of politics. This, at any rate, is the opinion of Butler's biographer, Anthony Howard. See Howard, *op. cit.*, pp. 341 ff. Butler's father had been Master of Pembroke College, Cambridge and there was a long academic tradition in the family.

22 *Op. cit.*, pp. 3–50.

23 A lament for the idea of consensus politics is to be found in Norman St John-Stevas (now Lord St John of Fawley), 'The disappearing consensus' in Anthony

King (ed.), *Why is Britain Becoming Harder to Govern?* (London, 1976). Lord St John's essay and the others in the same volume were published to accompany three television programmes shown on the BBC in the year of publication.

24 Philip M. Williams, *Hugh Gaitskell* (London, 1979), pp. 313 ff.

25 Heath was speaking to Anthony Sampson and the quotation is to be found in Mr Sampson's *The Changing Anatomy of Britain* (London, 1982), p. 37.

26 Philip M. Williams, *The Diary of Hugh Gaitskell 1945–1956* (London, 1983), p. 307.

27 The character of 'Mr Butskell' and the supposed doctrine of Butskellism was coined by the *Economist* in an article on 13 February 1954.

28 The constitutional convention, either during the process of nationalisation or of what is now called privatisation is that a 'vesting date' is named at the time of the Royal Assent. This is in order to give the industry in question, in whichever direction it is moving, time to adjust its affairs before legislation takes effect.

29 The Labour Party, largely because of its origins in the trade union movement, has always believed that manufacturing industry is in some way morally superior to service industries. In the early years of the Labour Party there were no trade unions representing workers involved in service industries. The party was created solely to represent in Parliament the interests of the manufacturing industry workers. See R. T. McKenzie, *British Political Parties*, (edn. 1963) pp. 386–412.

30 A good example of earlier nationalisation was the setting up of the Central Electricity Board in 1926. In 1933 the London Passenger Transport Board was established. The conviction in the twenties and thirties was that certain public utilities required central control.

31 The hotels, though not public transport, were denationalised by the Heath government in 1971.

32 See Michael Foot, *Aneurin Bevan: 1945–1960* (London, 1985), pp. 1–50. See also Mr Foot's illuminating essay on Bevan's wife, Jennie Lee in his *Loyalists and Loners* (London, 1986), pp. 19–43. Mr Foot's book on Bevan is perhaps not altogether to be relied upon for factual matters, since he (and this is his own word) worshipped Bevan and was later to succeed to Bevan's constituency of Ebbw Vale.

33 The first step toward vitiating Bevan's dream was made in 1951 with the introduction of prescription charges. On 7 January 1951 he resigned, followed by his (then) disciple, the President of the Board of Trade, Harold Wilson.

34 For the origins of the welfare policies of both major parties see Kevin Jefferys, 'British politics and social policy during the Second World War', in *The Historical Journal*, Vol. 30, No. 1 (Cambridge, 1987).

35 In 1969, when the then Lord Balniel (now Lord Crawford and Balcarres) was Shadow Secretary of State for Health and Social Services, I tried to persuade him to commit the Opposition to a refusal to fund any further advanced medical research. He declined my advice, and this is perhaps a good illustration of the willingness with which the Conservative Party embraced consensus as outlined above: the then Secretary of State, R. H. S. Crossman, was enthusiastic for every new medical idea, and tigerish in his fight for Treasury funds. On the 1942 Committee (called the Post-War Reconstruction Committee), see Jeffery's *op. cit.*

36 See Henry Pelling, *Origins of the Labour Party* (edn. 1965, Oxford), pp. 78–99.

37 Winston S. Churchill, *The Second World War*, Vol. II, *Their Finest Hour* (London, 1949), p. 12. Bevin after 'two or three days' of consultation with the TGWU Executive accepted the office of Minister of Labour.

38 Although Conservative governments were later to keep broadly speaking to the provisions of this Act, and even to amend it in a direction helpful to the workforce, coverage was never really complete. Even the Labour governments of 1964–1970 and 1974–1979 did not provide full insurance against industrial disease. A moment which dramatised one thing that was missing occurred in the hours leading up to the parliamentary vote of no confidence on 28 March 1979, which brought down the Labour Government headed by James Callaghan. Michael Foot was then Leader of the House, and desperate to procure the government's survival. He therefore offered Gwynfor Evans, the Leader of the Welsh Nationalists £60,000 to be placed in a fund for Welsh miners suffering from pneumoconiosis. This was something which many Labour Members had campaigned for over the years. In the circumstances, however, it was seen simply as a bribe, and Evans duly voted with the Opposition. See Patrick Cosgrave, *Thatcher: The First Term* (London, 1985), pp. 1–2.

39 See Peter Jenkins, *op. cit.*, p. 4. See also Anthony Howard, *op. cit.*, pp. 177 ff.

40 The USSR did not take the same attitude to the German territories which had been occupied by Russian troops. Whole factories were dismantled and shifted to Russia, and severe penalties imposed upon what was to become the German Democratic Republic.

41 On 27 November 1947 Attlee wrote to the Minister of Supply, George Strauss, refusing to permit the making of a public information film about the 'nonsecret aspects of the atomic energy programme'. Quoted in Kenneth Harris, *op. cit.*, p. 602. The peaceful development of nuclear energy was, in Strauss's opinion, potentially a first class public relations exercise for the government. But Attlee was paranoid about possible criticism of the atomic programme, rightly fearing that, after the bombing of Hiroshima and Nagasaki, important elements in the Labour Party would strive to frustrate a programme which he considered to be of vital national interest. The full details of the United Kingdom's growing capacity to wage nuclear war did not emerge until the 1950s.

42 The great expenditure of the Korean War had not yet come to haunt European governments, for the war did not start until 1950.

43 See above, p. 28

44 One could, possibly, add Hugh Dalton to their number, since, as Chancellor of the Exchequer, he had the ultimate responsibility for an economy at best fragile. But he had not had the same experience as the other two.

45 Churchill knew full well that the trade union movement harboured profound suspicions of him for his role in crushing the General Strike of 1926. See Winston S. Churchill, *The Second World War*, Vol. I: *The Gathering Storm* (London, 1948), p. 526.

46 Even as Foreign Secretary Bevin continued to exert a considerable influence on the trade union movement. Indeed, during the debate on the Trade Unions Act in 1946, which was unpopular in many trade union circles, he spoke to great effect.

It is unimaginable today that the Foreign Secretary would intervene in such a way in a matter of domestic policy. The Attlee government had, on the whole, relatively little industrial relations trouble during its time in office. There were, however, two dockers' strikes of brief duration in 1945, and Bevin was useful in coordinating the opposition of the rest of the trade union movement to them. The great majority of trade unionists were anxious not to rock the boat of a reforming Labour government; but the dockers, being Communist-dominated, felt no such obligations.

47 Sir Frank Roberts, 'Ernest Bevin as Foreign Secretary', in Ritchie Ovendale, *The Foreign Policy of the British Labour Governments, 1945–1951* (Leicester University Press, 1984), p. 22. Sir Frank Roberts was a diplomat of great talent and was entrusted by Bevin from 1945 to 1947 with negotiations between Britain and the USSR. Between 1947 and 1949, when ill-health forced Bevin to resign from the Foreign Office (he served in the non-departmental post of Lord Privy Seal until his death the following year), Roberts was Principal Private Secretary to the Foreign Secretary. His account not only of Bevin's policy, but of his personality, is invaluable. The major biography of Bevin is by Alan Bullock, published in three volumes, *The Life and Times of Ernest Bevin: Trade Union Leader, Minister of Labour* and *Ernest Bevin: Foreign Secretary* (London, 1960, 1967 and 1983).

48 It has to be remembered that, before the War, the Foreign Office was little concerned with economics and, in so far as diplomats were obliged to concern themselves with 'the dismal science' they accepted instructions from the Treasury and the Board of Trade.

49 See Kenneth Harris, *op. cit.*, pp. 262–5. See also Ben Pimlott, *op. cit.*, pp. 263–6.

50 Frank Roberts, *op. cit.*, p. 39.

51 Later, in 1957, to be transmuted into the Organisation for Economic Cooperation and Development.

52 Poland and Czechoslovakia initially joined OEEC, but were forced immediately to withdraw at the behest of Stalin.

53 There is a multitude of books on the subject of this intricate and eventually bloody post-war problem. The most recent is a brilliant and elegant book by Conor Cruise O'Brien, *The Siege* (London, 1986), pp. 309–333.

54 It is a curious fact to note from the vantage point of today that, in Bevin's time, it was the Republican Party which wished to withdraw from overseas responsibilities, and the Democrats which wished to assume them. However, the Republicans knew a winner when they saw one, and adopted General Dwight Z. Eisenhower as their presidential candidate in the election of 1952, which he won in a canter. As the former Supreme Allied Commander Europe in the closing stages of the War, Eisenhower was already certain that an American military presence on the European side of the Atlantic Ocean was essential.

2 THE CONSENSUS AT WORK

1 Baldwin was, in effect, the real power in the land. He was, however, more than willing to allow MacDonald to enjoy the trappings of office. See Keith Middlemass and John Barnes, *Baldwin* (London, 1969), pp. 305 ff.

2 Churchill was so determined in 1940 to be a leader above party that he insisted on Chamberlain remaining as leader of the Conservatives even though he himself had

become Prime Minister. This arrangement lasted until 7 October 1940 when a terminal illness forced Chamberlain's resignation. Even then Churchill was disposed to allow the Conservative Party in Parliament to select a new leader from among its members while he remained above the Party fray. However, his friends, notably Lord Beaverbrook and Brendan Bracken, persuaded him that, at a time when his virtually untrammelled authority was required for the war effort, he should not allow the emergence of a new and separate focus of power. Churchill therefore stood unopposed for the leadership of the Party. See A. J. P. Taylor, *Beaverbrook* (London, 1972), pp. 414 ff, and Charles Edward Lysaght, *Brendan Bracken* (London, 1979), pp. 181–2.

3 Mary Soames, *Clementine Churchill* (London, 1982), p. 382. Lady Soames's biography of her mother is at once both devoted and scholarly and it forms an invaluable part of the vast collection of Churchilliana.

4 For years the Conservative Party was deeply embarrassed by this electoral blunder, though from the 1970s onwards a new breed of Conservative came to believe that Socialism did, indeed, involve a degree of State control that was unacceptable to free men and women. On that belief rested the foundation of Margaret Thatcher's successes. All the circumstances surrounding the 4 June broadcast are described in Martin Gilbert, *Never Despair: Winston S. Churchill 1945–1965* (London, 1988), pp. 32 ff. There are later indications that, as he grew older, Churchill realised the unwisdom of his conduct of the 1945 campaign. He referred to his error in a discussion with the late Reginald Maudling on the text of his speech for the 1952 Budget. Maudling, then an officer in the Conservative Research Department, had done the first draft of the Prime Minister's speech. Churchill found it anodyne. He wrote in several what he called 'hurricane' passages. Maudling objected that these were 'unfair'. Churchill told his young interlocutor that fairness had nothing to do with politics. 'But, sir,' Maudling said, 'the people will think them unfair.' Churchill thereupon struck out his own passages and told Maudling that he did not want to make the same mistake again that he had made in 1945. Reginald Maudling told me this story in 1970.

5 See Donald McCormick, *The Mask of Merlin: A Critical Study of David Lloyd George* (London, 1963), pp. 159 ff.

6 See Chapter One above.

7 See Anthony Howard, *RAB: The Life of R. A. Butler* (London, 1987), pp. 140 ff.

8 *Op. cit., loc. cit.*

9 See Chapter One, note 1.

10 *The Gathering Storm*, p. 526. The continuing hankering after even the most modest form of coalition is well illustrated by his attempt, in 1951, to bring the Liberal Party into government by the appointment of their Leader, Clement Davies, to head the Department of Education: Davies's colleagues vetoed his initial acceptance. A very similar situation arose in February 1974 when Edward Heath tried to persuade the then Liberal Leader to become Home Secretary. As in the case of Davies, in spite of Thorpe's desire to accept Heath's offer, the Liberal Party said no. There was, however, a difference – the Department of Education in 1951 did not carry with it Cabinet rank for its Minister, whereas the Home Office, of course, did.

11 One of them, Lord Simmonds, would, of course, have been in the Cabinet anyway as Lord Chancellor. Although not formally a member of the Cabinet, I have included Earl Alexander as he held Cabinet rank.

12 In theory, Churchill was himself Minister of Defence, as he had been during the war.

13 See The Earl of Birkenhead, *The Prof in Two Worlds: The Official Life of Professor F. A. Lindemann, Viscount Cherwell* (London, 1961), pp. 277–95.

14 Iain Macleod, having made a devastating attack on Aneurin Bevan in Churchill's presence in the House of Commons in 1952, was immediately appointed Minister of Health – not then a cabinet post. There is no doubt that the speech won him the job, but Macleod once told me that Churchill had to ask for his name from the Chief Whip, Patrick Buchan-Hepburn.

15 Birkenhead, *op. cit.*, pp. 295 ff. Opinion was always sharply divided about Frederick Lindemann. Most people who had to work with him found him boorish and arrogant. Churchill, however, had the utmost faith in his ability as a scientist, and Clementine Churchill and the children, to whom he was unfailingly considerate, adored him. It is fair to him to say that he was invariably courteous to women and servants, and reserved his rudeness for his political colleagues and all other scientists. As to his merits as a scientist, one need only recall his clash, as Churchill's Scientific Adviser, with Duncan Sandys in 1943 over the question of German rocket capacity. In spite of the scientific evidence, he ridiculed the idea that the Germans were developing a massive rocket strike force and therefore opposed the idea of diverting Bomber Command to attacking it. Sandys opposed him and won the day. The attacks (successful) took place.

16 BBC Radio Profile, 28 June 1978, quoted in Howard, *op. cit*, p. 178.

17 Apart from being Secretary of State for the Dominions in 1939–40 (which could be considered a foreign affairs appointment) and Secretary of State for War for a few months in 1940, Eden's entire ministerial experience was within the ambit of the Foreign Office.

18 See Patrick Cosgrave, *op. cit.*, pp. 71–83.

19 There is evidence – see Martin Gilbert, *Never Despair*, pp. 653 ff. – that Churchill would have liked Woolton, a man with a long and distinguished career, to have been Chancellor. That was impossible, however, because the 1911 Parliament Act had laid it down that the Chancellor of the Exchequer could not sit in the House of Lords. This was because the quarrels which preceded the 1911 Act had been fundamentally about Money Bills. From 1911 onwards there has never been a Treasury Minister above junior rank in the Upper House, and his task is to attend only to minor details.

20 Whatever his qualities – and they were considerable – Salter was seventy and his appointment as Minister for Economic Affairs fuelled the criticism that the new Churchill Cabinet was over-weighted with the elderly.

21 See Bill Williamson, *The Temper of the Times: British Society since World War II* (London, 1990), pp. 40 ff.

22 There is a famous story, which I believe to be true, that, his Treasury civil servants having presented him with their preferred text for his 1952 Budget speech, Butler called for scissors and gum. He then cut up the text and rearranged

the paragraphs, explaining to them the while that he knew the sequence in which the argument should go in order to gain the approbation of the House. Whatever the facts as to its origins, the 1952 speech was a great success.

23 Anthony Seldon, *op. cit.*, p. 21.

24 See Anthony Seldon, *op. cit.*, p. 21. Sir Edward Bridges was Head of the Home Civil Service and Permanent Secretary at the Treasury; Sir Norman Brook was Secretary to the Cabinet.

25 Kenneth Harris, *op. cit.*, pp. 245 ff.

26 See Anthony Howard, *op. cit.*, pp. 178 ff.

27 Bridges was the son of the Poet Laureate, Robert Bridges, and shared his father's literary tastes. He had, however, been devoted to Hugh Gaitskell, and Butler initially regarded him with suspicion. Their common cultural interests provided a common bond that was to overcome this suspicion. Being also Head of the Home Civil Service, he was thus able to smooth the path of necessary retrenchment throughout Whitehall.

28 See Milton Friedman, *An Economist's Protest* (New Jersey, 1972), pp. 7 ff., a collection of articles originally published in *Newsweek* magazine. Professor Friedman has been both idolised and vilified throughout his career, and vilification continued even after he won the Nobel Prize. However, most economists now accept his view that fiscal measures take between nine and twelve months to take effect.

29 Anthony Howard, *op. cit.*, pp. 184–5.

30 Harold Macmillan, *op. cit.*, pp. 690 ff.

31 Though it can reasonably be said that Butler was not, in 1954, a candidate of such weight as he was in 1957 and 1963, he was still in the eyes of those who doubted Eden's capacity, the only possible alternative. In the campaign leading up to the general election of 26 May, Butler was the sheet-anchor of the Conservative Party. See Anthony Howard, *op. cit.*, pp. 215 ff.

32 'Floating' meant that the markets, rather than government, would determine what the value of sterling was, and that government would abdicate its role in this respect.

33 Up to then 1947 had been the worst post-war year from the point of view of the economy, since reconstruction costs and charges on health and social security were at their greatest.

34 See Anthony Seldon, *op. cit.*, p. 22.

35 At the time of writing, Russia has entered into an agreement with the De Beers Corporation to exchange a huge stockpile of diamonds for US$500 million. From 1986 to 1989 the Chancellor of the Exchequer, Nigel Lawson, followed a policy of 'shadowing' the Deutschmark. This he did by raising British interest rates as the pound slipped against the mark. High interest rates, while uncomfortable for the domestic consumer, attract foreign investment, which, of course, ensures that the currency remains buoyant. Mr Lawson was, thus, trying to have it both ways: the pound was a floating currency but, through manipulation of the interest rates, the Chancellor was trying to fix its value in relation to the mark.

36 See Anthony Seldon, *Churchill's Indian Summer* (London, 1981), *passim*.

37 See Anthony Howard, *op. cit.*, *loc. cit.*

38 It is instructive to record that John Major, when Chief Secretary to the Treasury, had portraits of both Gladstone and Goschen in his office. He took them with him to the Chancellor of the Exchequer's office, and thence to No. 10 Downing Street. Ministers are entitled to borrow portraits for their offices from the Crown Property Services Agency during their Ministerial tenure. He used a portrait of Goschen for his Christmas card in 1989, and thereby signalled the programme of financial austerity he began as Chancellor and continued when he became Prime Minister in 1990.

39 Anthony Howard, *op. cit.*, pp. 184 ff.

40 Howard, *op. cit.*, pp. 185 ff. and Seldon, *op. cit.*, pp. 160 ff.

41 See above, p. 45.

42 Butler spent his early, and formative, years in what is now Pakistan. In later years this meant that his sympathy for, and understanding of, Islam was much more marked than his sympathy for Hinduism.

43 *The Listener*, 16 April 1981. Mr Powell was reviewing my book *R. A. Butler: An English Life* (London, 1981).

44 The Conservative Party did not have formal elections for the Leadership until 1966, when Edward Heath beat Reginald Maudling and Enoch Powell in an election in which only Members of the House of Commons could vote. See below pp. 105–106.

45 Charles Moran, *Winston Churchill: The Struggle for Survival 1940–1965* (London, 1966), pp. 447 ff.

46 See my *R. A. Butler: An English Life* (London, 1981), pp. 45 ff.

47 See Anthony Howard, *op. cit.*, pp. 109–110.

48 Charles Moran, *op. cit.*, pp. 530 ff.

49 The Crookshank diary quoted by Martin Gilbert, *op. cit.*, p. 961.

50 Moran, *op. cit.*, *loc. cit.*

51 Moran, *op. cit.*, *loc. cit.*

52 John Colville, *The Fringes of Power: Downing Street Diaries 1939–1955* (London, 1985), pp. 707–709. Colville tells us that he wrote this entry in his diary immediately after the event. He says, however, that he did not date it.

53 Eden was in Washington at the time.

54 See Charles Moran, *op. cit.*, p. 556.

55 See Martin Gilbert, *Never Despair* (London, 1988), p. 1126.

3   THE FIRST BREAK IN THE CONSENSUS

1 See Chapter Two, note 17.

2 See Robert Rhodes James, *Anthony Eden* (London, 1986), pp. 362–3.

3 Harold Macmillan, *Tides of Fortune* (London, 1969), p. 688. This is the third volume of Macmillan's six fat volumes of memoirs which are accompanied by four further volumes of diaries. When Butler came to write his own autobiography, *The Art of the Possible* (London, 1971), he made a typically caustic remark in his preface about the tendency of politicians to glorify themselves by multi-volume autobiographies. He himself, he continued, had restricted himself to one volume, light enough to be read in bed with comfort and without falling asleep.

4 *The Art of the Possible*, (London, edn. 1973), p. 182.

5 See Anthony Howard, *op. cit.*, p. 217.

6 See my *R. A. Butler: An English Life*, Chapter Three.

7 Anthony Howard, *op. cit.*, p. 218.

8 James M. Buchanan and others, *The Economics of Politics* (London, 1978), *passim*.

9 Peter Jenkins, *Mrs Thatcher's Revolution: The Ending of the Socialist Era* (London, 1987), pp. 60 ff. Mr Jenkins's work is essentially a study of the successive governments headed by Mrs Thatcher. But, in order to give the historical background to her victories, he provides a valuable, if short, account of the period between 1945 and 1979. Its conclusion, as his title suggests, is that the burdens which I have already described of trade union privilege, high spending and inflation could not be carried into the 1980s. Mr Jenkins is no friend of Mrs Thatcher, but he believes that she was a necessary phenomenon and that her austerity measures, produced between 1979 and 1983, were absolutely necessary if Britain were to make any major recovery. The fact that, at the time of writing, the Labour Party, under the leadership of Mr Neil Kinnock, has adopted so much of Mrs Thatcher's programme as party policy sustains Mr Jenkins's opinion.

10 Philip M. Williams, *Hugh Gaitskell: A Political Biography* (London, 1979). Professor Williams's account of the Suez venture is a very full one, but the sequence of Gaitskell's actions is more succinctly summarised in his *The Diary of Hugh Gaitskell 1945–1956* (London, 1983), pp. 549–622. The Gaitskell diary was kept only intermittently, but Professor Williams has very usefully fleshed it out with speeches, letters and the texts of broadcasts. The pages of the diary to which I have referred thus give a valuable chronological account of Gaitskell's pronouncements during the Suez crisis.

There is an enormous literature on the Suez adventure. Hard though it is to make a selection of very good books, the two which I would choose for the British point of view are Hugh Thomas, *The Suez War* (London, 1985) and Richard Lamb, *The Failure of the Eden Government* (London, 1987). It is interesting that Mr Lamb was a Conservative candidate in Harold Macmillan's old seat of Stockton-on-Tees in 1950, and subsequently (and perhaps significantly) stood three times as a candidate for the Liberal Party. He was unsuccessful on all four occasions.

11 The extraordinary hot-house atmosphere in British government during the whole Suez episode was memorably summarised by Clarissa, Lady Eden (now Lady Avon) when she said, 'I felt as though the Suez Canal was flowing all the time through my drawing room.'

12 Lord Salisbury lisped. According to Lord Dilhorne in his *Memoirs* (London, 1968), pp. 4–5, his question to Conservative MPs whom he consulted was 'Are you for WAB or Hawold?'

13 Moshe Dayan, *Story of My Life* (London, 1976), pp. 180–2. Dayan gives a rather acid account of the negotiations between Britain, France and Israel in preparation for the attack on Egypt. 'Britain's Foreign Minister', Dayan writes, 'may well have been a friendly man, pleasant, charming, amiable. If so, he showed near-genius in concealing these virtues. His manner could not have been more antagonistic. His whole demeanour expressed distaste – for the place, the company and the topic.'

14 During the 1930s Macmillan was a rebel against the Chamberlain government, not only on appeasement, but on economic policy, and in 1936 resigned the Whip for a year over the lifting of sanctions against Italy. He wrote a book, *The Middle Way* (London, 1938), spelling out what he saw to be the advantages of Keynesian policies. To the end of his life Macmillan considered this rather pedestrian work to be an expression of a profound philosophical attitude. Thus, in 1966, he caused it to be republished by his family firm at the same time as the publication of the first of his six volumes of memoirs, *Winds of Change 1914–1939*.

15 Harold Macmillan, *Riding the Storm* (London, 1969), pp. 356–7.

16 See Patrick Cosgrave, *The Lives of Enoch Powell*, (London, 1989), p. 156. Alone among the Treasury Ministers Powell believed that sterling should be floated and that its value was something that should be determined by the market rather than by the government.

17 Until the election of 1979 these matters were determined by means of discussion in full Cabinet. Mrs Margaret Thatcher introduced a different system by which, if there was a dispute between a spending Department and the Treasury, the matter would be settled by a small Committee of senior Ministers. This Committee – Cabinet Committee No. 9 – is commonly called the 'Star Chamber'. See Peter Hennessy, *Whitehall* (London, 1989), pp. 22–3. The phrase 'Star Chamber' derives from Stuart times, when the Star Chamber was a Court meeting *in camera* which pronounced summary judgement on people deemed to be the King's Enemies.

18 See Patrick Cosgrave, *The Lives of Enoch Powell, loc. cit.*

19 It is the modern fashion that Treasury Ministers do not make public speeches on the economy between the beginning of financial negotiations with the spending Departments and the delivery of the Budget the following year. This rule did not apply in 1957.

20 Birch, as Chief Secretary, sat with the Cabinet.

21 This prudence did not make Gaitskell popular either with the trade unions or the left wing of his own party. Aneurin Bevan and Harold Wilson, indeed, had resigned from the government in protest against the Chancellor's introduction of prescription charges. But his troubles within his own party did not prevent him, with the support of Attlee, who had held on to the leadership in order to frustrate the ambitions of Herbert Morrison, the Foreign Secretary, from comfortably winning the leadership in 1955.

22 Philip M. Williams, *Hugh Gaitskell: A Political Biography* (London, 1979), p. 407.

23 Gaitskell's position was not immediately threatened and he stayed on as Leader until his death in 1963. Harold Wilson succeeded him, beating off challenges by James Callaghan and George Brown.

24 Vassall was a homosexual and had been suborned by the Russians as a result of his sexual activities while serving as an Attaché in the British Embassy in Moscow.

25 Quoted in Alistair Horne, *Macmillan: 1957–1986* (London, 1989), p. 236.

26 The same problems have continued to bedevil British governments up to the time

of writing. In 1989 Nigel Lawson and in 1990 John Major found the inflation consequent upon an expansion of credit – what Major called the growth of the 'plastic economy' – to be their chief headache. They were in a better position than Amory, however, in that public spending was under control. But for both recent Chancellors the principal instrument of reducing inflation was increasing interest rates, this being the successor to Bank Rate.

27 Horne, *op. cit.*, pp. 237 ff.

28 William Keegan's *Mrs Thatcher's Economic Experiment* (London, 1984), pp. 131 ff, provides an elegant defence of what came to be known as 'fine-tuning', which consisted essentially of juggling investment and employment figures with inflation. I am not convinced, however, by his argument and I think that the experiences of the 1970s and the late 1980s support me rather than Mr Keegan.

29 Sir Michael Edwardes has written an account of the rescue of British Leyland in *Back from the Brink* (London, 1983).

30 The following year Amory was made UK High Commissioner to Canada, and so passed for ever from the forefront of national politics.

31 Butler himself denied Macmillan's recollection to the effect that he had wanted neither the Commonwealth Office nor the Foreign Office. See R. A. Butler, *The Art of the Possible* (London, 1971), p. 231.

32 *Op. cit.*, p. 247.

33 Harrod's biography, published in 1958, is not, however, a very reliable source. He is, for example, exceptionally discreet both on Keynes's many misjudgements of economic trends and on his subject's homosexuality. The virtually definitive biography is Robert Skidelsky, *Keynes* (London, 1985).

34 Horne, *op. cit.*, *loc. cit.*

35 One of the major advantages of increasing Bank Rate (or, as we call it today, interest rates) is to attract foreign investment.

36 On 12 August 1957 Macmillan set up a Council on Productivity, Prices and Incomes. This was a first attempt to arrive at agreement between government, industry and unions on the three subjects of its concern. Voluntary wage agreements proved, over the years, to be ineffective. Both the Wilson and the Heath governments therefore introduced legislation to control prices and incomes. The intellectual case for government control of prices and wages is made by Aubrey Jones, *The New Inflation: The Politics of Prices and Incomes* (London, 1973). Mr Jones was elected a Conservative MP in 1950, and successively served as Minister of Fuel and Power and Minister of Supply. In 1965 Harold Wilson appointed him as first Chairman of the Prices and Incomes Board, and he resigned from Parliament.

37 Harold Wilson, *The Labour Government 1964–70* (London, ed. 1971), p. 25. It is interesting to observe that Macmillan and Wilson enjoyed the warmest of personal relations. A great tradition of political civility was lost when Macmillan retired. Wilson could stand neither Home nor Edward Heath. Mrs Thatcher could not stand Wilson, James Callaghan nor Neil Kinnock. Her dislike of them was returned in full measure.

38 For Churchill's reorganisation of government, see Martin Gilbert, *Winston S. Churchill: Finest Hour 1939–41* (London, 1983), pp. 3–22.

39 Robens had been a disciple of Ernest Bevin. He was thus of the old school of Labour politics, and he was distressed by what he saw as the increasing influence of the ideological left wing of the Labour Party. He was therefore pleased to be given both a traditional industry to run and a peerage. He took the job 'much to the annoyance of my own party', according to Macmillan as quoted in Horne, *op. cit.* p. 250.

40 *Op. cit.*, p. 253.

41 Horne, *op. cit.*, p. 335, quotes the view widely held at the time, that Lubbock, who made much of his service in the Welsh Guards, was the sort of candidate the Tories should have chosen. Instead, however, they chose a protégé of Butler's, Peter Goldman, who had been given a job by Butler in the Conservative Research Department after the war. Goldman was a man of extraordinary brilliance, but, though charming in private, he was cold in public. He was also Jewish, and the result was believed by Conservative Central Office to have been affected by the anti-Semitism of the voters. After the humiliation of Orpington, he left politics for good.

4 CONSENSUS AT HOME

1 One of Heath's rare ventures into humour in public was to say, in an interview with Robin Day on *Panorama* immediately after his appointment, 'I am neither a Lord, nor a privy nor a seal'

2 See F. S. Northedge, 'British foreign policy' in F. S. Northedge, (ed) *The Foreign Policies of the Powers* (London, 1968), pp. 150-85. The theory of the tripod was not a new one, although it was most elegantly formulated by Eden. The late Professor Northedge's major work, *The Troubled Giant: Britain among the Great Powers 1916-1939* (London, 1966) traces its origins as far back as the end of the First World War. See, in particular, pp. 223-47.

3 When the Heath government finally succeeded in its application to join the Common Market a transitional arrangement was made on behalf of New Zealand for her lamb exports. The terms of this agreement were never honestly kept by the EEC. Australia and New Zealand have, therefore, increasingly turned to Asian markets, as Canada has turned to the United States. American and Canadian cooperation culminated in the signing of the USA-Canadian Free Trade Agreement, which was signed in 1988 and became fully effective in 1991.

4 Macmillan lost Stockton in the 1945 General Election, but he retained such affection for it that when, eventually, he was made an Earl he took Stockton as his title.

5 George Hutchinson, *The Last Edwardian at No. 10: An Impression of Harold Macmillan* (London, 1980), pp. 83-4. Hutchinson died the day after the publication of this book, following a long and painful illness. Many others than Harold Macmillan had cause to feel gratitude to him. He was my mentor from the moment I started in journalism, and he was an unfailing fount of kindness and wise advice.

6 I once asked Enoch Powell who, first as a Minister of Cabinet rank and then as a Cabinet Minister, attended all the meetings at which Heath reported back to his

colleagues on proceedings in Brussels, what in his view were Heath's principal qualities. He replied that, in his judgement, these were Heath's incredible mastery of detail, which was combined with a capacity to speak at length and answer immensely technical questions without ever having recourse to notes or a brief.

7 Quoted in Horne, *op. cit.*, p. 428.

8 The full text of the Elysée press conference is to be found in *Major Addresses, Statements and Press Conferences of General Charles de Gaulle, May 19, 1958-January 31, 1964*, published by the Quai d'Orsay and distributed through French Embassies all over the world early in 1964. The answer to a question on the British application ran to rather more than four pages. See also Nora Beloff, *The General Says No* (London, 1963), pp. 11-19 and pp. 148-172.

9 Hallstein, who believed in the creation of a federal Europe, found himself in constant opposition to de Gaulle. As a result, France opposed his reappointment as President of the Commission in 1966. De Gaulle enforced his will on this appointment (which was regarded as a routine matter by the other partners) as well as on various other matters by the policy of the 'Empty Chair'. French politicians and diplomats simply stopped turning up for EEC meetings. The tactic worked. See John Newhouse, *Collision in Brussels: The Common Market Crisis of 30 June 1965* (London, 1967), p. 162.

10 Anthony Howard, *op. cit.*, pp. 288 ff.

11 This quotation is from Macleod's celebrated review of Randolph Churchill, *The Fight for the Tory Leadership* (London, 1964). It is reprinted in full in George Hutchinson, *op. cit.*, pp. 121-41.

12 See above, p. 68.

13 Horne, *op. cit.*, pp. 339 ff.

14 Butler's conduct on the occasion about to be described may well have been an important factor in Macmillan's determination the following year to prevent him becoming Prime Minister.

15 Butler was given the task of winding up the Central African Federation of Northern Rhodesia (now Zambia), Southern Rhodesia (now Zimbabwe) and Nyasaland (now Malawi). He did so to the satisfaction of white and black politicians alike. See Patrick Cosgrave, *R. A. Butler: An English Life* (London, 1981), pp. 107 ff. Butler's responsibilities at the time were staggering: apart from being Secretary of State for Colonial Affairs and Home Secretary, he was Leader of the House of Commons.

16 Eccles, as Lord Eccles, was to return to government in 1970, when Edward Heath made him Minister for the Arts. He is a highly cultivated man, with wide-ranging artistic interests. However, in the 1970 government he was saddled with introducing highly unpopular measures to impose museum charges and his arrogance in pushing the government's proposals (which were later withdrawn) earned him no friends.

17 In a later incarnation Deedes was to become Editor of the *DailyTelegraph*. He was given his peerage in 1988 on the recommendation of Mrs Thatcher.

18 It was to happen again after the General Election of 1964.

19 See Harold Wilson, *The Governance of Britain* (London, 1978), pp. 12-21.

20 It has been suggested by opposition parties throughout the post-war years that

governments can be overthrown if substantial numbers of Members from their own side either vote against them or abstain on a censure motion. The example usually mentioned is that of the fall of Neville Chamberlain in May 1940. But all that happened then was that the Prime Minister decided he could not go on and he handed over to another Conservative, Winston Churchill. Churchill formed a coalition, but he declared to the King, his intention, if the Labour Party would not cooperate, simply to form a new Conservative Government. Of his interview with George VI, when he kissed hands as Prime Minister, Churchill wrote 'The King had made no stipulation about the Government being National in character, and I felt that my commission was in no formal way dependent upon this point . . . If I found it impossible to come to terms with the Opposition Parties, I should not have been constitutionally debarred from trying to form the strongest Government possible of all who would stand by the country in the hour of peril, provided that such a Government could command a majority in the House of Commons.' See Winston S. Churchill, *The Second World War: Volume I The Gathering Storm* (London, 1948), p. 525.

21 Philip M. Williams, *The Diary of Hugh Gaitskell* (London, 1983), p. 591 footnote.

22 See above, p. 84.

23 See Anthony Howard, *op. cit.*, pp. 297-8.

24 Horne, *op. cit.*, p. 470.

25 Macmillan always believed that this Budget had no effect on the downturn in the economy, which began in the autumn of the following year. Most economists and historians now believe, however, that the very serious problems that Harold Wilson faced on assuming power in October 1964 were in large part of Maudling's creation.

26 *Op. cit.*, pp. 529 ff.

27 It was Hailsham who signed the Treaty in Moscow, in his capacity as Minister for Science.

28 In Macmillan's time the Leader of the Party attended the Conference only on the last day. Edward Heath introduced the innovation of attending the Conference throughout.

29 In his later years Macmillan, quite justifiably, complained that politicians could be damaged when a spy or traitor was captured, whereas capture should have redounded to the credit of the security services and the government.

30 A retiring Prime Minister remains in office until the Sovereign sends for his or her successor. While, theoretically, the Sovereign can send for anybody he or she chooses, in practice the governing party picks its Leader and informs Buckingham Palace, whereupon the new Leader is summoned.

31 The second volume of Alistair Horne's official biography of Macmillan, first published in 1989 and after revision reprinted in 1991, is disappointingly evasive on the subject of the succession in 1963. See the latter edition, pp. 527 ff.

32 Alistair Horne, *op. cit.*, (edn, 1989), pp. 556 ff.

33 The by-election was achieved by the resignation of the sitting Conservative Member, George Younger. The Party showed its gratitude to Younger by procuring for him the Tory nomination for Ayr, a seat which he won in the

General Election of October 1964. He was later to hold junior office in the 1970 government and high office under Mrs Margaret Thatcher.

34 Quoted in George Hutchinson, *op. cit.*, p. 133.

35 The 1922 Committee consists now as it did then of all Conservative back-benchers. Shadow Ministers – when the Party is in opposition – and Ministers when the Party is in power are excluded from meetings, unless invited by the Chairman of the Committee. Founded in 1922, the Committee initially consisted only of Members elected in the General Election of that year. Its power became evident, however, when the following year *all* Conservative back-benchers were invited to join it. On 23 October 1923 the Committee met at the Carlton Club and brought down the Coalition Government of the Lloyd George Liberals and the Conservative Party. 'Yet as all backbench Conservatives', as Peter G. Richards, in *Honourable Members* (London, 1959), p. 99, writes, 'can attend the 1922 Committee, it can claim to be fully representative of opinion in the Party. Such a Committee may seem inchoate, but it has often had profound influence on the direction of Conservative politics.' The historian of the Committee to whose work most attention must be paid is Philip (now Sir Philip) Goodhart, *The 1922: The Story of the 1922 Committee* (London, 1973), *passim*.

36 Lord Home, *The Way the Wind Blows* (London, 1976), p. 258.

37 It need hardly be said that, once in power, Harold Wilson conveniently forgot this undertaking.

5   THE PROMISE OF WHITE HEAT

1 See George Hutchinson, *op. cit.*, p. 133

2 See above, pp. 49–50.

3 There is a considerable literature on the whole question of the cost to the United Kingdom of Harold Wilson's determination to stave off devaluation. But I would cite, particularly, Wilfred Beckermann (ed.), *The Labour Government's Economic Record 1964–1970* (London, 1972), pp. 11–29. All of the authors in this compilation were sympathetic to the aspirations of the Labour Government; but they came to realise that the attempts to sustain the exchange rate severely damaged the government. At the time of writing, a Conservative government is seeking again to sustain the rate by membership of the Exchange Rate Mechanism of the European Monetary System. It remains to be seen whether this will prove as disastrous as were the attempts of the Wilson administration after 1964. In my view it will.

4 Harold Wilson, *The Labour Government 1964–70* (London, edn. 1971), pp. 21–40.

5 The first Wilson Government was guilty of creating a new Department without giving it the tools it required for the job in hand. It is difficult to mount any reasoned defence of the conduct of policy by the Department of Economic Affairs during its short life. However, in so far as the job can be done, it was done in typically robust fashion by George Brown, see his *In My Way* (London, edn. 1972), pp. 87–117. See also Peter Hennessy, *Whitehall* (London, 1989), pp. 182–3 and James Callaghan, *Time and Chance* (London, 1987) pp. 165–6. The Treasury in due course, aided by severe economic difficulties, squeezed the DEA so hard

that, in 1966, it was abolished. Wilson had the sheer gall to explain that the Department had been such a success that it was no longer needed.

6 See Harold Wilson, *op. cit*, p. 98. Sorenson was immediately given a peerage, as was Frank Bowles, who was, likewise unwillingly, persuaded to stand aside for Frank Cousins, the General Secretary of the TGWU.

7 See Harold Wilson, *op. cit.*, p. 31.

8 See Alan Bullock, *Ernest Bevin: Minister of Labour* (London, 1967), pp. 95–8.

9 Edelman's sexual indiscretions were notorious, and this meant that after the Profumo affair, of which he and his Security Adviser, George Wigg, had made so much, Wilson felt unable to give him a job in government.

10 The Cambridge literary critic, Dr F. R. Leavis, replied to Snow, and savaged him, in a lecture at Peterhouse, Cambridge, which was reprinted in the *Spectator* as 'C. P. Snow and the Two Cultures: A Reply', 3 August 1963. Slightly amended, this was published in pamphlet form as *Two Cultures?* later in the same year. It is amusing to note that the man who was to be Harold Wilson's scientific guru published all his works with the family firm of Harold Macmillan.

11 The Tactical Strike and Reconnaisance Aircraft, Mark 2, was probably the most original military aircraft produced since 1945. A fighter bomber, it could fly both at exceptionally low and exceptionally high altitudes. Production was cancelled by the Minister of Aviation, Roy Jenkins, in January 1965. For good measure Jenkins also cancelled the P1154, a Vertical Short Take-off and Landing fighter plane, and another V/STOL, a transport craft. The TSR2 programme was never reinstated, but the Conservative Government elected in 1970 did restore the V/STOL research programme. The programme led to the manufacture of the Harrier jet class, which proved so invaluable in the Falklands War of 1983.

12 The principal intellectual proponent of this policy of combined spending and control of prices and incomes was Antony Crosland. See his *The Future of Socialism* (London, 1962), *passim*. In 1974 Crosland produced a revised version of this book, *Socialism Now*, in which he retracted his views about inducing growth by public expenditure, though he retained his belief in prices and incomes control. The opposition to the Crosland thesis is expressed in virtually every publication by the Institute of Economic Affairs, but it is perhaps most pungently summarised in a collection of essays by the American economist, Milton Friedman, in *An Economist's Protest* (New Jersey, 1972), *passim*. The particular interest of Professor Friedman's collection of essays, which appeared in *Newsweek* during the sixties and early seventies, is that he offered predictions of how the American and, by extension, the British economy would behave. In all cases his predictions were fulfilled.

13 A poll was published in the *Sunday Times* on 7 January 1965 which suggested that three-quarters of Conservative backbenchers would have voted for Home.

14 The rules were changed in 1974, particularly to allow new candidates to enter on the second ballot.

15 The Labour Party has usually, though not invariably, selected its Leaders from men with either an academic or a trade union background. Exceptions are Clement Attlee, who came from a well-to-do business background, distinguished himself as a major in the First World War, and turned to Labour as a result of his devoted work in the slums of the East End of London, and Neil Kinnock.

Though Kinnock, the son of a miner, did take a degree he did not proceed in academic life, and his active trade unionism was vestigial.

16 Many Tories and some of the press made fun of a short, tubby, unathletic, middle-aged man attempting to model himself on Kennedy, but the satire never stuck.

17 The phrase is actually the title of the first chapter in the memoirs of Edward Short, *Whip to Wilson* (London, 1989). Short is now Lord Glenamara.

18 See above, p. 51.

19 See below, pp. 118–122.

20 See David Lloyd George, *War Memoirs of David Lloyd George* (London, 1938), pp. 32 ff. See also Geoffrey K. Fry, *The Growth of Government* (London, 1979), pp. 91 ff. Dr Fry's book is an invaluable guide to the phenomenon of government growth. It is only fair to say, however, that Dr Fry believes the growth of government to be entirely beneficial, while my view is that it was, in general, while not wholly harmful, very nearly so.

21 The Institute of Economic Affairs, which was created in 1948 by Ralph (now Lord) Harris and Arthur Seldon, was brought into being essentially to attack Keynesian ideas. Its boardroom is adorned by a photograph of Keynes, to which is appended this quotation. The IEA was the principal source of ideas for Margaret Thatcher after she became Leader of the Conservative Party in 1975.

22 Timothy Raison, *Why Conservative?* (London, 1964), pp. 28–45 and Chris Patten, *The Tory Case* (London, 1983), pp. 23–34. The reference I have given, Mr Patten's chapter 'Morality and Conservatism', outlines with great power the case for collectivist Conservatism. The interested reader can consult Austin Mitchell, *The Case for Labour* (London, 1983) and Alan Beith, *The Case for the Liberal Party and the Alliance* (London, 1983).

23 *The Road to Serfdom* (London, ed. 1976). In 178 pages Hayek demolished Keynes's work, which ran to 786 pages.

24 See Peter Jenkins, *Mrs Thatcher's Revolution: The Ending of the Socialist Era* (London, 1987), pp. 30–49. Jenkins is particularly interesting on the moral values of Socialism in the same way as Raison and Patten are on Conservatism.

25 The best account of the way in which the trade union movement created the Labour Party as its instrument is to be found in Henry Pelling, *Origins of the Labour Party* (Oxford, edn. 1963), *passim*.

26 Wilson was not the first prophet of efficient Socialism. This was Antony Crosland. See C. A. R. Crosland, 'The Future of the Left', *Encounter* (March, 1960). An interesting commentary on this issue is to be found in Samuel H. Beer, *Modern British Politics* (London, edn. 1971), pp. 210 ff. Wilson's own view of the matter is to be found throughout his account of the Labour government of 1964–1970, but especially in *op. cit.*, pp. 52 ff.

6   THE FAILURE OF A MAJORITY

1 'Full employment' does not mean what a literal reading would suggest but, rather, a low level of unemployment depending upon which statistical evidence is used. It is worth pointing out that governments of both parties have frequently changed the rules of evidence.

2 The view that there was something wrong with the country rather than the government of the day became very fashionable in the second half of the 1960s. There is a considerable literature on the matter, but that view is most succinctly expressed in Anthony King (ed.), *Why is Britain becoming harder to govern?* (London, 1976), *passim*. Professor King's work was based on a series of BBC radio programmes. For all that it was published a decade after the events described above, it represents a very general view of British politics from 1966 onwards. For an excellent general guide to the institutions of British government see Malcolm Wallis and A. H. Hanson, *Governing Britain: A Guide-Book to Political Institutions* (London, edn. 1975).

3 James Callaghan, *Time and Chance* (London, 1987), pp. 193 ff. In this discussion of his time as Chancellor, Callaghan tells an interesting story. One of his proposals in 1966 was to raise taxes on betting. He recalls that Iain Macleod, the Shadow Chancellor, sent him a copy of the Edgar Wallace thriller *The Calendar*. Macleod, himself a devoted gambler, was sceptical about the amount of revenue which could be raised from a betting tax, and he wanted his opposite number to read the novel, which is essentially a description of how the bookmakers avoided a betting tax imposed by Winston Churchill forty years earlier.

4 Callaghan, *op. cit.*, p. 199.

5 It is important, in the 1990s, to realise that the average level of inflation between 1951 and 1964 was under 3 per cent.

6 Harold Wilson, *op. cit.*, pp. 587 ff. Cp. James Callaghan, *op. cit.*, pp. 194 ff.

7 On page 589 of his memoirs, Wilson italicises some passages from his broadcast which were not so rendered in the press release.

8 Harold Wilson, *op. cit.*, p. 590.

9 The classical account of the attempt by the Labour government to reform trade union law is to be found in Peter Jenkins, *The Battle of Downing Street* (London, 1970), *passim*. Perhaps the most famous quotation from this book is Harold Wilson's remark to Hugh Scanlon, 'Get your tanks off my lawn, Hughie.' At this time, it should be remembered, Russian tanks were parked on the lawn of the presidential palace of Alexander Dubcek in Czechoslovakia. Wilson denied the truth of Jenkins's account of events. I, however, believe Mr Jenkins.

10 At the beginning of each parliamentary session the Parliamentary Labour Party elects a Chairman to present its views to the Leader of the Party.

11 This letter was widely reported, but my quotation comes from the *Daily Telegraph* of 17 June 1969.

12 Bernard Levin in *The Times* then and subsequently has used a delightful character, Mr Solomon Binding, who eternally enters into agreements which he has no intention of keeping.

13 Neither Jones nor Scanlon have written their memoirs. The subsequent careers of both men are, at least, entertaining. I lunched with Victor Feather towards the end of 1970. He predicted that Jones would never accept the peerage which he would certainly be offered when he retired from the TGWU. He was correct: Jones continues to live in his council flat in Brixton and campaigns for old age pensioners. Feather predicted, further, that Scanlon would accept a peerage as an act of reparation to his wife's family. Scanlon was a Communist when he married;

his wife's family were horrified since they were devout Roman Catholics. Scanlon, Feather believed, would make it up to them by taking ermine.

14 Edward Boyle, who died in 1981, always declined to write an autobiography, and no writer has ever taken up the task of writing a biography of him. This I regard as a great pity for, though he never held senior office, Boyle was a considerable symbolic influence on Conservative Party politics from the moment of his resignation from the government over the Suez War.

15 There is a full discussion of the consequences for all parties of Powell's speech in Patrick Cosgrave, *The Lives of Enoch Powell* (London, 1989), pp. 241 ff.

16 Wilson makes no mention of this collusion between his own private office and Powell in his memoirs. The Powell archive, and much anecdotal evidence, however, convinces me that such collusion took place. Wilson was a politician determined to win at all costs, but he kept his contacts with Powell confidential because of the continuing hostility of large sections of the Labour Party to Powell.

17 The elaborate proposals for trade union law reform were drafted, virtually single-handed, by Steven Abbott in the Conservative Research Department. Alas, Abbott, a man of great charm and generosity of spirit, did not live to see the full impact of legislation very similar to that which he designed implemented by successive governments headed by Margaret Thatcher.

18 I was one of those entrusted with briefing Heath for his morning press conferences. I, like others, became convinced that he had given up the ghost. It is greatly to his credit that he recovered his morale and fought back for the remaining ten days of the campaign.

7   THE UNQUIET REVOLUTION

1 Like Lord Home, Lord Hailsham, as Quintin Hogg now is, kept the title that he had had before, but with a different territorial designation. Lord Home, when he retired after the February 1974 General Election, took the designation of his home in Scotland and became Lord Home of the Hirsel. Quintin Hogg became Lord Hailsham of St Marylebone: St Marylebone was the constituency he had represented since 1963. In both cases the title was a simple barony. Since both men had renounced their hereditary peerages, and by law could not reclaim them, they had to re-enter the House of Lords at the lowest rank. Their sons, however, when the time comes, can, if they wish, assume the hereditary titles.

2 The present author was seconded by the Conservative Research Department to work with Macleod during the 1970 election campaign. He was in considerable pain throughout, and deeply distressed by the death of his mother at the end of the first week. I found him an entrancing and inspiring man, even though there were not many points of policy on which we agreed.

3 Michael Wolff remained close to Heath until his sad and untimely death in 1975. After the defeat of the Conservative government in the General Election of February 1974 Heath made Wolff Director-General of Conservative Central Office. He was dismissed immediately after Margaret Thatcher's election as Leader in April 1975.

4 Until we have Heath's long-promised memoirs, we will not know how he justifies the strange lethargy which preceded the October speech.

5 J. Bruce-Gardyne, *Whatever Happened to the Quiet Revolution?* (London, 1974), p. 5. The, alas, late Lord Bruce-Gardyne, in this short volume produced a moving, and often sarcastic, lament for the failure of the Heath administration to fulfil any of its major promises. The remark about production, distribution and exchange is deliberately taken from the stated aims of the Labour Party's constitution, and was designed to reflect Bruce-Gardyne's general, and often-expressed, contempt for Party Conferences.

6 Were negotiations to be satisfactorily concluded, it was necessary for the applicants to pass legislation conforming to the terms of entry. In Norway, however, a referendum on whether or not to join was required before legislation was introduced into parliament. Despite the vigorous efforts of the Norwegian government, the result of this referendum was an overwhelming rejection of entry into the EEC.

7 Canada was much less perturbed about the British application, for the great bulk of her trade was and is with the United States. In 1989 the two countries created a free trade area between them.

8 See Patrick Cosgrave, *The Lives of Enoch Powell* (London, 1989) pp. 256 ff. Since the Bill was a constitutional one, it had to be taken in a Committee of the Whole House on the floor of the Chamber. There was a further difficulty: by convention a constitutional Bill cannot be guillotined, that is to say that the government of the day cannot curtail debate.

9 Of those Labour pro-Marketeers, one, Roy Jenkins, was a frontbencher. He was Shadow Home Secretary, as well as being Deputy Leader of the Party.

10 Labour returned to power in 1974 and, in 1975, in accordance with an election promise, held a referendum on continued membership. But there was never much hope of British withdrawal.

11 Like most of Heath's administrative reforms, the responsibilities and structure of the Department of the Environment were laid down in very carefully drafted research papers prepared before the General Election. This meant that relevant legislation could be introduced quickly. The Conservatives took most of their proposals from the report produced by the Royal Commission chaired by Lord Redcliffe-Maud in 1969. It is pleasing to note that the man who drafted the Conservative document was Chris Patten, who was to become Secretary of State for the Environment nearly twenty years later.

12 The CPRS was abolished by Mrs Margaret Thatcher in 1983.

13 Emotions run high on any discussion on the affairs of Northern Ireland. To this day it is not clear whether or not the B-Specials were involved in the baton charge against a predominantly idealistic and youthful parade. In my opinion they were.

14 The events of 1968 and as they continue to this day have been described in many good books. From these I select two: Ed Malone and Andy Pollak, *Paisley* (London, 1986) and Chris Ryder, *The RUC: A Force Under Fire* (London, 1989). Mr Ryder's book is particularly valuable for the sensitive way in which he explains how it came about that young policemen, accustomed to a given structure, were taken aback by demonstrations against that structure.

15 Clauses 2 and 3 of the Constitution of the Republic of Ireland lay down a claim by the Republic to the sovereignty of the whole island. This claim is enshrined in

Southern Irish belief or, as it may be, mythology. The fact that a Republican Taoiseach (the word means Leader, but is most conveniently translated as Prime Minister) should visit Belfast in order to make an agreement was immeasurably dramatic for the Irish on both sides of the border.

16 See James Callaghan, *Time and Chance* (London, 1987), pp. 250 ff. Lord Callaghan wrote an earlier book, concerned essentially with Ulster, *A House Divided*. It is, however, far less interesting and less revealing than *Time and Chance*.

17 For the next few years the phrase 'security forces' encompassed both the Army and the RUC, the former being in complete control of the latter.

18 The 'temporary provisions' were extended in 1973 and remain in force to this day.

8   THE COLLAPSE OF THE 'QUIET REVOLUTION'

1 See Tony Benn, *Arguments for Socialism* (ed. Chris Mullin, London 1979), *passim*.

2 The only occasion in this century on which the Conservative Party was seriously, and even disastrously, divided was just before and just after the First World War. The dispute was about whether the United Kingdom should adopt a policy of Free Trade towards the rest of the world, or impose Imperial Preference, whereby the countries of the Empire would enjoy vastly more access to British markets than any other non-Imperial country. But, then, the principal proponents of Imperial Preference were the followers of Joseph Chamberlain, and Chamberlain was a former Liberal, who led his supporters out of the old Liberal Party in the nineteenth century when William Gladstone decided to embark on a policy of Home Rule for Ireland.

3 Harold Wilson, *The Labour Government 1964–70* (London, edn. 1974), p. 18.

4 Harold Wilson, *op. cit.*, p. 992.

5 As Lady Falkender recalls in Marcia Falkender, *Downing Street in Perspective* (London, 1983), p. 29, Heath took particular care to be generous to his predecessor. Initially, he occupied only the office space at No. 10, and gave the Wilsons ample time to move out of the living accommodation. Further – and this gave Lady Falkender particular satisfaction, since it made her work considerably easier – the new Prime Minister ordained that Wilson should have a car and driver, paid for by the state, *ad infinitum*. This practice has been continued by Prime Ministers of both parties from that day to this.

6 See Harold Wilson, *The Governance of Britain* (London, 1976), pp. 77–106.

7 The best account of the intra-Party Labour conflict over EEC membership is to be found in James Callaghan, *op. cit.*, pp. 294 ff. This account is highly self-serving but, nonetheless, illuminating on the conduct of foreign policy by the third Wilson administration.

8 This principle was most elegantly summarised not in British but in French politics in the 1930s, when a French Prime Minister, Léon Blum, stated that a Socialist Party – the one of which he was head – could have no enemies to the left. See Eric Heffer, *Never a Yes Man* (London, 1991), pp. 183 ff. Heffer applied the Blum principle to the two main extreme left-wing organisations, Militant and the Socialist Workers' Party. He did, however, draw the line at extending the hand of friendship to the Communist Party. He died just before this book, his autobiography, was published.

9 See R. T. McKenzie, *Angels in Marble* (London, 1972), *passim*. Professor McKenzie spent the last twenty years of his life trying to explain this singular fact of British political life. His work remains the definitive study of the phenomenon. To a Conservative, the angelic nature of the trade unionist is that he tends more often than not to vote Tory. The marble refers to his refusal to change his industrial practices.

10 Nearly all legislation introduced by a government of whatever party is prepared by a team of lawyers known collectively as parliamentary draughtsmen. The 1971 Act, however, was not referred, except for small technical matters, to parliamentary draughtsmen: it was wholly a Party political exercise.

11 Later head of the Freedom Association.

12 The Official Solicitor is one of the more obscure figures in the British legal system and rarely attracts public attention. He has, however, the right to intervene in the judicial process whenever he considers that wrong has been done or judges have given a decision against what the Solicitor considers to be natural justice.

13 To the end of his life R. A Butler regretted the fact that he had decided, when Chancellor of the Exchequer, not to float the currency. When a currency floats, decisions about its value in relation to other currencies depend entirely on the judgement of individual firms. If, however, a government decides to lay down a fixed exchange rate for its own currency in relation to other currencies it will, in the end, be obliged to subsidise fluctuations in the international market. See Patrick Cosgrave, *op. cit.*, pp. 85 ff.

14 The acronym for these bodies has passed into the language as QUANGO.

15 See Conor Cruise O'Brien, *The Siege* (London, 1986), pp. 530 ff. The 1973 rise in oil prices gave the oil-producing Arab nations, other than Iran, to understand that they could blackmail their customers; and so they did. Saudi Arabia, Iraq, and all the Gulf States realised that political ends could be pursued by money. The unfortunate nation left out was Jordan, which had no oil.

16 This was the first of two occasions on which Keith Joseph's friends were surprised that he was not made Chancellor of the Exchequer, the second being in 1979 under Margaret Thatcher. The Department of Health and Social Security was created by Richard Crossman in November 1968. In order to convey the impression that health care and social care was a seamless web, the political head of the Department was designated Secretary of State for Social Services.

17 Between 1906 and 1914 six Bills providing for Home Rule for Scotland were given their Second Readings in the House of Commons. None, however, reached the Committee stage. On numerous occasions from 1914 onwards petitions for some form of Home Rule for the Principality and Scotland received substantial support. In April 1945 the first Scottish Nationalist MP was elected to Westminster: he was defeated in the following General Election. It was not until July 1966 that the first Plaid Cymru MP was elected, and his success was followed on 2 November 1967 by an SNP victory. Both major parties endorsed the principle of devolution shortly thereafter, Edward Heath, doing so in what came to be known rather grandiosely as the Declaration of Perth on 19 May 1968.

18 Lord Redcliffe-Maud's terms of reference excluded Scotland and Wales, but

another Royal Commission – also appointed by Harold Wilson – headed by Lord Kilbrandon, reported on 31 October 1973 in favour of a directly-elected Scottish assembly.

19 William Whitelaw, *The Whitelaw Memoirs* (London, 1989), pp. 131 ff.

20 David Butler and Dennis Kavanagh, *The British General Election of February 1974* (London, 1974), p. 31

21 See Patrick Cosgrave, *The Lives of Enoch Powell* (London, 1989), pp. 347 ff.

22 It was Harold Wilson's initial temptation to claim victory on the night on 28 February. However, he accepted the advice of his Deputy Leader, James Callaghan, to remain silent until the Heath-Thorpe talks failed, which Callaghan was certain they would. Thus, on Monday afternoon Wilson was able to re-enter No. 10, Downing Street. See James Callaghan, *op. cit*, pp. 281 ff. and Roy Jenkins, *A Life at the Centre* (London, 1991), pp. 370 ff.

9 THE BEGINNING OF THE END

1 Callaghan, for all his failures in office, is the only politician this century to have held all four major offices of state. He was, successively, Chancellor of the Exchequer, Home Secretary, Foreign Secretary and Prime Minister.

2 James Callaghan, *Time and Chance* (London, 1987), p. 311. It is unnecessary to go into the tortuous details of what were essentially window-dressing negotiations, but the interested reader will find an admirably detailed account of them in Chapter 10 of *Time and Chance*. The budgetary problem was only addressed with resolution when Mrs Thatcher became Prime Minister in 1979. She was successful.

3 See Kenneth O. Morgan, *The People's Peace: British History 1945–1989* (London, 1990), pp. 3–28.

4 See Robert Blake and John Patten (eds), *The Conservative Opportunity* (Oxford, 1976). Lord Blake and Mr Patten (at the time of writing Secretary of State for Education and Science) detected the significance of the intellectual turmoil which overtook the Conservative Party between 1965 and 1979. In a memorable phrase Lord Blake observes, in his preface, 'Nothing is more powerful than an idea whose time has come'. Unfortunately for Heath, the truth of that adage was to be seen clearly only by Margaret Thatcher.

5 Within days of the defeat of October 1974 a meeting of a number of unsuccessful parliamentary candidates took place at Nicholas Ridley's London home. A strong but unfounded rumour was abroad that Heath was prepared to stand down immediately. If this had happened William Whitelaw would have been the undoubted favourite for the succession. Ridley and his guests were determined that in this event there should be an ideological challenger. One of their number was deputed to telephone me to ask me to find out what Joseph's position was. I did so, explaining the circumstances. He replied, 'You can tell them that I will be a candidate whenever a leadership election takes place.'

6 Nicholas Ridley, *'My Style of Government': The Thatcher Years* (London, 1991), p.6. For a full account of the battle for the leadership see Patrick Cosgrave, *Margaret Thatcher: A Tory and her Party* (London, 1978), pp. 30–74.

7 By 'our lot' she meant the economic Right. Because of her later career and long

years in power it is too readily assumed that in 1975 Margaret Thatcher was, herself, a leading figure among those who advocated the doctrine of monetarism – essentially a doctrine combining tight controls on public expenditure, low taxation and what has come to be called privatisation. It is important to remember that, though she was sympathetic to monetarist ideas, Mrs Thatcher was not intimate with any of the leading monetarists in 1975.

8 Patrick Cosgrave, *op. cit.*, p. 43.

9 Heath's contention was wrong. See Philip (now Sir Philip) Goodhart, *The 1922* (London, 1973), pp. 140 ff. Goodhart published a letter in *The Times* on 17 November 1974 reaffirming his undoubtedly accurate view that the authority of the 1922 Executive continues from one of its own elections to the next, whether or not a General Election has intervened.

10 The full Committee consists of all Conservative backbenchers. It is popularly believed that it was born out of a meeting of Conservative Members at the Carlton Club in 1922 which overthrew the Leader, Austin Chamberlain, and thus the coalition government headed by David Lloyd George. In fact it was initially merely a group of Members elected for the first time in the General Election of 1922. Its usefulness as a forum for backbench opinion became quickly evident, and it was therefore expanded to include all backbenchers.

11 William Whitelaw, *The Whitelaw Memoirs* (London, 1989), p. 141.

12 James Callaghan, *op. cit.*, pp. 272–8.

13 Michael Foot's position, when he was insisting on the abolition of all the trades union law reforms introduced by the 1970 Conservative government, was all the more powerful in that it was known that he could not be bought with office. In 1968 Harold Wilson had offered Foot the post of Home Secretary – with a free hand so far as legislation was concerned – provided only that he would support the British Government's backing of the American war effort in Vietnam. Foot turned Wilson down.

14 Collective Cabinet responsibility is a cherished part of the tradition of British politics. It was best expressed by Lord Melbourne, when he was Prime Minister in the 1830s. When division in the Cabinet had become known to the public, Melbourne said, 'Gentlemen, it doesn't matter what we believe, but we must all say the same thing'. The most elegant account of the Labour Party's difficulties on the European issue is to be found in Roy Jenkins, *A Life at the Centre* (London, 1991), pp. 307–26 and pp. 399–418.

15 See Bernard Donoughue, *Prime Minister: The Conduct of Policy under Harold Wilson and James Callaghan* (London, 1987), *passim*. 'Originally', Lord Donoughue, as he now is, writes in his preface, 'I had in mind to write a much larger, more detailed and comprehensive work on the 1974–9 Labour Government.' Lord Donoughue goes on to tell us that business preoccupations took up so much of his time that he felt he could not undertake the major work. So incisive is the slender volume that he has produced that every student of modern British politics will deeply regret that he could not find the time nor the energy to compose the larger study.

16 See Patrick Cosgrave, *Thatcher: The First Term* (London, 1985), pp. 1–27.

17 See *Staying Power: Peter Walker An Autobiography* (London, 1991), pp. 132–44.

Walker was dropped from the Shadow Cabinet immediately upon Mrs Thatcher's election as Leader, but brought back into government as Minister for Agriculture after her victory in 1979. It is greatly to his credit that he declined the title of Secretary of State, finding it to be excessively grandiose.

18 Robert Carr, the Shadow Chancellor under Heath, told her that he did not want to serve, and proposed to retire from politics when the next General Election was called.

19 The first was Reginald Maudling, appointed by Heath in 1965. In both cases the Deputy was the man who had finished second in the leadership ballot.

20 William Whitelaw, *op. cit.*, p. 143.

21 William Whitelaw, *op. cit.*, *loc. cit.*

22 Bernard Donoughue, *op. cit.*, pp. 126–7.

23 Natural wastage, or unexpected events, may, of course, do the job for the Prime Minister. In 1964, for example, the inability of the Foreign Secretary, Patrick Gordon Walker, to win a parliamentary seat, and the increasingly poor health of the Home Secretary, Sir Frank Soskice, gave Wilson an early opportunity to make changes.

24 Harold Wilson, *The Labour Government 1964–70* (London, edn. 1974), *passim*, but especially Chapters One and Three.

25 Roy Jenkins, *A Life at the Centre* (London, 1991), pp. 364 ff. In March 1974 Jenkins instructed Bernard Donoughue to tell Harold Wilson that he did not want to be "in his bloody government at all" – *op. cit.* p. 444.

26 Jenkins, *op. cit.*, pp. 444–5.

27 There is a full account of this remarkable adventure in Jenkins, *op. cit*, pp. 534 ff.

28 There were, as there are now, two Unionist parties in Ulster, one led by James Molyneaux and the other by Ian Paisley.

29 The last Speaker's Committee given this task was set up in 1908. Its report is still awaited.

30 An Order in Council, introduced in the House of Commons by the Minister whose Department it concerns, can be debated and even voted down, but it cannot be amended. Orders in Council are occasionally used to refine existing legislation on the mainland. Only in the case of Northern Ireland, however, is all legislation enforced through such Orders. This has the advantage for the government of the day of being able to introduce new legislation for the province late at night when the likelihood is that debate will be very brief. Successive British governments have argued that recourse to such draconian powers is necessary in the fight against terrorism.

31 See James Callaghan, *op. cit.*, pp. 451 ff. See also Patrick Cosgrave, *The Lives of Enoch Powell* (London, 1989), pp. 410 ff.

32 The original, and most enthusiastic, advocate of increased parliamentary representation for Ulster was Enoch Powell. It is therefore ironic that changes in constituency boundaries resulted in the loss of his seat at South Down in the General Election of 1987. Powell had foreseen that he would be in danger but, typically, refused to allow considerations of personal interest to stop him advocating something he saw to be right in principle.

33 It is extremely unusual to guillotine a constitutional bill, which this one was.

34 *op. cit.*, p. 506.

35 There was a great deal of collusion between Conservative and Labour opponents of the bill. Teddy Taylor, now MP for Southend East, but then Shadow Secretary of State for Scotland and Member for Glasgow Cathcart, was cordially detested in the Labour Party. He had been slotted in to speak in the debate against the Bill. However, a senior Labour backbencher advised Mrs Thatcher through an intermediary that an intervention by Taylor might well prevent Labour doubters from taking the opposition line. She therefore changed her plan, and asked Francis Pym, then Shadow Leader of the House, to open the debate for the Tories.

36 See James Callaghan, *op. cit.*, p. 507.

37 See Patrick Cosgrave, *op. cit.*, pp. 258 ff.

38 James Callaghan, *op. cit.*, p. 508.

39 See Peter Jenkins, *The Battle of Downing Street* (London, 1973), *passim*.

40 James Callaghan, *op. cit.*, p. 518.

41 Callaghan tells us (*op. cit.*, p. 559) that he was influenced in this decision by unhappy memories of ten years earlier when, as Home Secretary, he used a Labour majority to reject recommendations by the Boundary Commissioners which would have increased Conservative opportunities at a forthcoming General Election.

10   THE BREAKING OF THE MOULD

1 In 1970, at the Commonwealth Prime Ministers' Conference in Kuala Lumpur, Edward Heath evoked intense hostility on the part of his confrères by insisting upon the continuation of British arms sales to South Africa and upon the preservation of the Simonstown Agreement whereby ships of the Royal Navy could use Simonstown as a base for Atlantic and Indian Ocean patrols. This Agreement having been abrogated by the Labour government elected in 1964 was renewed by the Conservative government in 1970. It was therefore assumed by black African leaders that a Conservative government would, naturally, be hostile to their aims.

2 The then President of Tanzania, Dr Julius Nyerere, refused to attend the Conference on the grounds of his assumption that Mrs Thatcher would be opposed to majority rule in Rhodesia.

3 There is a full discussion of these matters in Patrick Cosgrave, *Thatcher: The First Term* (London, 1985), pp. 78 ff. and in – by the same author – *Carrington: A Life and a Policy* (London, 1985), pp. 146 ff.

4 Sir Ian Gilmour is a theoretician of middle-of-the-road Conservatism, that body of thinking most notably opposed to the views favoured by Mrs Thatcher. See his *Inside Right: A Study of Conservatism* (London, 1977), pp. 11–21.

5 Jim Prior, *A Balance of Power* (London, 1986), p. 154. The junior Minister was the Earl of Gowrie.

6 See Prior, *op. cit*, p. 157.

7 Norman Tebbit, *Upwardly Mobile* (London, 1988), p. 184.

8 Essentially, Scargill used his total control over the Executive of his union, and the support of important areas, principally Yorkshire and Scotland, to enforce the strike. Even so, miners from some areas, notably Durham and Nottingham,

refused to strike, and formed the breakaway union, the Union of Democratic Mineworkers.

9 See Peter Walker, *Staying Power* (London, 1991), pp. 140 ff.

10 See Patrick Cosgrave, *Carrington: A Life and a Policy* (London, 1985), pp. 126 ff.

11 See Max Hastings and Simon Jenkins, *The Battle for the Falklands* (London, edn. 1983), pp. 55 ff. This book, published within a year of the conclusion of the Falklands War, is exceptional in both its acuity and its authority. Jenkins covered political matters at home and Hastings, in the South Atlantic, covered the military details of the war.

12 On 19 January 1983, the report of the Committee of Enquiry, headed by Lord Franks, into the origins of the war was published. Not to put too fine a point upon it, the report was a whitewash job, exculpating the government, and particularly the Foreign Office and the Ministry of Defence, from all responsibility for the failure to anticipate Argentinian ambitions and military preparedness.

13 See Mrs Thatcher's introduction to the account of the Falklands War by the Battlegroup Commander, Admiral 'Sandy' (now Sir John) Woodward, entitled, *One Hundred Days* (London, 1992), p. xi.

14 William Whitelaw, *The Whitelaw Memoirs* (London, 1989), p. 203.

15 There is a curious parallel here with the debate on the conduct of the Second World War in May 1940. On that occasion the result of the vote in the House of Commons was so bad that the Prime Minister, Neville Chamberlain, decided to resign on the following day. But, in the House of Lords matters had gone well, and the Foreign Secretary, Lord Halifax, was astonished to learn from the Prime Minister of his intention.

16 See Admiral Woodward, *op. cit*, pp. 149–63.

17 There is a general discussion of the problems of this period in David Howell, *Blind Victory* (London, 1986), pp. 167 ff. A more detailed account can be found in Peter Walker's *Staying Power* (London, 1991), pp. 165 ff.

18 See Peter Jenkins, *Mrs Thatcher's Revolution: The Ending of the Socialist Era* (London, 1987), pp. 159 ff.

19 Peter Walker, *op. cit.*, p. 166.

20 Harold Macmillan once said that there were three organisations that no government should quarrel with. They were the Brigade of Guards, the Roman Catholic Church and the National Union of Mineworkers. All three have, at the time of writing, been defeated by government in specific areas.

21 *One of Us: A Biography of Margaret Thatcher* (London, 1989), p. 371.

II THE BITTER LESSON

1 James Callaghan, *Time and Chance* (London, 1987), p. 565.

2 Jill Craigie, the writer and television producer.

3 See Chris Mullin (ed.), Tony Benn, *Arguments for Socialism* (London, 1979), *passim*. By 'Parliamentary Socialism' Benn means the House of Commons. It has been a long-standing ambition of his to abolish the House of Lords.

4 Roy Jenkins, *A Life at the Centre* (London, 1991), p. 510.

5 *Op. cit.*, p. 518.

6 Labour Members of the European Parliament were later added to the electoral college and considered to be part of the Parliamentary Labour Party. Later, in order to avoid frivolous candidates, a provision was added that anyone standing for the leadership should have the initial support of at least 55 Members of the House of Commons.

7 The Parliamentary Labour Party elects the Shadow Cabinet, but the Leader allocates portfolios.

8 David Owen, *Time to Declare* (London, 1991), pp. 481 ff.

9 It is interesting to note that Jenkins and his wife had kept up their Labour Party subscriptions during his time as President of the European Commission.

10 *Op. cit.*, pp. 545 ff.

11 The trade union movement, principally through the medium of the Workers' Education Association, had a long and honourable tradition of setting up educational establishments for workers and their children, which were complementary to the state system. The difference between the 1970s and 1980s and previous generations was that the unions now wanted the government of the day to organise all education along lines preferred by them.

12 The number of votes given at a Labour Party Conference to a trade union is determined by the financial contribution made by that union to the party. Notionally this contribution is calculated on the basis of the per capita sum raised by the so-called political levy, but if a trade union leader so chooses, given the support of his executive, he may, and often does, inflate the number of members of his union and therefore enjoy an increased block vote at conference.

13 See above, p. 199.

12 THE DEMISE OF LABOUR

1 Until his death, Hugh Gaitskell had steadfastly resisted the idea of the United Kingdom joining the European Economic Community. His stance caused considerable pain to his acolytes, such as Roy Jenkins, Shirley Williams, Bill Rodgers and David Owen.

2 The task of the Election Court is to pass judgement on the rectitude in law and practice of election campaigns. The Court has the additional power to unseat an victor in an election campaign who fails to meet the legal requirements for being a Member of the House of Commons.

3 Eric Hammond, *Maverick: The Life of a Union Rebel* (London, 1992), p. 55.

4 Gill was speaking on Radio Four on 24 April 1992.

5 There is a very full, and entertaining, account of the birth of Wapping in Hammond, *op. cit.*, pp. 74 ff.

6 Hammond, *op. cit.*, p. 190.

7 For a full description of the Westland crisis, see Norman Tebbit, *Upwardly Mobile* (London, 1988), pp. 247 ff. 'I think that Michael's thinking is sometimes dominated by a single issue, making him somewhat myopic.'

8 The fullest account of Heseltine's reasoning is to be found in his book, *The Challenge of Europe: Can Britain Win?* (London, 1989), pp. 179 ff.

9 The Attorney-General of the day, though appointed by the Prime Minister, is responsible for the administration of the law, and as such can act on his own initiative if he suspects malfeasance

10 To win the Conservative Leadership, under the rules devised by Lord Home of the Hirsel, a candidate must win 50 per cent plus one of those entitled to vote.

11 See Bruce Anderson, *John Major* (London, 1991), pp. 220 ff.

Select Bibliography

Anderson, Bruce, *John Major* (London, edn. 1991).

Beckerman, Wilfred (ed.), *The Labour Government's Economic Record 1964–1970* (London, 1972).

Beer, Samuel, *Modern British Politics* (London, 1965).

Beloff, Nora, *The General Says No* (London, 1963).

Benn, Tony (ed. Chris Mullin), *Arguments for Socialism* (London, 1979).

Birkenhead, The Earl of, *The Prof in Two Worlds: The Official Life of Professor F. A. Lindemann Viscount Cherwell* (London, 1961).

Blake, Robert and Patten, John, *The Conservative Opportunity* (Oxford, 1976).

Brittan, Samuel, *Steering the Economy: The Role of the Treasury* (London, edn. 1974).

Brown, George, *In My Way* (London, edn. 1972).

Bruce-Gardyne, J. *Whatever Happened to the Quiet Revolution?* (London, 1974).

Buchanan, James M., *The Economics of Politics* (London, 1978).

Bullock, Alan, *The Life and Times of Ernest Bevin*, Vol. I, *Trade Union Leader* (London, 1960), Vol. II, *Minister of Labour* (London, 1967), Vol. III, *Ernest Bevin: Foreign Secretary* (London, 1983).

Butler, David. *The British General Election of 1951* (London, 1952).

Butler, David and Stokes, Donald, *Political Change in Britain* (London, 1969, revised 1971).

Butler, David and Kavanagh, Dennis, *The British General Election of February 1974* (London, 1974).

Butler, R. A., *The Art of the Possible* (London, 1971).

Callaghan, James, *Time and Chance* (London, 1987).

Churchill, Winston S., *The Second World War*, Vol. I (London, 1948), Vol. II (London, 1949) and Vol. VI (London, 1954).

Colville, John, *The Fringes of Power: Downing Street Diaries 1939–1955* (London, 1985).

Cosgrave, Patrick, *Margaret Thatcher: A Tory and her Party* (London, 1978).

Cosgrave, Patrick, *R. A. Butler: An English Life* (London, 1981).

Cosgrave, Patrick, *Thatcher: The First Term* (London, 1985).

Cosgrave, Patrick, *Carrington: A Life and a Policy* (London, 1985).

Cosgrave, Patrick, *The Lives of Enoch Powell* (London, 1989).

Crosland, C. A. R. (Tony), *The Future of Socialism* (London, 1962), revised as *Socialism Now* (London, 1974).

Dayan, Moshe, *Story of My Life* (London, 1976).

Donoughue, Bernard, *Prime Minister: The Conduct of Policy Under Harold Wilson and James Callaghan* (London, 1987).

Dudley Edwards, Dr Ruth, *Victor Gollancz* (London, 1987).

Edwards, Michael, *Back from the Brink* (London, 1983).

Falkender, Marcia, *Downing Street in Perspective* (London, 1983).

Finer, S. E., *The Growth of British Government* (London, 1975).

Foot, Michael, *Aneurin Bevan: 1945–1960* (London, 1985)

Foot, Michael, *Loyalist and Loners* (London, 1986).

Friedman, Milton, *An Economist's Protest* (New Jersey, 1972).

Fry, Geoffrey, *The Growth of Government* (London, 1979).

Gilbert, Martin, *Winston S. Churchill: Finest Hour 1939–41* (London, 1983).

Gilbert, Martin, *Winston S. Churchill: Never Despair 1945–1965* (London, 1988).

Gilmour, Ian, *Inside Right: A study of Conservatism* (London, 1977).

Goodhart, Philip, *The 1922: The Story of the 1922 Committee* (London, 1973).

Hammond, Eric, *Maverick: The Life of a Union Rebel* (London, 1992).

Hanson, A. H., *Governing Britain: A Guide-Book to Political Institutions* (London, edn. 1975).

Harris, Kenneth, *Attlee* (London, 1982).

Hastings, Max and Jenkins, Simon, *The Battle for the Falklands* (London, edn. 1983).

Hayek, F. A., *The Road to Serfdom* (London, edn. 1976).

Heffer, Eric, *Never a Yes Man* (London, 1991).

Hennessy, Peter, *Whitehall* (London, 1989).

Heseltine, Michael, *The Challenge of Europe: Can Britain Win?* (London, 1989).

Home, Lord, *The Way the Wind Blows* (London, 1976).

Horne, Alistair, *Macmillan: 1957–1986* (London, 1989).

Howard, Anthony, *RAB: The Life of R. A. Butler* (London, 1987).

Howell, David, *Blind Victory* (London, 1986).

Hutchinson, George, *The Last Edwardian at No. 10: An Impression of Harold Macmillan* (London, 1980).

Jenkins, Peter, *The Battle of Downing Street* (London, 1970).

Jenkins, Peter, *Mrs Thatcher's Revolution: The Ending of the Socialist Era* (London, 1987).

Jenkins, Roy, *A Life at the Centre* (London, 1991).

Jones, Aubrey, *The New Inflation: The Politics of Prices and Incomes* (London, 1973).

Keegan, William, *Mrs Thatcher's Economic Experiment* (London, 1984).

King, Anthony, *Why is Britain Becoming Harder to Govern?* (London, 1976).

Lamb, Richard, *The Failure of the Eden Government* (London, 1987).

Lloyd George, David, *War Memoirs of David Lloyd George* (London, 1938).

Macmillan, Harold, *Tides of Fortune* (London, 1969).

Macmillan, Harold, *The Middle Way* (London, 1938).

Macmillan, Harold, *Winds of Change 1914–1939* (London, 1966).

Malone, Ed and Pollak, Andy, *Paisley* (London, 1986).

McCormick, Donald, *The Mask of Merlin: A Critical Study of David Lloyd George* (London, 1963).

McKenzie, R. T., *British Political Parties* (London, 1955, revised 1963).

McKenzie, R. T., *Angels in Marble* (London, 1972).

Moran, Charles, *Winston Churchill: The Struggle for Survival 1940–1965* (London, 1966).

Morgan, Janet, *The House of Lords and the Labour Government, 1964–1970* (Oxford, 1975).

Morgan, Kenneth O., *The People's Peace: British History 1945–1989* (London, 1990).

Mullin, Chris (ed.), Tony Benn, *Arguments for Socialism* (London, 1979).

Newhouse, John, *Collision in Brussels: The Common Market Crisis of 30 June 1965* (London, 1967).

Northedge, F. S, *The Troubled Giant: Britain among the Great Powers 1916–1939* (London, 1966).

Northedge, F. S. (ed.), *The Foreign Policies of the Powers* (London, 1968).

O'Brien, Conor Cruise, *The Siege* (London, 1986).

Ovendale, Ritchie, *The Foreign Policy of the British Labour Governments, 1945–1951* (Leicester University Press, 1984).

Owen, David, *Time to Declare* (London, 1991).

Patten, Chris, *The Tory Case* (London, 1983).

Pelling, Henry, *Origins of the Labour Party* (Oxford, edn. 1965).

Pierson, Stanley, *Marxism and the Origins of British Socialism: The Struggle for a New Consciousness* (Ithaca and London).

Pimlott, Ben, *Hugh Dalton* (London, 1985).

Prior, Jim, *A Balance of Power* (London, 1986).

Raison, Timothy, *Why Conservative?* (London, 1964).

Rhodes James, Robert, *Ambitions and Realities: British Politics 1964–79* (London, 1972).

Rhodes James, Robert, *Anthony Eden* (London, 1986).

Richards, Peter G., *Honourable Members* (London, 1959).

Ridley, Nicholas, *'My Style of Government': The Thatcher Years* (London, 1991).

Ryder, Chris, *The RUC: A Force Under Fire* (London, 1989).

Sampson, Anthony, *The Changing Anatomy of Britain* (London, 1982).

Seldon, Anthony, *Churchill's Indian Summer: The Conservative Government 1951–55* (London, 1981).

Seldon, Arthur (ed.), *Rebirth of Britain* (London, 1964).

Shaw, George Bernard, *The Intelligent Woman's Guide to Socialism and Capitalism* (London, 1928).

Short, Edward, *Whip to Wilson* (London, 1989).

Skidelsky, Robert, *Keynes* (London, 1985).

Soames, Mary, *Clementine Churchill* (London, 1982).

Tebbit, Norman, *Upwardly Mobile* (London, 1988).

Thomas, Hugh, *The Suez War* (London, 1985).

Walker, Peter, *Staying Power* (London, 1991).

Whitelaw, William, *The Whitelaw Memoirs* (London, 1989).

Wiliams, Philip M. *Hugh Gaitskell: A Political Biography* (London, 1979).

Williams, Philip M. (ed.), *The Diary of Hugh Gaitskell 1945–1956* (London, 1983).

Williamson, Bill, *The Temper of the Times: British Society since World War II* (London, 1990).

Wilson, Harold, *The Labour Government 1964–70* (London, edn. 1974).

Wilson, Harold, *The Governance of Britain* (London, 1978).

Woodward, Admiral Sandy, *One Hundred Days* (London, 1992).

Young, Hugo, *One of Us: A Biography of Margaret Thatcher* (London, 1989).

Index